DARKEST VISIBILITY

A Journey into Self-In-Light-Meant

by

Pamela Nicole Murphy

To: Courtney
I really enjoyed
meeting you. I hope
that you enjoy my
journey.

Sincerely,
Pamela Nicole Murphy

First Edition: February 2020
ISBN: 9781661277482 (paperback)
Imprint: Independently published
www.darkestvisibility.com

This is a work of creative nonfiction. The events are portrayed to the best of Pamela Nicole Murphy's recollection. While all the stories in this book are nonfiction, some names and identifying details have been changed to protect the privacy of the characters portrayed. This book is faith-based, these captured experiences are about Pamela's evolved Christian's journey that are supported by her relationship with God and her faith.

DEDICATION

This book is dedicated to my grandmother and mother. My grandmother is no longer with us. She was strong, hardworking, and stern. A woman who did not allow anyone to control her. My grandmother had struggles in her life, and it's because of her I will learn how to face mine. I would not be the person I am today without the influence and strength of my grandmother. She taught me lessons that have impacted my way of thinking. My grandmother was a unique woman and she is truly missed.

Despite some of the traumas and experiences in my earlier childhood, my mother has been a stabilizing force in my life. Even though she was translating traumas and experiences from her upbringing, she has always unconditionally given me a fundamental love, that has allowed me to spread my wings. I have observed my mother's evolution towards her faith in God, and her love for her family. It is that uncanny strength that I inherited from her. And as I stand before her today, she has a strong testimony within herself. I love you mom.

CONTENTS

FOREWORD

Darkest Visibility is to capture the light of your inner most trauma and seeing it for what it is. Darkest Visibility allows us to salvage our most traumatic life experiences, while allowing them to become a beacon of resources towards Self-Discovery. It is often said that until you are faced with the darkest moment you don't know the true measure of your strength. And it is that process that the momentum of self-discovery will appear.

This book exemplifies how one's traumas, setbacks, and unwarranted events can lead you to the pot of Gold, which is Self-Discovery, anchored by faith, obedience while following the GPS (God's Principle System). Hannah embodies this system throughout her exciting journey towards her light. The reader will enjoy a roller coaster ride of Hannah's trials and tribulations, while being inspired by the magnifying lessons simultaneously, while gatherings of faith and light appear. Once Hannah obtains this light, she continues to navigate through her traumas only to use this formula towards her Divine purpose!

ACKNOWLEDGEMENTS

I would like to thank God who is primary in my life and without His encouragement and guidance this book would have never been written. I would also like to thank Nakachia M. Smutko who insisted that I finish the book because she felt connected spiritually and emotionally with my experiences. She was upset that the book was in its premature stages and she couldn't continue. I also want to give special thanks to Chaka Rosemin who shared with me her story which was just as inspiring as mine. She encouraged me to share my story with others when I didn't see the impact it would have. I want to give a heartfelt thanks to Renata Clyburn, Monica Richardson, Mae Best, Freda Brown, Benita Jay and Jessica Medina for being there for me during some of my darkest moments. They gave me support and reassured me that my book had purpose and meaning which motivated me to complete my book. I would also like to thank George Askew, Gail Gaines, Shelia Smith and Ada Joyner for reading my book providing me with the necessary feedback and sharing with me how it inspired them as well. Finally, I'm grateful for Bobby Ray Smith, my soul mate for guiding me through procrastinating periods, holding my accountable while cheering me on and assisting me with bring it all together.

INTRODUCTION

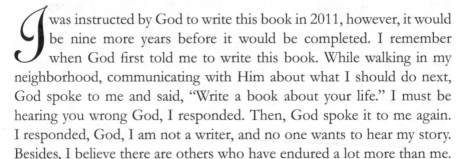

I was instructed by God to write this book in 2011, however, it would be nine more years before it would be completed. I remember when God first told me to write this book. While walking in my neighborhood, communicating with Him about what I should do next, God spoke to me and said, "Write a book about your life." I must be hearing you wrong God, I responded. Then, God spoke it to me again. I responded, God, I am not a writer, and no one wants to hear my story. Besides, I believe there are others who have endured a lot more than me. Knowing I had to be obedient, I thought to myself, I don't understand how God can expect so much from me. Well, he is God!

So, after my walk, I arrived back to my home, I grabbed a pen and some paper, all the time thinking, what do I possibly have to say? Repeating to myself in my head, English was my worst subject and now, I am expected to write a book. Continuously, I kept questioning God, in my mind like, "are you sure about this, what do I write about first, how do I even formulate my thoughts for someone to understand them. Without any more hesitation, I sat on my couch and began to write." Before I realized it, I had written the first 11 pages of my book within a few hours. It felt as though God had taken over my mind and body, using me only as a vessel to put it on paper.

Over the next few years, I would write more chapters in my book, then I would stop. Days, weeks, months and years passed, but I could not escape the feeling to finish it. The thought of being so transparent and exposing so much of my family was not an easy task. I would use the excuse, no one wants to hear your story, then, I would feel this pressure within my spirit to finish the book. Excuse, after excuse, my writing skills are of mediocrity and people will not understand my true message. No matter how hard I tried to escape it, I could not go a week without being faced with the question, when are you going to finish the book? I could hear that little voice saying, until you complete this book, you will never find what you are truly looking for. So, without any more hesitation here it goes.

The purpose of my book is to escort others to the light and out of the darkness as with my journey (self-in-light-meant). I deliberately made a decision to embrace the light. Through my experiences, I hope to bring awareness on how broken relationships can critically impact the future relationships of a child and how negative words can shape a child's self-esteem. To also show why it is important for a child to experience a real childhood. Furthermore, demonstrate how we often lack discernment and judge individuals based on outward appearances unaware of the pain inside. Lastly, to identify with why people sometimes choose death as a better alternative to living. Throughout my book, I attempted to show how these challenging life experiences have impacted my future and how I feel about them now. I was instructed by God to provide four different responses for each chapter. My perspective at the time, the message I am trying to convey, how this experience affected my future and my perspective now. As you read this book, you will notice the change in my perspective over time, which was influenced by spiritual growth and wisdom. My earnest prayer and desire is that, after you read my book that you will be spurred into action to view your own challenging life experiences, that may have left you with a negative perspective, can now be redefined more as a positive perspective.

Finally, I would like to encourage the individuals that I have portrayed in my book as people who have caused me misery, distress, anguish and agony in one way or the other in the past. The intention is not to bring attention to or magnify anyone's shortcomings or mistakes; it is the exact opposite. Hurt people, hurt people. We all had a role to play in this story, to bring it to the center and expose Satan's plots to keep us from reaching our true potential. This is about healing and giving hurtful and broken relationships closure. We have all made mistakes and wish we could change some of the decisions we have made in our past. Truly, I believe if it had not been for the individuals that caused me my greatest agony, I would not be the person I am today.

For we wrestle not against flesh and blood, but against principalities, against powers, against the rulers of the darkness of this world, against spiritual wickedness in high places. (Ephesians 6:12, King James Version)

CHAPTER

One

Illusion

For more than 30 years of my life I lived in an illusion which made me focus more on my limitations than my strengths. These were limitations I placed on myself because of my feelings of abandonment, rejection and unworthiness. As a child, it is hard to decipher what is true when you keep seeing adults live their lives in total contradiction to are teaching (do as I say not as I do). Although I was a child, I could distinguish right from wrong. I grew up hearing things about me that was not true. Words have a way of either encouraging you or discouraging you depending on who is saying it. People use the phrase "sticks and stones may break my bones, but words will never hurt me," but this is absolutely false. The negative words that were spoken to me as a child were uttered by people whom I loved and sought approval from, mentally paralyzed me in  my adulthood! Those words shaped and interfered with every aspect of my relationships throughout my life. I strongly believe that if I would have had more positive affirmations from influential people in my life at an earlier age then my life would have turned out differently. I would have experienced more peace, joy and happiness ultimately leading to a positive self-image. Now let's look at it from another viewpoint: It was those same life experiences that made me the person that I am today, and it also activated my desire to inspire others see their life from a different perspective.

The first lesson I want to capture in this book is that I have been living in an illusion. In the picture at the beginning of this chapter do you perceive two faces or one vase? Illusion may be defined as a thing that is or can be wrongly perceived or interpreted by the senses. We tend to believe what we see with our natural eyes while our spiritual eyes have been blinded by Satan. Therefore, we accept and perceive the natural eyes' vision of the condition, circumstance, situation or state we find ourselves in as the truth. You may be wondering what is the spiritual eye and how can one use it to see? Well, in the Garden of Eden before the fall, Adam and Eve only visualized good, evil did not exist for them. Also, when they communed with God, they understood him not with vocal words as we speak to each other today but through their spirits. This is why the serpent stated to Eve, "For God doth know that in the day ye eat thereof, then your eyes shall be opened, and ye shall be as gods, knowing good and evil" (Genesis 3:5, King James Version). It is obvious that Adam and Eve were not blind because they both could see animals, plants and fruit in the garden, so the spiritual eyes of Adam and Eve were already opened. However, it was their natural eyes that had never been opened that could only visualize both good and evil. Another demonstration of the spiritual eye and natural eye is illustrated in Mark 8: 23-25: " And he took the blind man by the hand, and led him out of the town; and when he had spit on his eyes, and put his hands upon him, he asked him if he saw ought.[24] And he looked up, and said, I see men as trees, walking.[25] After that he put his hands again upon his eyes, and made him look up: and he was restored, and saw every man clearly (King James Version). When the blind man saw men walking as trees, Jesus allowed him to see for a moment through his spiritual eye. Men walking like trees demonstrates how grand, strong and resilient we are viewed by God. And when Jesus touched his eyes the second time, he saw man clearly. This is how we perceive with our natural eyes. Through our natural eyes we see man in his current state. Once we view ourselves through our spiritual eye, fear will no longer be able to exist within us. If you truly desire to commune with God as Adam and Eve did in the Garden of Eden, pray and ask God to open your spiritual eye!

In order not to be continuously deceived, I learned to visualize through my spiritual eye and identify the voice that is speaking before I act on it. God communicates with me through my spirit and Satan communicates to me through my mind. While the Lord wants me to disregard my feelings/emotions and to believe his word, the devil on the other hand wants me to be distracted by my feelings/emotions and believe what I see as reality. God knows that if I could just grasp hold of the fact that he has given me all power, that there would be no reason for me to fear, doubt or lack anything. With God's way I would do the following confidently: 1) believing without seeing; 2) living with expectations; and 3) and manifesting into existence what I desire. Satan believes that if he can present a situation to me that emotionally affects me that he can get me to do the following with no qualms: 1) cause me to doubt my faith; 2) believe my situation to be an absolute truth; and 3) and consequently, through my belief, I will manifest the situation in my reality. I accept that Satan will utilize the people (family members, friends, acquaintances, associates, supervisors, co-workers and so on) that are closest to deceive me, but it's still just a distraction. It may be a hurtful distraction, but it's still a distraction, nonetheless, the aim is to take me off course. And it is through distractions that Satan had successfully hindered me from reaching some of the blessings that God has in store for me. I hope that by reading this book you will be able to identify the schemes that work to distract you and veer you off course to keep you from reaching your true purpose.

The year 2011, I was at my wits end fed up with the negative thoughts trying to pull me deeper into the darkness realizing that the light I was embracing was getting dimmer and dimmer. It was the next event that would trigger me into self-discovery mode of why? AAs I was driving down the road, headed to my house in Richmond, I was pondering over ideas of a business I could start up when I heard the words, "You are going to be homeless." I immediately recognized the voice; it was Satan speaking to me. I had just recently closed the business I had for three years that brought me a substantial income and I had no idea what I was going to do next. I was also still getting over all the issues that came along with my then-recent divorce. Trying to hold everything together, those last couple of years had been a stressful time for me. At this time, I became furious with the devil and then with myself, "How can I even entertain these thoughts?" God had just made it possible for me to return to my marital property that had been occupied by my ex-husband

3

Canaan for the past two years. Canaan had refused to pay any portion of the mortgage for the entire time he had possession of the property. Therefore, I was solely responsible for paying the entire mortgage for a residence and he was confident that I would pay the mortgage because he knew I would not default on my credit. He remained in the property until the judge finally ordered him out.

The home I lived in with Canaan for six years had been empty for four months now. I was currently living in my other home in my hometown of Freetown. I had contemplated moving back to Richmond, but no final decision had ever been made. It was a business meeting with my business associate, Lot that prompted the eventual move. Lot had asked me, "When are you going to move back to your house in Richmond?" I had responded, "In a few months," but truly I just wanted the house sold. He followed up with the question, "What is holding you up?" I drew a blank at that time since I really did not have a valid excuse. The conversation occurred on a Monday and Lot advised that he was going to help me move on Wednesday. I smiled not thinking he was serious but what was my excuse? The following day I reserved a moving truck and packed all my items up in one day. While I was packing, I knew I had made the right decision because of the peace I felt while I was doing it, and I was not even fazed about doing it all by myself.

Wednesday came and we packed the 26-foot moving truck with no room to spare. I had some large furniture to move, not to mention all the boxes I had in a storage unit. Once all the furniture and boxes were loaded, we headed back to my house in Richmond. I knew my helpers were tired, but I could not think of one person to help them once we got back into the area. I had been away from that area for more than two years, so I prayed to God for some help. I was about five miles away from my house when I noticed someone, I thought was an old associate by the name of James playing basketball in his yard. I called James and told him I had just passed his home and noticed him outside. He said it was not him but his son. I explained to him that I was moving back to the area and I needed help moving my furniture my helpers were about to pass out. He agreed to help and promised he would be there shortly. Meanwhile, my helpers began moving the furniture in the house. I could see that they were exhausted from moving all my oversized furniture. I began praying to God again, asking him to please send help soon because I just knew they were going to either pass out, drop the furniture or hurt themselves.

After about 30 minutes, James arrived. Upon arrival, he told me he owned his own moving company. That was music to my ears because I was confident that my furniture had a good chance it would make it upstairs in one piece and my helpers would not get injured. Once all the furniture and boxes were moved in and the guys had eaten, I informed them I had to run an errand. I told them I had to go to Lowes and purchase a refrigerator. Canaan had sold the one in our home, so my plan was to buy another refrigerator on credit. James stated that he had a refrigerator in his garage and only used it for storage, and that I could buy it if I liked it. Later that night I went by his house, saw the item: a stainless-steel black side-by-side refrigerator. It was a perfect match, better than the one I originally owned. He sold it to me for $350 and I was so thankful. God was in the move from beginning to finish. He provided me help to move, peace during the move, and the appliance I needed after the move. Therefore, I became so frustrated with the devil and myself, because I knew the devil was lying, but I was angry at myself for entertaining it, especially after God had done all this for me. But of course, this is what the devil had done to me for years, but I was determined to put an end to it that night. That night I stopped by my neighbor's house, the husband and wife are both pastors. I felt as if I was insane. Whenever something good would happen in my life, instead of having joy, I could only focus on the negative. I explained my frustration to Mrs. Rebekah. I asked why I could not appreciate what God had done for me and why I always felt like God was going to take everything from me any minute. Mrs. Rebekah said to me, without a second thought, "Someone took something from you when you were young." I left their home and walked two doors over to my house that night determined to be delivered from the burden that had plagued me for so many years.

The Lord had blessed me so much! I had opened and closed several businesses; I had done well for a kid from a small town like Freetown. Over the years, I had lived in nice homes, taken several vacations, had a generous income, and bought my dream car: a black convertible Jaguar. Still, I could not explain my feelings, such as why was I so susceptible to the devil's comments. Why could I not resist him? I knew that God would not return me to my home only to watch me to lose it, unless he has something better in store for me. I thought about the story of Moses, the Israelites and Pharaoh in the Bible. If I doubted God, I would be no different than the Israelites who doubted Him on the Red Sea even after he had delivered them out of Egypt (Exodus 14). The Lord opened the Red Sea for them, so I just had to believe he would do the same for me in my situation. I had to believe what God did for others he would also do for me. Acts 10: 34-35 reads, "Then Peter opened his mouth, and said, of a truth I perceive that God is no respecter of persons: 35 But in every nation he that feareth him, and worketh righteousness, is accepted with him."

I immediately went into my house, rushed to my prayer room and began writing down all the things that I needed to thank God for. I figured if I focused on my blessings that it would open the door to identify the cause of my negative thoughts. My list became lengthy, but I still found no answer or relief. God then spoke to my spirit and told me to write down what I feared from Him. I began to write down my thoughts in elementary form; it was almost childlike. All those years I had been hoarding feelings with no knowledge that they even existed towards God. I had never realized the events of my childhood had that much effect on me until I penned down my feelings on paper that evening. Without hesitation, I wrote what I feared most about God.

First, I feared that God might change his mind about me.

Second, I feared that God was going to take everything away from me.

Third, I feared that God did not love me.

Fourth, I feared that the words in the Bible applied to everyone else but me.

Tears ran down my face knowing what I had just written was not true, but rather a trick of the enemy, a feeling, a distraction. However, those subconscious thoughts plagued me. I knew it was not true, but I couldn't shake off that feeling or fight it. No matter how hard I tried to fight it, I could not. I could feel in my heart (spirit) that God loved me, but my mind constantly contradicted it. It was at that moment that God revealed to me the truth behind my fears. My fears came from a place of hurt. They were the result of others that had a vital role as an authoritative figure in my life and absolutely had nothing to do with God. And those hurtful memories that coincided with the fears hindered me from building a closer relationship with God and believing his word to be absolute truth. I asked God to forgive me because I had held him to the same standards as man. In the past, people I placed in high esteem failed to measure up to the standard I had placed them on, and subconsciously without realizing it, I had parallel God to the same unfulfilled results.

At that moment, I prayed for and forgave everyone, that was involved in those painful memories, that impacted my life at such an early age. I realized during that revelation that instead of having faith in God and believing God had all the power and all the answers, my faith was in my experiences. I had given my power to the ones that hurt me. From that moment onward, I placed my faith back into the rightful all-powerful hands of God and regained my power through forgiveness.

My perception then:	My achievements were often overshadowed by my fear of losing it all. I was preoccupied with getting more before I lose what I have already accomplished. This internal conflict is what kept me feeling unfulfilled for a long time in my life.
Message:	Satan targets and speaks to our vulnerabilities which usually nests in our mind and what we see. God communicates with us through our spiritual eyes and the ears of our hearts. This means He breaks us, to awake us, not to forsake us.
How the experience affected my future:	My approach to future issues that jolted me was this; I focused more on it being a call from God, than a hug from Satan. Satan wants us to be comfortable and untested, God wants us to embrace opposition and allow Him to be our strength in between the chaos.
My perception now:	God is never in a competition with Satan, it is us who choose to let go of the standards of God and become enticed by Satan. This is when we feel that strong current of disobedience, which is translated into insecurities, loss of self-worth, and despair.

CHAPTER

Two
Innocence Gone

I was overflowing with joy when I looked out the window and scrapped the paint off the window seal in our new home. I was so excited, and I found the greatest pleasure in just scrapping those window seals and cleaning up the paint particles off the floor. We were finally in our new house, with so many big rooms and I felt like we were rich. We had a living room where our company could sit privately away from everyone else. We had a dining room, kitchen, laundry room, and I even had my own bedroom, but my favorite was the family room where my stepfather, Jonathan, would play with me and my brother. I never realized how much this meant to a three-year-old little girl and the impact it would have on her until now.

I had my own bedroom filled with Winnie the Pooh paraphernalia, a bedspread, record player, stuffed animals, toys and books. My favorite book was *Little House on the Prairie* by Laura Ingalls Wilder. The book was very thick, but I was determined to read it. The reason I was fond of *Little House on the Prairie* was because of the love that the character Charles Ingalls showed to his children. For me, Jonathan represented  Charles Ingalls. He married my mother, Rachel, and he treated us just like he was our biological father, actually better than our biological father. We knew our biological father, Levi, but he was never really interested in having a conversation with us when we were young. Therefore, Jonathan was the only real father figure that we knew and loved. If only Jonathan knew how much we loved and admired him I believe in my heart, he would have handled things a little differently.

I loved and enjoyed the first years of my life; I do not believe any child loved to work more than me. At a very early age, I was always trying to prove that I could do it, whatever it was. I would sweep and mop floors, dust furniture, clean cabinets, clean bathrooms, as well as wash and iron clothes as amusement. When it was time to wash the dishes, I was too short to reach the sink, but I would pull up a chair and stand in it. I was determined not to let anything stop me, not even my height. And when it came to ironing, I lowered the ironing board just low enough for me to iron. As a little girl, I believed I could do anything if given an opportunity.

For a two-year-old and three-year-old, my brother Ishmael and I were living the life. I can remember my first birthday party: it was my day, *my* special day. I could hardly wait; the anticipation drove me wild and I could barely get any sleep the night before. The time finally arrived when all my friends were gathered around the large dining room table waiting to be served the Neapolitan flavored ice cream, and of course, my favorite, chocolate cake. I felt like a queen. A party was thrown for me. It was one of the most memorable days of my life. Who knew then that it would be another 30 years before I would have my next birthday party?

Of course, Christmas was like a fantasy. I would hear my mother and Jonathan talking while they were wrapping our gifts and putting them under the tree. Then after a while they'd be complete silence. So, I would tip toe into the living room and look under the tree, and break into a smile so big it revealed every tooth as my eyes spread wide open in glee. There were so many presents I could not believe it; I thought Ishmael and I were the luckiest children in the world. Back in the bed I was not able to sleep a wink. My little heart was so full of joy that sometimes I felt like it was going to burst. I would lie in bed counting the hours as it passed with the biggest smile on my face. On Christmas Day, Ishmael and I often rushed to the tree tearing open the presents, playing and laughing uncontrollably. As for me, I had everything that a young girl could ask for.

Ishmael was 13 months younger than I was so I would always try and tell him what to do. I acted like I was years older than him. But there was one thing that I did not try to stop him from doing and that was getting excited about Jonathan returning home from work. We would run back and forth to the window waiting for Jonathan to pull up in the driveway. At the time, he was in the army stationed in Fort Ville, which was over an hour from our home. In my eyes, Jonathan was perfect, and we had the perfect family, but of course that is from a child's perspective. My mother was 18 years old when she gave birth to me and 19 when she gave birth to my brother. She married my father, but things just did not work out for the two of them. She is in her second marriage and has a man that loves her and provides stability.

Whenever we spotted his car coming down the road, Ishmael and I would hide behind the door anticipating its opening, waiting to jump on Jonathan's back as soon as he stepped one foot in the house. I think he always had a feeling we would be waiting because every time he came home, he would have that special treat for us, those Keebler chocolate fudge striped cookies that we loved so much. He would smile and laugh as we almost knocked him down trying to jump on his back. I did not realize as a child that he was on the road driving more than two hours a day and then worked 8 to 10 hours a day. How tired he must have been daily after work. Looking back now I am sure he must have been weary when he came home from work, but he never showed it. He just played with us as if he had just woken up full of energy, he was the best dad in the world to me.

Day after day we would follow this same routine, waiting at the door for Jonathan to come home. As time went by my mother became pregnant and we had a new little brother, Joshua, my stepfather's biological son. We were living the life and from a child's point of view, we had it all. Even with the birth of Joshua, things did not change, as Jonathan continued to show us the love, we so desired from him. One day the news came that Jonathan had to leave. All I can remember is that one minute he was there and then the next minute, he was gone. I'm not sure where he was deported to at the time, but I think it was Germany. I remember talking to him on the phone and saying "over" at the end of each sentence. I just wanted my dad back home. I never wanted to imagine my life without him because I missed him so much. Why did he have to leave? I know it was his job, but things would never be the same again.

Being a young mother and an Army spouse can put a strain on any relationship as it did with my mother and Jonathan. While Jonathan was gone, my mother's commitment to the relationship began to fade. Absence did not make the heart grow fonder, as they said. Things just unfolded rapidly, and the marriage could not withstand its current. The comprehension of a child should never go unnoticed. Adults must be role models of what they expect a child to display, rather than display a negative image and expect the child to develop a positive picture. I wanted to intervene between my mother's feelings of despair and any potential of someone taking Jonathan's place but I could not do anything because I was only a child. I could not stop what was predestined to happen.

My maternal grandmother Deborah found out about the inevitable and things went from bad to worse. I have always witnessed my mother showed Deborah the utmost respect despite how my grandmother interacted with her. I can remember this one incident quite clearly. Deborah called my mother on the phone unleashing a great deal of profanity and assassinating her character. My mother reluctantly replied, "I am grown now." She then gently laid the phone down without hanging it up. My mother feared my grandmother, however she still loved and respected her. I could hear the trembling in my mother's voice and see the anguish on her face as she told me to hurry up and get in the car to leave our home. We both knew what would be occurring next. My grandmother's house was less than four miles away from our home and we knew it would only be a matter of time before she showed up at our house. I was so afraid for my mom because she was terrified, to say the least.

We both jumped into the car and left the house in a rush. I thought we had made it, but less than two miles from the house, my grandmother flagged my mother and told her to pull over. Now as an adult I wonder why we did not go a different route. We went the exact route that my grandmother would use to drive to our house. Anyway, as my grandmother approached the car, I told my mother to "hit the gas pedal and go" but she did not dare disrespect her mother. Instead, she just froze. My grandmother attacked my mother. I wanted to do something to protect my mother, but I was helpless. As a child, I only thought children received such punishment. As I watched her physically abuse my mother, I became both confused and enraged. I could not do anything to stop it, but I decided that day that I would not allow it to happen to me. It seemed like hours had passed before it finally ended, as a patch of hair was thrown into my mother's lap with tears streaking down her cheeks. Afterwards, we drove off silently as we were both in a state of shock. A while later I did discover that my mother had taken all the hair that was pulled out of her head and placed it in between pages of her Bible. It was a reminder to me of my mother's pain.

I'm not sure how much time passed by when Jonathan finally returned home. Because of the things that I had witnessed and been exposed to, I knew things would never be the same again. My life of innocence had been shattered and my eyes were opened to what was happening in the real world. It was a world of betrayal, hurt, abuse and lies. Jonathan found out that my mother had emotionally disconnected from him due to his absence and her insecurities. Yet, he told my mom that he was willing to recommit to the relationship. It seemed that the explosion had been avoided but someone else had some ammunition in storage. My mother had mixed feelings because she was ashamed of her actions but nevertheless, she also wanted to make it right. But the person that she expected to be her pillar of support had instead taken up the role of the nemeses.

Jonathan had forgiven and accepted all that was done during his absence, but with him being constantly reminded of the past, by other influential characters, placed a strong strain on the foundation of the relationship which had already been weakened. My grandmother should have been more of a refuge for my mother oppose to being the nemeses. As I witnessed all of this, I could only imagine the shame my mother felt. Where was she supposed to find comfort when the source of her hurt and oppression was her mother who was supposed to be there for her? I could not understand why my grandmother would treat my mother in such a way. I am still haunted by some of the inappropriate and hurtful comments she made about my mom back then. Children are like sponges because they soak up everything adults say and do. So, it is imperative that a person be a positive role model and be careful what one says in front of children because it will have lasting effects.

Jonathan had a lot on his plate: a wife that he truly loved and a mother-in-law constantly reminding him of the past practices of my mother. Jonathan and my mother divorced. My life, my mother, and my brothers' lives all took a drastic turn. I wish I could say it was for the better.

My perception then:	I was living the happiest life any little girl my age could have imagined, then I watched it all slip away and I was so powerless and could do nothing to keep my family together.
Message:	Adults should never underestimate children's abilities to comprehend situations and how their actions directly affect children's lives.
How this experience affected my future:	After witnessing my grandmother's physical abuse towards my mother, I decided at that moment I would never allow anyone to physically abuse me without standing up for myself.
My perception now:	My stepfather and mother made the best decisions for their relationship based on their situation. They had no idea that the demise of their relationship would emotionally impact my brothers and my future. I understand that my grandmother thought what she was doing was the best for all of us because of her past experiences. However, it was translated usually through physical and mental abuse. Trauma lives vicariously in all of us. Whatever trauma we are exposed to, if proper interventions are not applied, no matter how big or small, the people closest to you will be subjected to your previous traumatic experiences.

CHAPTER

Three
Love Lost Its Meaning

I do not know how things got so messed up for this eight-year-old little girl. Ishmael, Joshua and I are now living with our maternal grandmother, Deborah. Why did my mother allow Deborah to talk her into letting us stay with her? Deborah told my mother she would keep us until she could find somewhere for us to live, me and my two brothers. She convinced my mother that she would make sure that we were alright and would stay together. What my mother did not know was that Deborah was secretly working behind her back in alliance with Jonathan. Jonathan, expectantly so, was upset by the separation between him and my mother, therefore, he was secretly seeking to get sole custody of my younger brother, Joshua, unknowingly to my mother.

Before long, Jonathan was showing up daily at my grandmother's neighbor's house, Phoebe. He would tell Joshua, to come over, but not Ishmael or me. I finally realized that the feeling he had towards us had changed. I was young but I understood that we no longer meant anything to him because we were not his biological children. I loved him

14

as my father even though he was not my birth father. What I could not understand, however, was how his feeling had changed so quickly. For me, the blood parent did not determine my love, it was the parent that showed me love. How could I be so stupid to think he truly loved us? But I could not understand why he would pretend to if he really did not. My feelings for Jonathan were so strong and I never thought I would have to imagine or live my life without him in it.

By this time, Jonathan had started dating Ms. Phoebe's niece, Leah. I watched him visit Leah almost every day from across the paved road. He would not even come over to at least say hi or visit us or even speak to us when he would see us playing outside. Parents are supposed to love their children and be role models for them, because if they lie to us who then will we look up to? It felt like my little heart was being broken over and over each time he visited next door and ignored us as if we never existed. What had happened to the man we had loved and revered so much, was it all a lie? Why did he hate us now? How could you love and treat someone so good today and treat them so badly the next day? My little heart had been broken into tiny pieces and then crushed. Someone had stolen my stepfather's body and the man I would see almost daily across the street was someone else. The man that was my stepfather would never do this to me. I wanted to know how he had disposed of his love so I could do the same with mine because holding on to mine hurt so much. It was at that moment that I discovered that love could change without warning. I could not understand how he could stop loving us, but we could not stop loving him too. No one was there to comfort us or even explain to us what was going on. I was only eight years old when I stopped trusting in love. The words I love you stated to me, meant nothing to me from that point on.

One of the good things that I can remember about being at my grandmother's and living across from Ms. Phoebe's house was that she had two grandchildren who also lived with her. Their names were Tamar and Absalom. Tamar was around the same age as me and in the same grade as me. Ishmael and Absalom were one year apart in school. We had a lot of fun playing together as kids. We would always play together and be over at each other's house. Except when Tamar and I would get into an argument and stay mad at each other for about a day then makeup. But I cannot really remember if Ishmael and Absalom fought except of course when Ishmael would try to practice the wrestling moves, he had seen on television on Absalom. But overall it was great having kids my own age to play with because we had to make our own entertainment back then.

So, after months had passed, Jonathan had gained full custody of my brother. My mother found herself in the position where she felt greatly betrayed by her mother again. Jonathan had taken my younger brother away from us. Now to me, my loving Jonathan had become the devil. He had turned his back on us and now he had taken my little brother also. The pain of being separated from my younger brother was so awful, I had taken care of him every day like he was my little baby. I felt so helpless and hurt that there was nothing, I could do to keep him with us. I wanted to die my little baby was gone. And after Jonathan finally received sole custody of him, my little brother would often go over to Ms. Phoebe's house with Jonathan, just across the street from us. Each time I would hear a car, I would run to the door to see if it was Joshua coming over to Ms. Phoebe's house. But when Jonathan would come over, he would forbid Joshua from crossing the street to visit us at our grandmother's house. This put me in an awkward position because I would often go over to Ms. Phoebe's house but now, I felt uncomfortable going over there when Jonathan came to visit. Every time Jonathan and Joshua came over to visit at Ms. Phoebe's I would stay in my grandmother's yard or sit on the porch and just watch my little brother. I would just stare at Joshua and he would be staring back at me. But as soon as no adults were around Joshua would sneak over to be with us every chance he got. There were a few times Joshua would come to Ms. Phoebe's with Leah and on a few occasions with Leah's sister and they would not allow him to come over and see us either. This was my baby brother whom I had fed, rocked to sleep, changed his diaper from the day he was born. At times I felt like he was my little baby because I loved him with all my heart. What sense did it make to keep our brother from us, we had done no wrong? He was my flesh and blood. If they were trying to punish my mother, she was not there living with us. What sense did this make, why in the world would adults do this to innocent children? I could not figure out what I had done wrong to deserve this type of treatment. Literally, I wanted my heart to stop beating, it was the only way I felt, I could avoid the pain and disappointment.

The first Christmas was the hardest and maybe you could understand better if only you knew how things got so whacked up. There were a few presents under the tree but not many for my brothers or me. I had tried everything I could to keep my mother and Jonathan together, but it was not enough, and I felt so worthless. This would be our first Christmas

16

morning since the separation of my parents. On that Christmas morning, Jonathan came over but he was empty-handed, not one gift for me or my brother. He did not even say Merry Christmas to us. He came over to use the telephone. I watched him as he made the phone call and then walked right past me out the door, not even saying goodbye. This is the man that had lavished us with cookies, toys, hugs and love. Charles Ingalls was dead to me. I would never be the same after that day and unknowingly I would carry that hurt for the next 40 years of my life.

Jonathan married Leah. Then some months later they moved, Jonathan had a new assignment. I knew the day of waiting and listening for the cars hoping Joshua would come over was a thing of the past. When they left, I had no idea where they were taking my little brother. All I knew was that my little brother was gone, and I could no longer protect him. But later because of Leah, Ishmael and I would know exactly where they were living. Across the street at Phoebe's house, what do I see to my amazement? Tamar and Absalom on the front porch modeling their Korean sweat suits with their names imprinted on the back hood for Ishmael and me to witness. Leah had sent her great niece and nephew the monograph sweat suits. Tamar and Absalom were so excited about their new outfits. I tried to smile on the outside but on the inside, I felt like I was dying. I tried to be happy for them. But I could not truly because they were reaping the benefits of the man that was once our father. Afterward, I went back into my grandmother's house with no one to confide in about what had happened and how badly it hurt me. Jonathan and my little brother were gone, and I had to face that fact. But now, I had to be reminded of what we lost, every time, Tamar and Absalom wore their sweat suits. Our little world had already been turned upside down and now having to endure even more heartache. I really do not think adults truly realize how much they can affect a young impressionable child and the impact it can have in their life.

I often thought about Joshua and prayed that one day we would be reunited. But once we were separated by the distance, our relationship with Joshua would never be the same again. The closeness that sibling usually share would be destroyed by manipulative, self-serving adults. After the move, Jonathan would usually only allow Joshua to visit us once a year during the summer. It seemed like we were raised in two different worlds. I found out during my childhood that adults were so consumed with their own wants, desires, and spitefulness that they never stopped for a second to consider how it would affect the children involved.

Over the years I had always wanted to ask Jonathan so many times what Ishmael and I did to him to make him stop loving us. Even though he and my mother divorced, I felt like that had nothing to do with the bond we had with him or so I thought. Over the years he would regularly come back to town to visit. Every time I would see him during his visits in our hometown on holidays or funerals, those feelings of rejections would consume me all over again. He would speak to me casually, acting as though we never had any type of close relationship. Maybe if I had gathered the nerve to ask him back then I could have gotten some type of closure. I understand now that so many times these feelings have hindered me from being as successful as I could have been. Because of this mistrust, I had experience in my early childhood, I questioned every compliment and declaration of love expressed towards me. I wish I could say how Jonathan treated me did not affect me, but it did both in my childhood and adulthood. As a child, I felt abandoned and rejected. As an adult, I said I wanted and desired to be love, but the truth is, I really did not believe in love anymore.

As I explained in Chapter 1, God spoke to my spirit and ask me to write down all the things that I feared about him. The first thing I wrote down was that I feared he was going to change his mind about me. But as I wrote it, God opened my eyes and it became clear to me why I felt the way I did. It was easy for Satan to convince me not to trust anyone, after Jonathan had abruptly changed his feelings towards me. I had been holding God accountable for my stepfather's actions, but I could not see it until he revealed it to me at that moment. I had suppressed all the pain and hurt for so many years that I was not even conscious of what I was doing. Now, I realize my subconscious mind always pondered on what I had done wrong to cause Jonathan to change his mind about me and stop loving me. But my conscious mind often reflected on all the mistakes I had made in life, so I just felt I had given God enough reasons to change his mind about me.

I did not realize until years later that I had abandonment issues. Who knew that my stepfather distancing himself from me could have such a major impact on my life? Most people would think well he was just your stepfather not your biological father, but he was my world and the only father I knew. There are no words to express how much I really loved him or to explain how much his actions hurt me. But what I was left with was a fear of rejection and abandonment. Rejection and abandonment for me was the fear of not being loved and that the people who do love me will eventually get tired and leave me. Rejection for me resulted in me trying to shield my heart. If I did not allow anyone into my heart, then no one would have to stop loving me or reject me again. In the presence of others, I could maintain a pretense of being a happy young girl. And when I did allow someone to get close, I would question their motives and keep them at arm's length. But inside I had no self-worth and low self-esteem. I felt a lot of guilt, like a burden and I often blamed myself for everything. And these emotions affected every aspect of my adult life. Even though I had to deal with a lot of those negative emotions as a child, during adolescence and adulthood it was those same emotions that allowed me to have compassion for others.

Believing that Jonathan changed his mind about me was the root of my first fear. After God revealed it to me it was so evident, and I even questioned that. Since it was so obvious why did I not just figure that out years ago and saved myself so many years of agony? The problem was that I had so many illusions based on my experiences that it became hard for me to decipher the truth even when it was as clear as day. Jonathan had just gone through some major life changes and his world was now in turmoil. The woman he thought he would spend the rest of his life with divorced him. He was single again and now had a young son that he was now responsible for. And let's not minimize all the self-serving people in his ear giving him malicious advice regarding his life and relationships. What Jonathan endured would have injured the strongest spirit. Looking back now, I realize that I was never rejected or abandoned by my stepfather. Instead, I was an innocent bystander caught up amid hurt adults unable to effectively deal with their own pain, fears, and struggles.

After identifying the root of my problem, I had to find a way to heal. The first thing I did was to ask God for forgiveness for holding Him accountable for the actions of someone else. Next, I asked God to remove anything from my heart that I was holding against Jonathan. Once I finished praying, I felt an amorous presence over me and then suddenly had a desire to press on. Then I began to see vivid scenes from my childhood when I felt like I was all alone with absolute clarity. In the scenes, I could see God's presence. As He showed his presence to me, it felt as if he was inundating my heart with love to the point, I felt like it was going to burst. He allowed me to see that I was never alone that he had been there with me all the time.

Because of my feelings of rejection and abandonment forming secure attachments in my childhood directly affected me in forming a healthy relationship in my adulthood. An attachment disorder begins at the early life events of a child and manifests itself over time into adulthood in a more severe form. There are four distinct styles of attachment: fear-avoidant, dismissive-avoidant, anxious-preoccupied and secure. John Bowlby was the first to introduce the attachment theory and that a child's intimacy and sense of security with their primary caregiver plays a crucial role in how secure they will be as an adult.

- Fear-avoidant: I want to be in a relationship but what if I get hurt.

- Dismissive-avoidant: I do not need anyone; I'll depend on myself.

- Anxious-preoccupied: I want a connection with someone special but they do not want me.

- Secure: I am fine with someone and I am fine without.

The two styles I faced in my adulthood were fear-avoidant and dismissive-avoidant. I desired a relationship and engaged in them, but I was too protective of my heart and never truly opened my heart to anyone. And I decided at a very young age to give up depending on adults. I was determined to make it on my own and never trust anyone again. But I could never truly get the real meaning out of life if I did not trust again and allow someone into my heart. Yes, opening my heart can make me susceptible to hurt and pain but the heart is a resilient organ, it can take it. Instead of closing it, I decided to keep it open for someone deserving of it. No matter how hard we try and deny it we all need somebody. The beliefs that I established at a young age were not valid. Yes, it is true the pain I endured was heartbreaking, but if I had been given the opportunity to form more secure relationships, then my opinion and beliefs would have been different. So, now I must remind myself daily, that I am deserving of good things, which is not an easy task to do, but it is something I must so for absolute healing. I became so attached to the wrongs that have been done to me that I found it hard for me to let them go. I was afraid to believe for better in fear of facing disappointment, so I stuck to what I knew. What I fear I create! Fear draws more fear!

Lastly, from one adult to another, if you get in a relationship and you introduce your child to those experiences, the child endures the emotional attachment of each of those relationships and their loss. Often, adults vacillate from one relationship to another not considering the emotional disorder of the child. It is those experiences that lead us to the seeds of attachment disorder that challenges the child's future relationships due to trust, insecurities and low self-esteem. Any changes in our relationships should be explained to the child so there's minimal trauma reenactments from previous scars! Therefore, I sympathize with you to muster up enough strength to sit down with your children and explain the situation to them. It is important that you give them much assurance that even with all the changes that they are still loved, and nothing will change that.

My perception then:	Never trust anyone that tells you they love you. Love is just a word with no deep meaning.
Message:	Parents, stepparents, guardians and authority figures never underestimate how much children need your support, guidance, and love. Abandoning/rejecting a child by leaving or by being preoccupied can root the fears of being unloved and unworthiness. Children will believe that they are unworthy and powerless and will internalize this as they cannot rely on others to protect them. When giving gifts or giving attention to children in the presence of other children, it is imperative that you do not show preferential treatment between the two. It may create animosity and bitterness between the children. Children are emotionally unable to perceive the personal connection with the relationship of giver to receiver. Unresolved childhood attachments issues leave adults susceptible to difficulties in forming healthy adult relationships. And the patterns of attachment disorder are usually passed from one generation to another.

How this experience affected my future:	For most of my life, I found it difficult to trust people motives for showing me affections through words or actions. I did not trust love, therefore, I was not able to receive love throughout most of my adulthood. Whenever I purchased gifts for my granddaughter in the presence of her sister, and on holidays and birthdays I also made sure I brought gifts for her sister also.
My perception now:	Jonathan was dealing with his own grief and challenges (hurt people hurt people) and never realized the emotional impact that he had on my life. He had no idea how much he was loved and admired by my brother and me and how his emotional absence would affect our lives.

CHAPTER

Four
Fears Takes Root

What had happened to my Little House on the Prairie family? One day as I sat in my 3rd grade class crying within I came up with an idea about how I was going to get my family back together. I figured if I just went back to my old home somehow things would work out, I had to do something. So, after school that day instead of getting on the bus to go to my grandmother's house I got on the bus to go to my old house. As I got on the bus the bus driver spoke to me like nothing had changed. And I acted accordingly. When I arrived at my old home, I got off the bus as if I still lived there. I knew I could not get in the house, so I didn't even try. I just walked to the backyard and sat on the back porch wondering what I could have done differently. I tried to stay strong and hold back the tears, but I was overwhelmed with sorrow of how my life got turned upside down. After crying for what seemed like hours, I put my book bag under my head, made a wish and laid down hoping that when I woke up  everything would be different. I so desired to have my fairy tale life back but when I woke up things were the same someone had taken me back to my grandmother's house. It would be forty years later, that Jonathan would tell me that he was inside the house on that day. I had no idea he was there. I guess he just couldn't face me. The little girl he had held in his arms comforting so many times before and now he could not do it anymore. He admitted he was inside the house crying also. He said he was heartbroken and torn up on the inside having to see me suffer and not being able to do anything about it.

Now just a passing memory, my little house on the prairie family. I wanted to live with my mother, but I knew she had a lot of challenges to deal with at the moment. I realized that this situation was hard on everyone and I prayed to make it better, but it did not happen. I guess my mom thought it could not get any worst, but it did. Once we began living with my grandmother she made it almost impossible for our mother to see us. So, our mother would make unannounced visits to our school to visit my brother and me without my grandmother's knowledge. Of course, we kept it a secret for fear of what she might do to her if she found out. My grandmother refused to relinquish her control over my mother as if she were still a child. I would hear my grandmother on the phone complaining to people that our mother was neglecting us by not calling or giving her any money to support us. I knew I had to do something. I had to find a way to get some money and give it to my grandmother so she could stop slandering my mother's name. It hurt me so much to hear her talk down on my mother in that manner when I knew my mom was suffering already. In my mind, I was determined to find a way to stop it.

I can remember this incident just like yesterday. It is a memory that has stayed in my mind for so long that I cannot forget even though I want to. During this one specific time, Deborah had sent several requests for my mother to visit. My mother had refused to come and to my grandmother, this was a sign of disrespect and justification for retaliation in Deborah's eyes. I could sense that my grandmother felt she was losing her dominance over my mother. My mother after receiving all the messages would always secretly contact me within a short period of time and ask if everything was OK. I would let her know that we were all fine. I understood clearly why my mother did not visit us at our grandmother's home, if I was in my mother's shoes, I would not have come around either. I knew my grandmother's only reason for contacting my mother was to make her conform to her rules. And when she did not respond the way my grandmother wanted her to I knew trouble was around the corner. After that night, I lost all the respect I had for my grandmother's role forever. I could sense in my spirit that trouble was approaching, and I felt something bad was going to happen. My grandmother had sent a message through my mother's now sister law, Julia, and told her that I and my brother were sick. Oblivious, my mother did not know this was a lie. My mother put aside all her legitimate concerns and rushed to my grandmother's house fearing we were sick. That night we had a few people in the home, my grandfather, my grandmother, Uncle Haman, Ishmael, me and two friends of Deborah. My mother and Julia stepped into the home unaware of the chaos waiting for my mom. Immediately, Deborah accused my mother of not speaking when she walked into the house which was untrue. My mother responded, I spoke, and before the words fell off her tongue, my grandmother became physically violent towards my mother. Everyone stood around in awe, it was like a movie; no one could believe what their eyes were seeing. I think everyone was in shock. No one was expecting that. Not even me, even though I had witnessed the car incident this was even more intense. I think my grandmother had forgotten that she had guests. She became ashamed not by her actions but only after she had realized that her friends had witnessed her in a rare form. Of course, all the family members were accustomed to my grandmother's domineering ways. After I witnessed this altercation between my grandmother and my mother, there was no way I could ever respect my grandmother the same way again. My mother had not done anything to deserve this type of treatment.

I cried all night thinking about how my mother must have felt. For the second time, I had witnessed my grandmother abuse my grown mother. With every tear, I cried grew the resolution in me. With every fiber in my body, just like I knew my name was Hannah, I knew I would never allow anyone to abuse me like that regardless of who they were. It was clear to me why my mom made some of the decisions she had made in life. I could not help but imagine what my mom's childhood must have been like seeing her in her adulthood now. Who was there to support her when she was just an innocent child? Who was her role model? How could she have possibly felt loved? Even though I witnessed the abuse I was never afraid for myself because I had made a promise to myself that my grandmother would never do that to me. Ephesians 6: 2-3 states "Honor thy father and mother; which is the first commandment with promise;3 That it may be well with thee, and thou mayest live long on the earth." After that night, I believed my mother had sealed her stay on this earth for a while because throughout it all, my mother never once disrespected my grandmother.

Repeatedly, "You know Rachel has not sent me any money for these kids as much as they eat!" Every day the same conversation on that telephone. I guess she thought the people she was talking to was going to give her some if she kept complaining. My grandmother deserved an Emmy for making me feel like a burden to the point that I was truly convinced that I was a burden. I had a plan to fix things and I could hardly wait until summer. I believed at the time that she did not love us because she complained daily about having to take care of us and plus, she never said, "I love you." But I was going to get a job so I could pay my grandmother for room, board, and food. It was evident to me that she valued money because she talked about it every day and when someone gave her some, she would have the biggest most radiant smile on her face. So, in my little mind, I figured if I gave her some money, she might start loving us and stop talking about us to other people.

Finally, the summer came, and I had gotten a job driving the tractor pulling a harvester in a tobacco field. I was so excited. Now my mother would not have to struggle so hard to send my grandmother money and I would take care of me and Ishmael. The first day on the job the owner said I would get paid $1.50 an hour for driving the tractor and I knew the tobacco croppers and tiers handlers were paid $3.00 an hour. That entire day all I thought about was how I was going to make $3.00 also. From that day and each day thereafter, I could hardly look ahead driving up the tobacco rows from looking back watching the croppers crop the tobacco. I knew if I just got a chance I could do it too. I could not wait to get to the end of the row when we would have to break for a few minutes. I would jump off the tractor and crop one of the cropper's rows on foot as far I could until it was time for me to get back on the tractor. I did that over and over at the end of each row, trying to prove to the owner that I could do just as well as those older workers even though I was only nine. I would make at least $60 a week and, of course, some weeks I made more. I would give my grandmother some money and keep a few dollars for myself to buy my school clothes. I still wanted to make more money. After several weeks of following this same routine, the owner told me I had done a good job, but he did not need another cropper right now. I asked him if I could be a cropper next summer and he said I could have the position of a tier handler and I was overjoyed. I thought to myself that I got this summer job locked down for next year and now I must find a winter hustle.

For the next couple of years, until I was 15, I would work in the fields all summer long. I would pick blueberries, peppers, cucumbers and work in tobacco fields whatever field I could do to make money. Around 15 years old, things changed I was no longer able to work during the summer due to my schedule. Every summer I was either involved in a basketball, academic or college prep camp. By the age of 15, I had picked up three other hustles doing hair, baking cakes and cleaning houses. I was making $50 to $100 on a Saturday. My grandmother had taught me at the age seven how to bake cakes and at a very young age, I realized I had a gift to organize and clean and doing hair. Looking back now I enjoyed working as a child, but I worked too much. Every child deserves a childhood and I do not feel like I had one. I was too busy trying to learn how to make money that I never stopped to enjoy life. These experiences made it extremely difficult for me to trust God and surrender to him as an adult because I was under the illusion, I had been taking care of myself since I was a child.

When we moved in with my grandmother, my grandfather, uncle, and cousin were also living there. My uncle, Haman, is 10 years older than me and my cousin, Dinah, 4 years older. The house had only three bedrooms. Therefore, Haman shared his room with Ishmael and Dinah shared her room with me. Before I came Dinah had her own space and now, she had to share it with her younger cousin. I'm sure she hated the fact that after having her own privacy she was now forced to share, but who could relate better than me. How did I get here? My life was perfect once and now I'm sharing a room with my cousin who hates me. But what can I say? I have invaded her space! I did not mean to be a problem I just became one because of my circumstances. I looked up to Dinah and I could not comprehend why she treated me so awfully. I wondered why she could not see that I was hurting. I felt like I was dying on the inside. I had just lost my world and if there was anything, I could do to change it I would have done that. I accepted my fate and realized that the old Hannah was dead. And for the next few years while living together under the same roof with my cousin I felt as if she detested me. Dinah would say some things to me that would make me cringe inside. After a while it became the norm for me, no one else loved or appreciated me why should she be any different. After dealing with my relatives I concluded that I could not depend on anyone but myself for love.

My uncle, Haman, on the other hand, was nice to us. He was the best uncle anyone could ask for. He was only 10 years older than me and he had a full-time job. He showed us love and affection. He was so young, but it was obvious to me that he was just good at heart. His personality was so inviting, sweet and kind. He was like an angel to us. He never made me, or my brother feel like a burden instead he did the exact opposite. He treated us like we were his children. I can remember him buying Ishmael and me bikes for our second Christmas after we moved in with them. He tried to do as much as he could for us throughout our stay. My uncle had thrown me a lifeline. He was always doing nice things for us. I remember when he paid for me to go to 4-H camp when I was around 11 years old. I was so excited because it was also an opportunity to get away for a bit. It was my first time away from home. While there I learned to shoot the bow and arrow, paddle canoe, and swim. A couple years later he paid for me to go to my first basketball camp. I do not think he understands how much that meant to me. During those years I was feeling unloved and unimportant, but he brought a sparkle of hope.

Revisiting my childhood memories as an adult, I do not believe that my grandmother was a bad person. She was just ruled by a controlling spirit and she loved us in her own twisted way. I believe that at some point in her life that she was hurt and mistreated, and the spirit of control took domination over her life to ensure it would never happen again. I also concluded that my grandmother was never shown love which was why she was not able to show love. While I was growing up, I didn't see my family show a lot of physical intimacy towards each other, like hugging or kissing as a sign of endearment. I never really heard any kind words spoken about another person in our home by my grandmother. What I did hear was a lot of negative comments about other people and myself included. I recall hearing things like; they have a nasty house, I would not eat their food if I was starving, they are so lazy that they will not hit a lick at black snake, tell your (our friends') mom to buy you some soap so you can wash, and so on. I would hear those negative comments almost daily as though they were lyrics to a song that was on repeat in a jukebox. I wondered if these people knew what was really being said about them how would they feel, or would they even come over anymore? Even though I was exposed to a lot of negatively, I realized it was not right. From a very young age, I recall having a strong desire to do good, knowing clearly the difference between good and evil. Regardless of my experiences during my childhood, that desire kept pushing me to continue even when things looked hopeless.

I could remember my grandmother buying me something and within the next couple days she would get mad at me and take it back. This happened repeatedly, buy and give me something, get mad, and take it back. After a while, I just got used to it. I knew if she brought me something, I knew not to get too attached. But this one time I let my guard down. My grandfather had gotten sick and we were going back and forth to the Veterans' hospital. During one of his checkups, it was around my birthday. I had seen the most beautiful gold watch in the hospital's gift shop, My grandmother had asked what I wanted for my 16th birthday and I told her the gold watch. She said I was not going to get it because it cost too much. But every time we passed that gift shop, I would find myself staring at that beautiful watch. Others may have been disappointed about not being able to get it, but I decided years ago, I would work to buy whatever I wanted myself. To my surprise, on my birthday she had brought me that gold watch it was even more gorgeous on my wrist. I was thrilled that I now owned what I thought was the most exquisite watch ever. I could not believe that Deborah had spent that much money on me. I was in awe and thinking that maybe she had finally changed. A glimmer of hope shone over me and I began to think that she must really love me to buy me this gift. The excitement was short lived. She took the watch back from me the very next day. I cannot remember what I did to make my grandmother mad at me. It did not take much. I just hoped she would calm down and give it back. It never happened she took my beautiful gold watch back to the gift shop in exchange for her money. Trust me, I had not done anything to deserve to have my watch taken back. Why would my own grandmother, flesh and blood, always do this to me? After that incident I never wanted her to ever buy me any gift again. After this incident, I made up in my mind to try and never ask for anything and whatever I needed I would figure out a way to get it for myself or go without.

Back in Chapter 1, when God spoke to my spirit and ask me to write down all the things that I feared from Him, the second thing I wrote down was that I feared he was going to take everything from me. But the moment I wrote it down, God opened my eyes and it became clear to me why I felt the way I did. It was the gifts that my grandmother had given me and taken back that created a deep-rooted fear of loss in me. So, I was subconsciously holding God to the same standard. I had no issue believing God had blessed me with everything, I was given, but unconsciously, I believed that if I messed up and was not perfect, he would take it all back. And of course, my life was nowhere near perfect in my opinion. I had made lots of mistakes, so I felt it was bound to happen. So, I just lined my thoughts up with my past experiences and expected the worst. I had accepted losing things as a part of life; therefore, I grew accustomed to it happening and it became a part of my belief system.

The root cause of my second fear is evident. The taking back of the gifts had caused to me to conclude that I was not deserving of good things. I had formulated my thoughts to believe I was incapable of holding onto anything good. And when good things did come for me, I would expect for it to be taken away just like I expected the sun to rise the next morning. I allowed the outcomes of my experiences to form a permanent fixture in my mind as if they were the gospel truths. Because of the frequency of the activities I allowed it to become my truth when it was all deception. Looking back now, I believe that my grandmother felt I was deserving of the gifts. My grandmother's action had nothing to do with me instead it was more about her need for control. At a very young age, I took some of her control over me by working and acquiring things for myself. Therefore, I believe she gave me the gifts as a punishment with the sole purpose of instilling the fear of loss in me to regain that power she felt she had lost. I realize now, I deserved every good gift and good thing that I am given. I must accept that some people give freely and some people give with strings and motives. However, regardless of others' actions, it is no reflection on who I am but a representation of that person's character, heart, and insecurity.

My perception then:	I did not feel a sense of security with my family because I had witnessed too many boundaries that had been crossed. It is my responsibility to provide for myself as a child. I was a burden and a nuisance to my family.
Message:	Mental or Physical Abuse cannot be justified. If you decide to allow children or anyone to reside in your home, make them feel welcomed. The individuals especially children involved usually already feel a sense of abandonment and at your mercy. Young children should be allowed to work but it must be done in moderation. Children deserve and must have the opportunity to behave and interact as children in order to slowly mature as a mentally healthy adult. Giving and then taking away from a child can create a false sense of security and low self-worth.

| How this experience affected my future: | At a very young age, I started relying on myself and only me for my support. I believed that no one had my best interest at heart. I found employment at a young age so I could be financially independent.

If someone did a nice gesture for me I would find a way to pay them back, I was not able to just accept their gesture as a gift or act of kindness.

In conversations that I needed advice, I would always talk fast under the assumption I was wasting the others person valuable time. Subconsciously, I felt as if I was a burden and a nuisance. |
| My perception now: | We all need someone and there are trustworthy people in this world.

There are truly good people that show acts of kindness and expect nothing in return. I believe now that I am not a nuisance; I am an asset. |

CHAPTER

Five
The Facade

During most of my childhood I focused on becoming financially independent so I could depend solely on myself. I often thought about what I could do to change my situation, but I always came up blank. I felt like I had no one. I often questioned my mere existence. All I wanted was for someone to welcome me in their arms, hold me, squeeze me, kiss me, and say I love you. But that never happened, at least, not to me. However, when I would visit my friends, I noticed as their parents pampered them making sure they had everything they needed.

I would witness my friend's parents hug and kiss them and say things like, "be careful", "call me if you need me", and "I love you". Why could I not hear those same words from my family to me? What was wrong with me? When situations like this occurred in my presence I felt like crawling in a corner and withering up. I literally felt like I was dying inside. I envied the love and affection that my friends  received from their parents. And times I wished I could trade places with them but came to internalize the belief that I was the problem therefore even if that happened, they would not love me either.

34

My grandmother did not show us lots of affection, but she did not physically abuse us either. I know you would probably assume so because of the way she treated our mother, but she did not. She yelled a lot, but most parents do. I could deal with that. If my brother and I got a spanking, we probably deserved it. Dealing with physical pain is not my story. What I allowed my Deborah and Dinah take away from me at such a young age was mentally. I allowed them to strip away my self-worth which, in turn, impacted most of my adulthood. They constantly spoke negatively about me in my presence and after a while, I started believing it. As a child when I looked in the mirror all I saw was an ugly little girl with a pale face, big forehead, and buck teeth. It finally started making sense why they did not like me. I could now envision what they saw: an ugly girl. So, during my youth, that is how I viewed myself internally. I always tried to keep a smile on my face in hopes that it would hide some of the ugliness. Because the smile was a façade of being happy therefore my friends and teachers were unable to see that anything was bothering me. So throughout middle and high school, I should have been nominated for best actress in addition to the title that I actually received as best all-around student. I played the role of a lifetime a happy young lady refusing to show anyone how I truly felt on the inside and this continued throughout my adulthood. Those malicious remarks verbalized against me stayed with me and was a primary factor in developing my distorted belief system. How is a belief system formed you ask? A belief system is usually formed by a child's experiences and since in most of my experiences with my family I felt unwanted and unloved I formed the belief that if your own family does not love you then no one else will. So, it was hard to think positive about myself when for the most part of my life I've only heard negative things about me from the people that were my flesh and blood and were supposed to love me. And once my family was no longer able to directly criticize and belittle me, I took over the role of doing it to myself. In the absence of my grandmother and cousin, I started treating myself the way they had treated me. I became my own worst critic. Hannah in my eyes was never good enough, smart enough or pretty enough. And if I ever needed the validation of my inadequacy, those negative comments spoken over me decades ago continued to replay over and over in my head as if they were a broken record. Sometimes I wished my grandmother had just physically beaten me a least I know those wounds would have been healed by now.

I recall this one occasion when I was in elementary school all the kids were outside playing and the adults were sitting on their perspective porches talking and just enjoying a nice summer day. My grandfather, Charles, had an old green pickup truck that he did not drive faster than 10 miles per hour we could walk faster than he drove. On this one particular day, he allowed us, the children in the neighborhood, to ride on the back tailgate of his truck. About five of us were all sitting next to each other laughing, talking and smiling with our little feet hanging down wagging in the wind. And yes, that was fun for us back in the days before video games. Then one of our neighbors told my mom and grandmother that I was dragging my feet on the road which was not true. This lady was known for starting up unnecessary confusion, but back in those days, if another adult told your parent you did something wrong, they asked no questions. You got spanked or some other form of punishment regardless of whether it was true or not. My mom and grandmother told me to get off the truck and come there. I believed that my grandmother was not going to ask me what happen but spank me based on someone else's allegations against me. I obeyed part of my mom and grandmother's request. I got off the truck. But when I got off, I did not approach them. Instead, I started running for what I thought in my little mind was my life. I ran around my grandmother's house past the garden and then around my aunt's house and no one was able to catch me. My mom was pregnant with my brother, Joshua, so she did not even try. I kept running as if my life depended on it. On my second trip around the houses, I was determined I was not going to be caught and be punished for something I did not do. I had made it successfully again around both houses again and no one able to catch me. However, on my third trip around the house, I started wheezing, I had asthma as a child, and I was slowing down, but they were still not able to stop me. I was determined I was not going to get caught. By this time my grandfather had parked his truck and was chopping in his garden and he had been watching me run with all my might. On my fourth trip around I was running on fumes and when I tried to run past the garden my grandfather stuck out his hoe and I ran right into it. I was completely exhausted; tears were running down my face and my heart beating so fast and I had no strength left to try and defend myself. I just knew I was going to get a whipping. My grandmother came over to the garden and picked me up and my grandfather said, "You better not whip that girl!" My grandmother carried me in her house as I cried hysterically in her arms. She did not say anything to me but then something amazing happens. She sat down in a chair with me in her arms holding my head up against her breast and rocked me to sleep. My little heart melted when my grandmother embraced and rocked me in her arms. I felt a sense of affection and security that I had never felt before and immediately I fell asleep. At that moment, I felt a glimpse of hope, was it possible that my grandmother loved me. For the first time, I allow myself to believe there was a possibility that she might like me. I only wish I could have experienced more moments like this with my grandmother. She obviously had it in her to show affection, but something was blocking her from revealing them. After that day, I cannot recall ever having this same feeling again as a child with my grandmother.

People expect others to just read their minds and know how they feel but that is impossible. It's important that we not only articulate how we feel but convey it also. We go through life thinking a person feels a certain way about us, but in truth, they feel differently. I understand that most adults were hurt as young children and mimic those hurts towards others in their adulthood. Others have even openly admitted to me that they treat their children just the way their parents treated them, but that does not make it right or give them justification to treat someone else horribly. If you were a victim of mental or physical abuse, I'm sure that you did not get any pleasure in it so why inflict that same pain on anyone else. It's time that we break these bad habit and curses that have been passed from one generation to another. We need to learn to communicate, listen, and love more. "Love never fails....." (1 Corinthians, 13:8). Why would you want anyone to grow up with an empty space in their heart and miss the greatest gift of all love like I did?

My grandmother was obsessed with keeping a clean house. She would make all of us work and clean up except for my brother, Ishmael. Ishmael had a way with my grandmother he could talk his way out of anything with her. Needless to say, he did not do a lot of cleaning around the house or anything else. In my eyes, he was an up and coming con artist but in a good way. I could remember one day at 4 o'clock in the morning my grandmother was yelling, "Get up, get up every one of you." I looked at the clock and thought to myself only three hours before must get up for school. We all dragged ourselves out of bed, Dinah, Ishmael, and me to see what in the world was so important that we had to get up at this time of the morning. Well, we found out. Unwashed dishes had been left in the sink. I'm not sure whose turn it was to wash dishes because we were accustomed to washing all the dishes up the moment we finished eating.

We were not even allowed to sit and digest the food before we were expected to clean up. So, I am not sure how those dishes were left in the sink. But anyway, she made us participate in washing the dishes, sweeping, vacuuming, dusting, and pretty much cleaning up the entire house. By the time we finished, it was time to get ready for school. I can remember this as if it just happened yesterday. However, in most of my adulthood, I found it hard to just sit down and savor and enjoy a meal. Instead, I ate so fast as if I was inhaling my food because I was so focused on cleaning up afterward. The first time I ever went to sleep leaving dirty dishes again in my sink was when I was in my thirties. At the time when I was young, I never viewed this incident as a positive experience. However, because of this experience as an adult in my workplace, it always taught me to double check and make sure the job I had done was done well. I have my grandmother to thank for this skill that I have today. I only wish that she could have shown us more love amid these great lessons that she taught us. The reverence I would have had for my grandmother if only she had shown some type of affection, positive reinforcement or validation.

During a couple of my childhood years, my grandmother was a bootlegger, a person that sold beer out of her home. My grandmother was the owner, bartender, and bouncer. She was all three in one; she was a woman to be feared and someone to be respected. Grown men feared the presence of my grandmother because they had seen her in action. They had witnessed her grab men with her bare hand by their neck, collar, or whatever she could grasp and throw them out of her house as if they were a bag of trash and not even break a sweat. However, I never feared my grandmother in this way as others did. I think it was because I made up my mind after witnessing her beat my mother that I would not allow her to treat me that way, so I had no fear in that area. I feared more about not being accepted and loved by her. Well, back to my grandmother's profession at the time. Even though we had a lot of traffic in her home we still had the cleanest home on the street, probably even in the town. It was a good thing for me because I discovered as a child, I was allergic to dust and if there was one thing, I was good at and enjoyed doing it was cleaning. Later as an adult, I realized my cleaning behaviors were characteristics of someone with OCD, obsessive-compulsive disorder, but I think I was a mild case. I recall this one guest of my grandmother, named Ms. Hagar that would come over almost daily. She was a really nice, mature, soft-spoken lady but constantly had a cigarette in her hand. I despised the smell of smoke and the sight of ashes. She would make the comment before I can put the ashes from one puff to another in the ashtray, I would have it cleaned and put back. I had become an absolute neatness freak. Mrs. Hagar was really impressed with me. She would always compliment me on how smart and pretty I was in the presence of my grandmother. My grandmother would say do not tell her that before it gets in her head. I could not understand why my grandmother did not want others to compliment me. It was enough that she did not. No matter who would come to my grandmother's home, they would usually say I was a smart and pretty little girl. Again, she would say, do not tell her that she is grown enough already. If only my grandmother could have agreed. I had cleaned up and done everything she had asked me to do, and even did the extras. Almost, every compliment I have ever received from someone in either my grandmother's or cousin's presence was followed by a negative rebuff from them. But it appeared to me after a while I would never do enough to get any praise from them, so I stopped looking for it. So, from that point on when someone attempted to compliment me, I would interrupt them before they could finish the comment. I felt like I just could not win. Every approval I got was always overshadowed by disapproval.

My grandmother did allow me to take part in extracurricular activities. She also let me borrow her car to use to get back and forth to practice and games. She made it clear I could play sports if I kept up my work around the house. So, a typical day for me was getting up in the morning, driving the school bus, picking up students to transport them to school, and then going to class. After school, I would drive the school bus transporting the students back home. Once I got home from school, if laundry was hung out on the line, I would take them in, change my clothes, jump in the car, and drive the 25 minutes to commute back to practice. When I returned home from practice, I would fold up clothes, clean up the kitchen and do my homework. On weekends, we had to clean the house from top to bottom. And after all that was finished, we had to iron all our clothes for the entire school week. Having to complete all these tasks in a short period of time caused me to become very organized and structured. So, throughout my adulthood, it was hard for co-workers to compete with my organizational skills and work ethic. I was usually able to work circles around them. Again, these are other skills I have, thanks to my grandmother, she is one of the reasons I am so structured and organized today.

Another important thing that my grandmother instilled in my life that I am very grateful for is attending church. We had to attend church every Sunday. First and third Sundays we would attend the Baptist Church, second and fourth Sundays we would attend the Methodist Church and if there was a fifth Sunday in the month, we would attend the Holiness Church. I wish I could say I enjoyed going to church every Sunday, but I did not. They did not have children's church like they do today. Maybe if they did, I would have enjoyed it more, instead, the children received the same message as adults. And most of the services the children were fighting hard to stay awake. So, we complained almost every Sunday about having to go, so my grandmother gave us a choice. This is my grandmother using her wisdom at best which she imparted into me. She gave us two choices: the first one, go to church, or the second one, you do not have to go but if you do not go you have to stay inside all day. I recall the Sunday I decided not to go to church, sleeping in until the late hours of the morning. Wow, it felt great. I woke up feeling so refreshed not having to get up so early. I thought to myself this is not such a bad trade-off; I made the right decision. Around noon I got up took a bath, got dressed and ate. Once I finished eating, I looked outside, but the street was bare, and the porches were empty almost everyone in the neighborhood was in church. So, I decided to sit down on the couch and watch a little television, but nothing was really on. Back in my days we only had five television channels to choose from at the time they had not incorporated cable or satellite television. But later that afternoon church was over, and everyone had returned home. Ishmael came in, changed his clothes and then ran right back outside to play. A few minutes passed, and I looked out the front screened window and saw Ishmael, Tamar, Absalom, and other kids from our neighborhood outside playing. My face was pressed up against the screen door watching every move they made and trying to listen to everything that they said. Then a little more time passed and Tamar and Tabitha came over to find out why I was still in the house. They were all curious as to why I was not outside playing with them. I explained the trade-off I had made by not going to church and they both just shook their heads. They felt sorry for me, but they knew when my grandmother said something, she meant business. So, Tamar said, "Tabitha, we better leave before Mrs. Deborah makes us go in the house." So, they left and went back to playing with the other children. Afterward I just continued to watch them play through the window and thought about the choice I had made. This ended up being a pretty miserable day for me. All rested up with nothing to do. I would have freely traded off a spanking to get outside and play that day. As I continued to look out the screen window watching them play, the degree of the fun they were having seemed comparable to a day at Disney World in my eyes. I regretted ever making the choice to stay home over attending church. That was the last day that I ever missed church intentionally. The memories and lessons of that day still reside in me today. Now, even as an adult, if I do not go to church, I find it difficult to leave home and partake in any other activities that day.

On Saturdays, sometimes I would help my grandmother clean the church for a little extra cash. While cleaning up I would play around: imitate singing, playing piano and preaching. I did it all. I know I sounded horrible singing and playing piano, but I did not let that stop me. But I thought I did well on my mini-sermons. One of the elderly ladies in the church even encouraged me to keep singing and playing the piano stating that God might bless me one day with the gift. I just smiled. It never happened but I kept trying, anyway. It's a funny thing, my grandmother, just let me be me when I was in church. She never really said anything about me acting like a drama queen. But I really enjoyed helping my grandmother clean up. I believe subconsciously I was still trying to get her approval. One Saturday, as I was cleaning the podium, inside the bible I came across a poem that reminded me about the day I stayed home from church. I wanted to memorize it so I could recite it in front of the whole church on a Sunday. It was important to me that both parents and children heard it because of my experience. Every Saturday that I helped clean the church I memorized a little bit. It only took a few Saturdays before I had the entire poem memorized. I still can recite it to this day, "Mary Had A Little Boy." The author is unknown, but these are the words to the poem.

Mary had a little boy, His soul seemed white as snow. He never
went to Sunday School,
"Cause" Mary wouldn't go!
He missed the Bible stories, That thrill the childish mind. While other
children went to class,
This boy was left behind.
As he grew from babe to youth, Mary, to her dismay saw the soul that
once seemed white,
Was turning dingy gray.

Knowing now that he was lost, She tried to win him back. Alas,
the soul of the boy she loved, Had turned an ugly black.

Now Mary goes to Sunday School And stays for preaching too. She begs
and begs the preacher "Isn't there something you can do?"
He tries and fails, and then he says, "We're just too far behind." "You
warned me years ago," she said, "But I would pay no mind."
And so another soul is lost, That once seemed white as snow. He
would have gone to Sunday School, But Mary wouldn't go!

This poem is so true in many ways. Going to Sunday school every
Sunday laid the foundation for me as a child. As an adult, I stayed away
from the church for a few years because a part of me had lost hope. But
because I had been grounded in the word of God in Sunday school, I was
able to find my way back.

I only wished my grandmother knew how to show me, love. She
taught me so many important lessons and skills over the years that could
have left me with a good impression of her but all the things she did was
overshadowed by her need for control and her inability to show love and
affection. My grandmother taught me how to can grape jelly, apple jelly,
and peaches. For all those that do not know what canning is, it is making
and preserving food in a can or jar. What I loved most was when she
allowed me to clean the hogs after just being slaughtered. We would store
up plenty of meat from the hogs like a pork chop, tender loin, bacon,
sausage, liver pudding, and so on. I loved to try new things. I always took
the job no one else wanted, which was cleaning the chitterlings. People
did not like to clean the chitterlings because of the smell and they often
complained it was hard to get them cleaned. But I loved a challenge and
I would always take the job every chance I got. She taught me how to
bake cakes at seven years old along with remodeling rooms. When the
bar needed to be torn down in our house, we did it. When the vanity and
commodes needed to be changed out, we did it. When ceiling fans had
to be changed, we did it. If the walls in the house need to be painted, we
did it. Whatever needed to be done we did it. Now as an adult, there is no
task in my home that I am afraid of tackling. In my first home, I changed
out the vanity and commode, put up ceiling fans, installed light fixtures
and removed and sanded down the wallpaper, and painted all by myself.
In my second home, I painted most of the rooms in my house, installed
the garbage disposal, installed ceiling fans, changed out dryer plugs and
assembled most of the furniture. And when my friends needed something
done in their homes, they would call me. I had become a jack of all trades.
These are other skills that I learned from staying with my grandmother.

But I was never able to appreciate them because of the resentment that I carried in my heart for her always putting me down. I felt more like Cinderella with the evil stepmother but in my case grandmother.

Prior to my grandmother's homegoing, she deeply desired to be shown love and affection from her offspring. Yet she never showed any of these feelings toward us. However, she expected us to demonstrate those emotions towards her. How did she know if we are even capable of it? Where were we supposed to learn it from? It's not like she illustrated it. During the writing of this book, it became evident to me that my grandmother had also been exposed to negative experiences in her childhood which shaped her into the adult who didn't show love and affection. It had been passed from one generation to another generation. I believe with those deep-seated emotions; it was difficult for my grandmother to just get over her feelings and show affection without any acknowledgment or treatment. It's obvious that my grandmother had not formed the secure attachments necessary for healthy development in a child, therefore, preventing her from passing them on to us. Instead, she passed on what she had learned. She portrayed the common symptoms in the attachment style, fearful-avoidant. The fearful-avoidant attachment style is characterized by a negative view of self and a negative view of others. Those who fall into this category view themselves as unworthy and undeserving of love. Additionally, they feel that others are unworthy of their love and trust because they expect that others will reject or hurt them. Given their negative view of self and their view that others are bound to hurt them, those with a fearful-avoidant attachment style tend to avoid close involvement with others in order to protect themselves from anticipated rejection (Bartholomew, 1991).

As I wrote the above paragraph my blind eye was opened; the spiritual eye. It was like a flash of light came into my presence and lifted a weight of me. All those years when I was a child and I felt like my grandmother did not love me were all cleared in that one moment. She was only mimicking what she learned as a child. I began to wonder how she must have felt as a little girl and the pain she must have endured growing up. And I started pondering these questions in my heart. Did anyone show her love and affection? Was she complimented or made to feel important? Who was there for her when she needed someone? My grandmother was a product of her environment and she did the best she knew how to. The only way she knew how to show her love was to be stern with us and give us the skills we needed to survive in life.

There was no possible way that she could have given us what she did not have. People may say she could have treated her children better than she was treated but here is the problem with that: Yes, we can all change and not imitate the lessons learned from our environment, but first we must realize that we have an issue and need to change. Most people are blinded by their own deficiencies and never come to the realization that they need to be transformed. Now, I can truly admire my grandmother for who she is. A black woman that lived in a time black people still faced a lot of oppression and she raised her children to be polite, hard-working, God-fearing adults. Yes, she has many faults and flaws, as we all do. But she did a great job with what she had to work with and that is something to be admired. It's important that we do not go through our entire life focusing on the negative outlooks and disregarding the positive ones. The experiences in my life that I once viewed as a disadvantage, I now, interpret as an advantage. For instance, all experiences that involved my grandmother that I once viewed as negative and the ones that I viewed as positive, the truth is an event or experience in life is neutral, however, how you look at it that makes it a negative or positive one.

My perception then:	I grew up believing that I was unimportant unworthy of unconditional love. I placed focus on financial stability and put value in others rather than myself.
Message:	Adults understand the power you have over your children. Words have power, use them to build and not to destroy your children's hope. Wisdom presented in animosity is never well received. If you want your child to learn and respect the life lessons you are trying to teach them it is vital that parents and guardians not only show discipline but love and affection also.
How this experience affected my future:	I viewed myself through other people eyes. I allowed my insecurities to dictate my actions which created more doubt and uncertainty. My success in life is a result of the skills I developed and the lessons I learned through life.
My perception now:	The business sense that I possess today was honed indirectly from daily experiences taken from my grandmother's parenting skills. My grandmother was a product of her environment and imitated the experiences she had been exposed to. She gave us the necessary tools and skills in life for survival. I can attribute many of my skills to my upbringing. It was the structure that allowed me to achieve success as an adult. People are not perfect and experiences are neutral. It's how you view the situation that makes it positive or negative. Positivity is all around us we just have to adjust our focus to it.

CHAPTER

$\mathcal{S}ix$
Pointless

From junior high throughout high **school**, I played sports every season. During the Fall I played volleyball. **Winter**, I played basketball. **And in** the spring, I played softball. It became evident to me during junior high that basketball would be my sport of choice. I became interested in sports at a very young age. I was five years old when I began watching my Uncle Haman play basketball. Nothing could be more exciting than being at an event and the person performing is someone in a **close** relationship with you. He was a point guard and I regarded him as a superstar. I was excited on the nights that we had home games because I knew I would get a chance to see my uncle in action. On game days from the time I woke up until I arrived at the gymnasium my little heart felt so much enthusiasm. In my **eyes**, he was undeniably the greatest uncle and basketball player in the world. I was so proud that he was related to me and I wanted everyone to know that he was my uncle.

Before the games even started the noise was so loud that you could hardly hear yourself thinking in anticipation of the players running out of the locker room. It was such a thrilling experience for me. The cheerleaders were cheering and holding the newly made banner with the bulldog mascot drawn on it. The banner that I'm sure it took the artist days to create would be torn into pieces in less than a few seconds. We could hear the bulldogs barking and it was only a matter of time before they would run out of the locker room. Then the moment we had all waited for, my uncle leading the pack breaking, running through the beautifully made banner. As my uncle and the rest of the team set up for warm-ups, I would jump up and down on the sidelines with so much excitement in my little body. I could remember waving my hands and hollering his name, "Uncle Haman, Uncle Haman" so he would know I was there to cheer him on. At that moment, no one could have stolen my joy even if they tried. My uncle had skills he could dribble, pass and shoot the ball very well. Throughout the entire game, I stood up and cheered with the cheerleaders every chance I got. Each game I would go through the same routine, running up and down the bleachers, waving my hands, calling my uncle's name and cheering as he ran up and down the court. And when he made a shot or made a fancy pass or stole the ball you would have thought I had lost my mind the way I was screaming and hollering. Watching my uncle Haman play gave me such a rush. When the game was almost over, I would go and sit on the bottom bleacher waiting for the buzzer to go off to end the game. And once that buzzer went off, nothing or no one could stop me from running to jump on my uncle. You talk about being a happy little girl, there are truly no words to describe how I felt during those games and the moments in my uncle's arms. I left the basketball games with the impression that I would become a cheerleader when I grew up. I could hardly wait to become a Freetown Bulldog cheerleader, or so I thought. But that dream would never come into fruition. A few years later our high school was closed, and we had to merge with another high school, Reigning High which already had their mascot, the Mustang. So, my dreams of becoming a Bulldog would never transpire.

My first impression of Reigning High School was that their basketball players looked like giants. I was a little afraid of our schools having to merge. And now with the redistricting of seven different communities attending the same school being transported took a long time just to get there. I wondered if I would have to focus on my education or my security. The rivalry between the two schools was undisputable and now they expected us to socialize and learn all under the same roof. At Freetown High School, everyone knew everyone, we all lived in the same small town, and it was truly like family. No one really wanted to make the transition. It would still be a few years before I would be in high school, but I had family that had already merged. So, this allowed me the opportunity to experience the ambiance of the school before I enrolled. I would attend most of the athletic events there watching Dinah play basketball. Once I started attending the events, I realized that Reigning High School was also a family-oriented school just with a lot more family members. And a lot of the students at Reigning High School worked with their parents and friends on farms to help with harvesting for their family's source of income. So, we all ended up being more alike than different and together we created a strong sense of confidence. Our school may not have had the most updated facility; and may not be in an ideal location or had only an enrollment of about 600 students but what we had there that superseded other schools was pride. There was something about Reigning pride. It had an aura that other students would envy and desire. In retrospect, I have come to learn that the biggest obstacle we all face in life is usually resistance to change. It's amazing how illusions can create such a false sense of reality so instead of fearing the unknown I feel it is important to embrace it with expectations.

Now, Dinah was playing basketball and she was just as good as my uncle and only 5'4 in height. She was the Mustangs' shooting guard she could dribble, block, rebound, and shoot. She wore the number 25 on her Mustang's jersey. I never wanted to miss a game. It was something to see when those women come out of the locker room. They did not perform like typical women, they played like men. These women could steal the ball, pass, shoot, dribble, rebound and some could almost dunk. They were the defending champions and they played hard non-stop throughout every game. I was so proud to say that Dinah was my cousin, even though I did not feel the feelings were mutual. She scored double digits in points and rebounds almost every game night. My family would all cheer her on. I would sit on the bottom bleacher so I could get a good look at every move so I could rehearse the moves later. By this time, I had realized I wanted to be a basketball player instead of a cheerleader. In junior high, I would play basketball during the girl's game and I would cheer at half time during the boy's games. How I was able to cheer is absolutely hilarious to me now because I have absolutely no rhythm. So, it was not a hard decision for me to choose basketball as my sport of choice. Anyway, I could hardly wait to get to high school and be just like Dinah. I wanted to hear those same cheers for me. After each game, I would brag to my friends about my cousin's stats for that night, and I told them I was going to do the same thing when I got there.

Dinah was only four years older than me, so she graduated one year from high school then that following year I started high school. A couple of months after I started high school it was time for basketball tryouts. On my first day at basketball tryouts, I told the coach that I had to have my cousin's number before I had even made the team. Another player was also interested in the number. I explained to the coach that the number had a lot of sentimental value to me and I had to have it. Well, he stated that I had to make the team first. So, each practice I would go the extra mile. I would run harder and exercise harder because I was determined to make the team and earn Dinah's respect. I know I had to go up against some hard contenders with me being a freshman and last year players already had their starting positions, but I did not allow that to deter me. Finally, after weeks of extra training, the practice paid off and I made the team. I was so excited about making the team, but not for the reasons most people would think. I knew how much my Dinah revered the sport of basketball and the great athletes she played along with and against. I concluded that if I made the team and became a great player then I would be able to penetrate her heart and I would finally get her approval and she would love me.

It was the day I had been anticipating. We were going to get our assigned jerseys. I was full of anxiety and my heart was palpitating I did not know how this day would end. My coach had no idea how important it was that I had my cousin's jersey but for me, it was a matter of life or death. I had concluded that if I did not get Dinah's number our relationship was as good as dead, and it would be impossible for me to get her validation. As I stood there waiting to get my jersey, my mind was racing with thoughts. The most memorable being that this is my last opportunity to prove to my cousin that I was worthy of being loved. My heart was racing as he threw out the jersey to the first five starters, but none had the number 25. So, still shaking I had made it past the first hurdle, thinking to myself if I do not get this jersey, I am doomed. Finally, he called my name and I could see in his hand a jersey which number was not the number 25. He imitated throwing me the jersey he had in his hand, and I was overwhelmed with the feeling of failure. I thought to myself, I will never get Dinah's approval now. Then suddenly, my coach said, just kidding, and he threw me the number 25. My sad face brightened up as if I had won the lottery. Now I had a chance to change everything. There was no possible way she could still hate me now. All I would have to do now is be the best player on the team and it would be impossible for her not to think highly of me then.

My freshman year I started as the sixth man. The sixth man means that when a starter comes out of the game, I was the first player to go on the court. My first game, I cannot recall any of my family members coming. It was just the first game. I had plenty more and I was sure they would attend. As I continued to play, I earned starting position in my freshman year and remained as a starter until I graduated. Each game, I would look up in the stands and not one of my blood relatives was there to cheer me on. However, by this time I had a lot of other fans cheering for me, my classmates, my friends, and their families. My family members never found the time to come out and support me. My mother had just recently gotten saved and the members of her church told her it was not Christian-like to go to basketball games. My uncle's job required him to work second and third shift, which conflicted with most of my games or I know he would have been there. Dinah was just living her life, no different than most young people in their twenties. I really did not expect my grandmother to come, I cannot recall if she went to my uncle or cousin's games either. My grandfather was too sick by this time to get out. But I would look in the stands and see my teammate's relatives standing up and cheering for each of them. I would just use my imagination and envision that the people in the stands cheering were my relatives.

As games and years went by, I could no longer put forth the effort that I had previously given to this game and I no longer tried to be acknowledged by my family. The gratification that came with receiving the trophies and rewards was nullified. It was during my last year in high school that a part of me gave up on being accepted and I conceded to defeat. I felt like my family whom I looked to for approval for all these years had abandoned, discarded, and just deserted me. My self-esteem slumped even lower. And this brought about an almost dramatic change in my life which would be one of the most powerful illusions that would drastically alter my belief system. I had tried for years to get validated by family members but time after time unknowingly they rejected me and my desire for their approvals. Afterward, I internalized their rejections and began to doubt my personal worth and I started undermining my own view of myself. During my adulthood, I emerged as my greatest enemy and I judged myself more harshly than the toughest critic. Nothing I did was ever good enough; it was almost impossible for me to give myself credit. I often criticized myself for being what I perceived as incompetent and inadequate. Satan had recognized this weakness within me and used it to distract me to derail my future. I had allowed the devil to infiltrate my mind and exploit one of my deepest insecurities and he played me like a puppet. For years the devil was able to manipulate my every move, the access I had given him gave him the power to create even more inner self-destruction. The confidence and joy I once embodied as a young girl were now personified by a woman who exemplified traces of insecurity, low self-esteem, depression, anxiety, and uncertainty.

Basketball was not the only thing I gave up on in life. Every other challenge that I would face, from that point on, would be dealt same manner, but not consciously. I was not aware that the same decision I had made about basketball years ago would directly affect every other situation I would encounter in my adult life. When I found myself at the pivotal point in life when it was time to go to the next level, I felt restricted by this unknown force. Subconsciously, I felt like it was pointless making an effort to achieve anything with the hope of being commended. My conscious mind was not even aware that I was doing this. Others may look at my situation and say I did achieve a lot of goals in life but there was more to the story. The accomplishments that I had made in life required little effort on my behalf, so I do not take credit for them. All those abilities came naturally to me because they were gifts from God. God had blessed me with the ability to do a lot of things so naturally, that anything I did within my gifting I was great at it. However, when I would be faced with situations that were not in my gifting, the insecurity that had been created within me prevented me from even trying. I would not even allow myself to pursue the opportunity. Subconsciously, I was holding on to the belief that hard work, dedication, and persistence would never lead to validation or approval, so it was useless putting in so much effort. This had become my new belief system, my new way of thinking. Satan had temporary achieved his purpose intent in my life to disapprove of myself and once he accomplished that the power of influence God had given me would be silenced. How could I ever inspire or encourage anyone else if I felt inadequate myself? Therefore, if I continued with this mindset, I would never fulfill my destiny and acquire the blessings that God had in store for me.

Graduation day, another memorable day for me, that added fuel to the already blazing fire. I was the president of my class and had served in the position for all four years of high school. I was so nervous about having to give the final speech for our graduating class, but I was proud to do it. My family came and my cousins, Anna's immediate family came also. My cousin, Anna had moved from Upstate and stayed with us for her last year of school and she was also graduating. I was happy that most of my family members had shown up to share this day with me after them having a non-existent presence during most of my high school years. Despite them not being there in my past I was excited about them being there on this day. I thought to myself, maybe I had been unfair to my family and all those thoughts and feelings I had for them all these years were not warranted and only a distortion of my imagination. For a few short moments, I was able to experience the feeling of being honored and valued and a glimpse of hope surfaced in my heart but those feeling would be short-lived. Abruptly, my feelings were interrupted and ruined by the lack of thought and consideration by my family members. No one in my family thought enough of me to savor this day for me by bringing a camera. The class president and the overall best student, MVP in basketball and volleyball, and an upcoming freshman at the University at Chapel Hill was not worth the cost of a disposable camera. This was long before the invention of cell phones with cameras. My cousin, Anna's mother, who was my great aunt, was obviously proud of her. She took picture after picture of Anna and pictures of us together but the glow on my great aunt's face was electrifying. So, on my very last day of high school for a few moments, I felt like I was important to my family but then reality came full circle those feelings of being insignificant and worthlessness surfaced, and they were more powerful this time.

Reflecting, God's presence was always with me and he was supporting my every endeavor. He put me in positions and ensured that I excelled and shined for everyone to see. God had protection over me which prohibited anyone from seeing the emotional turmoil that was on the inside of me. I was unknowingly anointed by God. Because of the glory of his presence in my life others perceived me as a strong and confident individual. I was so caught up in the emotional pain that I only focused on what I was not getting in life; validation and approval from my family. I never stopped for a moment to focus on all the great things I was already capable of doing on my own without even having their validation. God had already given me everything that I needed to succeed but I was just too blind to see. My success was never a consequence of their approval instead it is a result of self-validation and God's approval. I discovered in my adulthood that I was giving too much attention to the negative things that I never stopped to appreciate the good things.

I got so caught up in looking for external forces to complete me that I overlooked the fact that I already had everything within me. God had anointed me at a very young age and given me all the confidence and abilities I needed to strive in life. But because of other people's treatment I allowed my emotions to consume and distract me from appreciating all the good that encompassed me. Instead, I surrendered my confidence and minimized my talents to fit the expectations others had of me. For years I had lost my confidence, joy and hope all because of lack of validation. Validation for a child is extremely vital and will likely result in him or her being able to self-validate and walk in confidence in adulthood. And a child without validation will likely end up seeking approval from the wrong people.   From my childhood to my youth, I made good grades, was respected by my peers, favored by my teachers, and excelled in sports, member of student council, invited to college summer academic programs, worked at the Governor's Mansion, and so on. So, my family members were unaware of my need for validation and approval. It was impossible for them to address my issues because God had blessed me in everything, I attempted, so there were no obvious signs of distress only signs of success. I guess in their eyes I did not need any help because I was doing fine on my own. I never complained to them about how I was feeling. I just internalized it. I really did not feel like anyone cared enough so I just kept it to myself. So, I asked, why would God allow me to be treated this way? God made it clear to me that he was my direct source for communication and the only validations that I needed would come from him. I was sent here for His purpose and my purpose would be carried out without external influences and if he had allowed my family members to validate me, I would have been emotionally vulnerable to them and then probably incapable of fulfilling my destiny.

"There are certain core needs shared by every person on the planet," stated the article "Who Needs Approval?" on advancedlifeskills. com. "Some of the needs are physical such as food, water, and air. We also have emotional needs. Once our physical needs are met, filling our core emotional needs becomes our number one priority in life. Whether we choose to acknowledge it or not, the desire for validation is one of the strongest motivating forces known to man." From the time we are born we seek validation. There are two types of validations, internal and external validation. Internal validations are validations in which you demonstrate a sense of high self-esteem and confidence and you recognize your value and your worth. External validations are validations you desire from others.

Sequentially, external validations expose your emotional vulnerability and cause you to relinquish your uniqueness and self-worth to others. Children require external validations from their parents. Children that received validation from their parents tend to foster more confidence and tend to be mentally and socially strong adults not vulnerable to changing waves of external validations. Children that lack validation, on the other hand, tends to suffer from low self-esteem, sense of unworthiness and ultimately self-disapproval. These children, in their adulthood constantly seek out external validations but due to their own self-disapproval no external force of validation will be able to change that person's image of themselves and no matter how much they achieve in life it will never be enough. And adults who have no internal sense of worth who depend on external validations for approval are often in for a rude awakening, this is the blueprint for being a miserable and an unhappy adult.

In order to take back control of my life, I developed my own self-worth by learning to self-validate. This is not an easy task to complete however we are all worth the effort. Combined with living in the spirit and believing, here are a few steps used to assist in the process of validating myself.

- Start valuing myself and stop judging myself.
- Use positive words to describe myself.
- Set goals that I want to accomplish.
- Participate in the activities I enjoy.
- Build a healthy and loving relationship with my inner child.
- Give myself a pat on the back for tasks and jobs done well.
- Look in the mirror and smile at myself.
- Treat myself to something special.
- Boast to myself about me.
- Have an expectation of being blessed.
- Focus on my talents and gifts.
- Counter all negative thoughts with positive ones.
- Treat others the way that I want to be treated.

These are just a few things that I made as a daily practice that accelerated my growth in creating my own self-worth and transforming my mindset.

My perception then:	No matter how hard I tried it was never good enough. My accomplishments were never acknowledged or complimented, therefore, higher achievement was pointless.
Message:	Children must be validated and approved. Children need continuous affirmation, support, and encouragement from childhood until they reach the age of adulthood. If given to them throughout their childhood, the child is more likely to have self-confidence when they become an adult. These children will also have the ability to self-validate when they reach maturity. However, children who lack validation will more likely possess traits such as low self-esteem, sense of unworthiness, self-disapproval and they may also lack self-confidence which will carry over into their adulthood. Everyone needs someone to support, encourage and make them feel important.

How this experience affected my future:	I had accomplished many goals in my adulthood but when I would get to a pivotal point I would not put in the effort to try harder to achieve the next level. I was holding on to the belief that hard work, dedication, and persistence would never lead to validation or approval so putting in any effort was pointless if there would be no positive outcome. Subconsciously, I felt it was pointless trying to make an effort when it would never be commended.
My perception now:	Those experiences were just a trick of the enemy to distort my thoughts and deter me from operating in my purpose. Life experiences are supposed to make us wiser and stronger not weaker. God will supply and restore anything that I had lacked or did not receive during my childhood. Giving up is no longer an option for me. My family was unaware of how much their validation and approval meant to me. I believe because of my achievements they believe I was strong and confident and didn't need attention.

CHAPTER

Seven
The Landlord

The very next week after graduation I traveled to UNC Chapel and enrolled into the summer bridge program. This program allowed new freshmen a head start with taking classes and getting familiarized with campus life before the fall semester would begin. I just knew my family would finally be proud of me because my grades had been good enough to get into a great college. I had been accepted into one of the largest and best universities in the country. I was proud of myself coming from a school of fewer than 600 students attending a university with over 20,000 plus students. I remember my freshman year the fall when all new freshmen had arrived. Now I'm here at one of the most prestigious colleges in North Carolina and flat broke because I did not have a chance to work and save money because I had attended the summer program at UNC. But I knew in a matter of a few weeks that my financial aid would come through and sustain me for a few months.

However, before the semester would end, I would be on limited funds. I would go home on holidays and sometimes on the weekends but none of my family members would offer me any financial support, so I did not bother to ask. I just could not bear being let down anymore. However, I witnessed a totally different relationship with my roommate and college friends and their parents. When my roommates and college friends would return from home, I would notice that their parents and families accompanied them back to the campus. Their families would help them lug up into their dormitory rooms all their food, supplies and clothing they had purchased for them. And then they'd inquire if they needed anything else. And when their parents would depart, they would give them a long warm embrace with kisses and a mandate that they call if they needed anything. I witnessed this year after year happening for my roommates and friends. It was during those years that I allowed the spirits of self-pity and envy to set up and residence in my heart. I desired to have relationships with my parents like the relationships with their parents. I wanted to experience the love and attention that was being shown to my roommates and friends.

For the next three years, I supported myself with a part-time job, which was only a few hours a week, and credit cards, once the financial aid ran out. When I maxed out my first credit card, I got a second one to pay for the first. Once I maxed both the first and second card, I got a third to pay for the first and the second card. Then once all three cards were maxed, I got a fourth to pay for the first, second and third card. Now I had reached my limit with all the credit cards. The only option I thought I had was to ask my family. So, I arranged a way home one weekend hoping someone would give me enough money just to buy some food, hygiene products and to wash my laundry. I visited both my mother and grandmother and neither of them offered me a penny. The four-hour round-trip home yielded no fruit. I was now worst off than when I started. I arrived back at my dormitory with tears in my eyes, trying to figure out why God would allow my family to treat me in such a way. What had I done so wrong to deserve this? What was wrong with me? I thought I cannot hold them accountable if I have not even asked. I said to myself, "Hannah, give them one more chance." So, I gathered the nerve and I contacted both my mother and grandmother explaining to them the issues I was facing in college and that I needed their help. My mother just listened without really a word. My grandmother told me to drop out and come back home and get a job at the town shirt factory. There was no way that I was going to return home. I felt like I had no home or real family. I was merely a lost soul with no one to turn to for guidance or help, not even God. I just wanted to disappear into thin air. I had become so bitter and defeated that I allowed my emotions to consume me. And it was around this time that I allowed the spirits of resentment, rejection, and confusion to set up residency in my heart.

During my three years, not only was I a student facing tough class schedules, demanding professors, and financial debt, I had become the landlord for self-pity, envy, resentment, rejection, and confusion with no profit in return. Once I became the landlord for these spirits, I was blinded from seeing the truth; I saw only what these spirits wanted me to see. They helped me focus on every negative situation and circumstance in my life that had occurred. They convinced me that I would never be validated or approved so there was no point for me to keep trying or wasting my time. They provided me with supporting evidence by making me revisit all my childhood memories and now my current experience of getting into a prestigious college with no encouragement or support. These spirits had proven their case in my mind. Once they had control of my mind, I was like I was a string puppet with absolutely no control of my emotions. I did not have the capability to make a rational decision regarding my situation. I started making one bad decision after another while in college. My will to succeed had been taken captive by these evil spirits that had taken residence in my heart and control of my mind. I could no longer encourage myself and my grades dropped so much that I had to quit even though I had only one year left to complete my degree at UNC-Chapel Hill.

My college years should have been some of my best experiences in my life such as gaining new friendships, enrolling in new activities, joining clubs, attending games and events and most of all completing my degree. Instead for me it was just another place to try and fit in and survive. In college I felt like a whale out of water even with the opportunity within my grasp, I did not have the inner strength to force myself to go just a little longer and not give up. It would have been great to receive the validation and approval from my family, but I really did not need it to succeed. God had already equipped me with all the skills that I needed to be a success, but I chose to focus on what I did not have and gave in to self-pity. I wasted a lot of time and energy focusing on the negative things that were going on in my life while I was in college. I was so consumed with getting some type of validation that I lost focus on my true goal which was to get my degree and become the first in my family to finish college. I never even gave myself credit for getting into such a prestigious university. I was so busy seeking for everyone else to validate me and I had not even validated myself which is not an easy task if you do not know what that looks like. However, I should have focused more on the positive factors in my life such as the fact that I was smart enough to get into UNC, I had received some financial aid, my tuition, room, and board was paid, I have a lot of skills to make money on the side, and I'm a survivor. I believe with all my heart that if I had focused on these positive things in my life that God would have open doors for me to finish college. And why do I believe this? Because in my adulthood when I finally comprehended and executed this revelation, God had allowed good things to happen in my life that originally appeared impossible to me.

I was now officially a college dropout, a real failure in my eyes. I was now convinced that my family did not care for my well-being at all and that they didn't care if I was alive or dead. I felt like I had no real family, no real home to return to, and I was all I had in the world. I did not want to return home and face the people in my town that had so many high expectations for me. I just wanted to disappear as if I never existed. I hated that I was ever born. I was broken, afraid, and I had no clue as to where I wanted to go to from this point. Home was not an option for me. I could not bear the thought of being hurt anymore believing it would have pushed me off the edge. My only chance of redemption was to run and get away as far as possible from home. My plan was to not return until had I become a success. This was when I opened the door for more tenants to include the spirits of guilt, shame, and loneliness to set up residence in my heart also.

This was when I made the decision to try and find success in another state. I had a brother named Seth that lived in the city and he said that I could come and live with him and his wife, Priscilla. Seth and I had the same father, lived in the same town, went to the same school but grew up in different homes. This opportunity was my chance to keep my failure a secret until I could redeem myself. So, I packed my clothes in my white Mustang GT and set out for the 11-hour trip. As I was driving down the highway, I thought about the day I purchased my mustang and how excited I was to get my childhood dream car. My mother and stepfather Nathan had co-signed for me to get it. I was happy they had really come through for me this time. I started reflecting on when I knew the Mustang was my dream car. It was back when I was living my fairytale life. Jonathan had purchased my mom a 67 green Mustang as a gift. I thought it was the most beautiful car in the world and I fell in love with the car on the spot. I was only about 6 or 7 years old, but I knew what I wanted, and I had to have this car. I asked Jonathan if he could buy me a Mustang when I was old enough to drive and he said, "yes, baby." I did not doubt him for a moment. I believed with all my heart that he would buy me one because he loved me and he had proven that, but I was so wrong. I thought about how naïve and stupid I must have been. I had believed in someone and trusted my own feelings, and I had ended up setting myself up for harm, therefore, I deserved to suffer. I was at fault, but I had no intentions of allowing anyone to get that close to me again.

My thoughts began to change as I arrived in the city thinking that the change in environment would make all the world of difference and this would be a fresh slate. But I had no idea what I was in for. After a few weeks of being there, I realized I had left a state where I could greet a person with a smile or wave and their response was usually welcomed and precipitated to a state where people would retort the same gesture with an unwelcoming, antisocial, and snobbish reaction. I felt like an outsider. I was used to being friendly and cordial towards people, but I found that here an act of kindness was depicted as an invitation to deceitfulness. I had to make the best of this. I had no other choice in my mind, and if I failed at least I would fail where no one knew me. I was more than determined to make this opportunity work or die trying. And that was exactly what almost happened.

My first challenge was to find a job and I did so within a short period of time. I was hired to along with several others to open a Home Improvement Store that had just recently been built. The store was completely empty except for shelves. I was hired alongside 29 other ladies. Our job was to stock all the items on the shelves and label them. The supervisor let us know on the first day of work that one of us would be selected as the fourth head cashier, three other head cashiers were already veterans in the company. So, realizing that I had an opportunity to be a lead cashier and make more money I knew the plan of action I would put into place. I would come to work and give 110 percent. I never slacked off and never missed a day of work like some of the other employees. But I found myself being resented by the other ladies. I had previously tried to build a rapport with them, but they were distant and appeared uninterested in building a friendship. However, there were a few associates that I would converse with, but I remained focused on doing my job and doing it well. The lesson my grandmother had taught me years ago dealing with the dishes in the sink was a constant reminder to make sure I completed my job and did it well. And I did just that. We could finally see the results of all our hard work; the store was almost completely stocked. We were less than one week from opening and it was rewarding day. I can remember so vividly sitting on the bleachers in the store wondering in excitement about the award I would get. The supervisor called out the first award and that co-worker's face lit up like a light bulb. The supervisor called the second award and that co-worker's face appeared to be even brighter. The supervisor called out the third award and I was sure this was going to be mine but again it was another co-worker. And you could see their excitement also as they cheered running down the bleachers. The supervisor called out the fourth award, my name was not verbalized. Then the fifth award was announced and there still was no mention of my name. The last and final award would surely be mind, I thought. I knew my work was impeccable and could not possibly go unnoticed. The last name was announced, and it was not mine. Disillusioned by what had just occurred, the thoughts, "You got nothing" ran through my mind repeatedly like a broken record. I was so disappointed that I felt like I had been cheated out of something again. How could I have been overlooked? I had worked so hard; I knew my work ethic was untouchable. I had worked harder, put in more forth more effort and had remained focused until the very last day. All I could think about now was getting out of sight fast because the floodgates of tears would not be held for much longer. I did not want anyone to see the disappointment on my face, so I hurried towards the bathroom to regain my composure. As I approached the bathroom door, I could hear voices, so I immediately changed my frown and put up a smile, I had practiced this for years. I did not want them to see my disappointment. Two of the women in the bathroom were the veteran head cashiers. I walked in and greeted both ladies and then proceeded towards the stall. I could not get to the stall fast enough. I did not know how much longer I could hold back the tears. But before I could make it into the bathroom stall, one of the head cashiers smacked her lips and with a tone of discontent and said, "Hannah! You know you are the other head cashier, right?" I responded no, I did not. I heard what she said but in her delivery of the news, she minimized the position and the honor associated with it. Now, instead of rejoicing and focusing on the fact that I had the head cashier position, I focused on how she delivered it to me. I had been rewarded with the position based on my hard work which should have felt like a great achievement being selected from a pool of 30 women, but because of the way it was presented to me, I allowed it to discredit my accomplishment and dampen my spirit.

God had already equipped me with everything I needed to succeed but, I was too focused on looking for external recognition to appreciate it. I had believed my work ethic was untouchable; I had worked harder and put forth more effort so regardless of anyone else's acknowledgment I should have applauded myself. God expects us to compliment ourselves whether others commend us or not, and whether we are rewarded or not. I was still seeking validation, trying to find someone, anyone who would agree I was worthy. Constant validation from outside sources can be very disturbing. The need for these validations empowered others to control me. It is important that we all learn to self-validate and compliment ourselves, and in turn, we will establish an internal structure within that is not easily swayed by others coupled with the lack of appreciation or acknowledgment.

The living arrangements were not going so well with Seth and me. His brother-in-law, Peter and I were around the same age and he knew I did not know a lot about the different parts of the city. He agreed to help me explore the neighborhoods to become better acquainted with traveling around the areas. Later, I discovered that Peter had a girlfriend named Delilah, with whom he had two children and that they had a turbulent relationship. I finally met Delilah and during our first encounters, she appeared to be pleasant and forthcoming. We met at Peter parent's house. We seem to be hitting it off based on great conversation. She conducted herself in a very friendly manner. She tried to bring me up to speed up her and Peter's relationship and everything they had been through together all in one visit. She pretty much portrayed Peter as being a lying, cheating scoundrel whose parents always took up for him. On the other hand, the brother-in-law's family had described Delilah as a jealous, obsessive woman that was out of control. Mostly, I just listened to them all; everyone was new to me and in my opinion, all their sanities were in question. I did not know who to believe and really it did not matter, or so I thought. I just assumed they were like most young couples needing to mature to help ease some of the arguing and fighting. Really, I did not concern myself with their relationship, it was not my business. I just wished them and their children well. I could not have invented what is about to happen next, all I will say is that it should have mattered. Peter had discussed with Delilah that Seth and I were having problems and that it was best if I moved out. On the few occasions that Delilah and I had met, she seemed like a nice lady. She called me and welcomed me to stay with her until I could find a place to live. I cannot remember the month, but I remember it was snowing during that time of year because my Mustang had already slid several times in the snow and ice with me just merely avoiding two accidents. I moved in late that evening and stayed my first night. Delilah acted like an angel; she was so welcoming and hospitable. I could not have asked for a more pleasant person to be around.

She had a two-bedroom apartment which was beautifully decorated. In her living room, she had a couch and a chair with a coffee table in the middle. As we sat in her living room on the second day facing each other, she began drilling me asking me a lot of questions about Peter. I informed her I had no idea what she was talking about and, as for myself, I had no interest in Peter. I suddenly discovered that her main reason for offering me a place to stay was to know if I had any relationship with Peter. I tried to convince her that there was nothing going on between us, but I could not understand why she would ask me to move in if she thought I was having an intimate relationship with her man. She told me about all the medication she had to take blaming Peter for her stress and the reason she was on her meds. She began in vivid details explaining to me how she had cut his tires, retrieved a knife while demonstrating with the knife in hand, how she did it because he would not return her calls one night. She continued to boast about how she busted out his windows, keyed his car, broke into his mother's house and stalked him on several occasions. She then looked directly into my eyes and told me she would hurt any woman that he was involved with by cutting their throat. I could see the evil in her eyes. I knew I had not convinced this lady after seeing her transformation. In a second this woman had transformed from an angel to Satan, himself. It was obvious that she had not taken her medications this day. I thought to myself, Delilah is a psycho and I should have listened to them, it was now clear to me. They were absolutely 100 percent correct by saying this woman was out of control. She continued to engage me in conversation while still holding the knife in her hand. Now, this conversation was going on well into midnight and it was snowing outside. I was trying to remain calm and not appear defensive, but my anxiety level was at an all-time high. I would have to actually fight this woman, I thought to myself. How am I going to explain if I take this knife from this lady and cut her in her own house? No one is going to believe that this was self-defense. If she cuts me, no one really knew I was here. All I could think of was, "how am

I going to get my belongings and get out of here without incident?" There was no way I was closing my eyes in that apartment that night. I kept repeating in my head that this is not going to turn out good if I do not get out of here soon. I began looking for an escape route waiting for any distraction to make my move. Finally, a noise in the kitchen and Delilah went to check on it. I ran to the back bedroom grabbed my suitcase and clothes basket and then ran back through the living room out the front door as fast as I could. I almost slipped and fell on the snow running to my car, but I did not know if that psycho was behind me or not. I could not look back as the story of Lot's wife turning into salt flashed in my mind. I kept running until I reached my car. Finally, I had made it to my car, I opened the door, threw my clothes in and jumped in locking the doors behind me. A sigh of relief came over me as I drove off into the night. I had no idea where I was going, and I had no one to turn to. I came up to a McDonald's and with no money and nowhere else to return I slept in my car. It was so cold, but I had blankets to cover up, but I do not recall being afraid of sleeping in the parking lot that night. I was more afraid that one of us would have been a fatality if I had stayed in that apartment one more minute.

Looking back now, God had sent angels to watch over me when I did not have the astuteness to do it myself. A twenty-year-old young woman, country girl, whose life had just been threatened, now living on the city streets in her 5.0 Mustang GT, a magnet for thieves. My insight and good judgment had been completely distorted. Blinded by the spirits they set up residence in my heart that I could not see the destructive path they were leading me down. By concentrating so much on the negative experiences in my past, and giving no credit to the positive ones, I identified with and associated with spirits whose only goal was to have my soul. Through these spirits, Satan had set in motion his plan to take my life and access was granted with my permission.

My perception then:	I was a failure and the best way to disguise my shame was to leave and not return until I had redeemed myself.
Message:	Focus on the positive experiences in life and give very little attention/energy to the negative incidents. By focusing on what you perceive as negative experiences, you set the stage for more negativity to exist. Do not allow evil spirits to enter your heart because once they do, they are hard to evict. During their stay, they will create nothing but total chaos in your life. Do not allow Satan to distract you from your blessings and the joy that comes with them. Regardless of the situation, always look for the positive in it and the gift of the lesson that you receive.
How this experience affected my future:	I made decisions that were not in the best interest of my future and put my life in danger. I allowed myself to go from what I had perceived as a bad situation to worst.
My perception now:	Failure is the pathway to success. Life experiences may not be comfortable and may cause some pain, but it is the resilience that is important. I believe that no matter how bad a situation may seem it is just a distraction. God will provide me with a way to escape.

CHAPTER

Eight
Motives

*J*esus warns us of Satan's motives. "The thief comes only to steal and kill and destroy" (John, 10:10, New International Version). His first tactic is to send his evil spirits to infiltrate our minds using experiences of abuse as a gateway into our souls. Once he gets access, several different spirits can inhibit our mind depending upon the type of abuse you may have suffered. Such spirits of rejection, abandonment, self-hatred, loneliness, guilt, shame, jealousy, resentment, disbelief, fear, suicide, and so on may occupy our souls. The moment negative spirits enter, we begin to feel worthless as human beings, undeserving of love, and incapable of receiving love. If Satan can stop us from believing in love then it will be impossible for us to feel love, show love, and receive love; and therefore, separating us from God. God is love. Thus, to have a relationship with God, we must believe in love. "Whoever lives in love lives in God and God in them" (1John 4:16, New International Version). Love had lost its meaning to me years  ago and the illusions that created those irrational beliefs was the final act Satan needed to create mayhem in my life. The prince of darkness, Lucifer, had clear motives for my life which was to steal my dreams, destroy my relationship with God, my family and kill me.

The strategic plan Satan used to carry out his motives in my life was really very simple. Satan intentionally selected specific members of his workforce. His crew consisted of individuals that have been previously hurt, abused and traumatized. Weaken vessels on board; Satan is sure to attempt to carry out his plan without hesitation. Do you want to know who his workers are and how to recognize them? Ok, here is the tricky part. It could be your parents, grandparents, siblings, friends, associates, supervisors, co-workers, employees, neighbors, and so on. A lot of times these individuals will have strongholds in their lives that they have suppressed and are not even aware of but everyone else can see it. Their denial can blind them from circumstances based on inner thoughts and cause them to find fault in others yet, not identifying with their own issues. Once Satan has established this darkness in their illusions, it is easy for him to infiltrate their minds, feed them with lies and justify their thoughts and reasons for carrying out his plan. Stop for a moment and meditate on this for a few minutes. No really stop, please. Do not read another word until you meditate for a few minutes. Now, answer this question. Are you or have you at any time been a part of Satan's workforce?

I woke up at daylight after tossing and turning all night parked in the McDonald's parking lot. I looked around to see if anyone had noticed me sleeping in my car. I gathered my personal hygiene products and put them in my purse and discreetly walked into the McDonald's restroom to freshen up. For the first time since I began working at my job, I called into work that day and informed them that I would not be in. I shared with one of the head cashiers that I had grown close to about my situation of having nowhere to stay and little money in my possession. I rode around town the rest of the day not knowing where I was going to lay my head that night. The thought of returning home crossed my mind but it was quickly dissuaded when the thought of being a failure surfaced. I could not go home as a failure and have people look down on me and criticize me even more. I had a good job and I was determined to make it work. So that evening, I went back to the same McDonald's and again parked in the lot for the rest of the night. I would crank up the car and turn on the heat throughout the night to stay warm. To save gas I was only able to run my heat for a few minutes before having to turn it off. It was hard for me to sleep so most of the time I would just rest my eyes afraid to fall in a deep sleep. The next day at daylight, I got up and again I was able to freshen up in the McDonald's restroom, but I did not have access to electricity for my curling iron. So, a few hours later, I called out of work again. I could not go into work because my hair was a mess it looked like a wreck and it would have been obvious to others that something was wrong. Later that evening, one of the head cashiers called and informed me that her sister had an extra room for me. I immediately got the address to the sister's home. I did not even ask a lot of questions. All I could think of was getting to sleep under a roof tonight and off these dangerous streets. I arrived at her home tired, exhausted, and we talked for only a few minutes before I fell asleep. I was so tired that the next morning I slept past my shift and did not call in by the appropriate time to call out. I knew my job was in jeopardy now, but I was too exhausted, stressed and frustrated to even worry about it.

The sisters' name was Michal and I had met her on a few occasions when she came to pick up her sister, the head cashier, Phoebe, from work. I really did not know her well; as a matter of fact, I did not really know anyone that well. I felt like a stranger in this unknown land, but it was a better tradeoff than home. So instead of returning to something familiar, I took a risk and moved in with a complete stranger. I was so driven by the belief that I was a failure that I failed to see that I was putting myself in danger. I felt so unworthy as if my life did not matter so whatever happened to me meant nothing. My self-esteem was so low and my ability to think logically was gone. I continued this downward spiral to make one bad decision after another. It was as if I had lost all sense of reality. I was so consumed with misery and anguish that before returning home as a failure, I would rather return to home in a box. I was a depleted case of hopelessness, without reasons to live.

Michal was a single mom with three small children. She lived in a low-income area and was struggling to take care of her children on her own. I was grateful to have a place to lay my head and to take a bath, but I soon found out that everything comes with a price. For Michal, I was a dream come true. I was a babysitter that could watch her children while she graciously strolled out to enjoy a nightlife. I did not enjoy the nightlife; it never appealed to me as a teenager or as an adult so staying at home was fine by me. One day Michal suggested that I meet her boyfriend Jairus's best friend, Benjamin, to see if there was a connection. I was bored with absolutely no social life, so I said what the heck. Finally, I met Benjamin and realized that he was not my type, but circumstances have a way of helping you lower your standards. He was a slick talker, lived home with his mother, drove a school bus and had one son that lived with him. This man had nothing to offer me but physical touch and a little conversation, and my low self-esteem caused me to settle. He would come over, only to stay a little while during weekdays and on weekends he was at the night club. He invited me out to the club, but I had no desire to follow him even if it meant the only way, I could see him. This pattern of dating went on for a while and I compromised my standards and continued it just to have some companionship. He was not my type, he did not treat me well, and we had nothing in common, and yet I continued to see him. It is amazing how it is so easy to settle for someone that is obviously bad and unhealthy for you just because you want to have a "somebody" in your life.

On this one night, I overheard Michal talking to her other sister, Orpah, on the phone planning to go out that Friday night. I had a puzzled stare on my face when I heard her tell Orpah that Benjamin would be there. Why would she be telling Orpah that Benjamin would be there, especially when Michal had gone out of her way to ensure Benjamin and I met? When I told her I was not interested, she continued to invite him over, so he could interact with me. But later, I would discover that the only reason Michal had set me up with Benjamin was so her boyfriend, Jairus would visit her more often. Jairus would always make a date with Michal but would very seldom show up. Benjamin and Jairus were always together, so she figured if Benjamin came to see me, then Jairus would surely come. The night after Michal left for the club, I could feel the bottom of my stomach turning. I felt manipulated, deceived, bewildered, and uneasy. There was no way that I could fall asleep after what I had heard. I had to know if what I suspected was true or not. There was a nagging feeling that all my suspicions were true, and I knew my shelter would be in danger again. But I could not just overlook the churning feeling in my stomach. So, after a few minutes, I called the next-door neighbor to come and babysit. I got dressed and headed out for the club. I really did not know the directions to get to the club, and Benjamin had only shown it to me once. My adrenaline was flowing and in my subconscious memory the directions had been stored, I drove straight to the club not missing one turn in my white Mustang GT.

Once I arrived at the parking lot of the club, I parked the car and then got out to approach the entrance of the club, at which time, Orpah was exiting the club walking towards me at a fast pace while hauling insults at me. Orpah and I had only met a couple of times in passing when she would visit her sister Michal. I noticed that she was somewhat distant when I was around, but I did not think much of it because most of the people I met were standoffish in this state. I knew at that moment it was exactly what I was suspecting, a relationship between her and Benjamin that I had not been forewarned about. It was clear to me now that her frosty attitude towards me was as a result of jealousy. I was infuriated that I did not consider my surroundings or the consequences; I went full speed ahead ready to engage in a physical altercation. There was never even a discussion of why I was there. It was obvious that my presence alone was not welcomed. I had walked into unknown territory without contemplating all the harmful scenarios that could have been my current reality. Blinded by hopelessness, rejection, loneliness, and betrayal, nothing mattered to me anymore. As Orpah and I approached each other in haste, Jairus proceeded to grab Orpah and ushered her to her car and Benjamin grabbed me and led me into the club. It was shocking what had just happened. I thought to myself these people are loco! The jukebox was on playing loud, but I could hear him clearly when he admitted that he and Orpah used to date and that she wanted him back. All I could think about was why Michal so selfishly set me up with one of her sister's ex-boyfriends. I realized at that moment that things would never be the same for Michal and me after that night.

It is around two o'clock in the morning as I was walking out of the club. When I approached my car, I noticed a long-indented scratch on the driver side of my Mustang. It was never a question of who did it. I thought to myself how Michal could put me in this situation and then sit back and watch her sister key my car. I was a friend, a good roommate and a babysitter for her children. By the time I arrived at Michal's apartment, she had thrown most of my possessions out on her front porch and kept a few valuable items for herself. I questioned myself, what had I done to deserve this? I was an innocent bystander misled into a relationship that did not have to happen. I was tired, sleepy, frustrated, mentally exhausted, and homeless again with nowhere to go and it was almost 4 o'clock in the morning. Again, I had no place to lay my head for the night, so I considered driving all night until daylight. No idea what I was going to do next the only thought was not returning home until I had made something of myself. I drove around in my car for a few hours crying and thinking about all that had occurred over the last few months and how terrible this situation ended.

Before daybreak, I received a call from Jairus telling me that he had a place for me to stay. Jairus had another girlfriend named, Rhoda that he was in an intimate relationship with that agreed to let me stay with her for the night. I had no other choice. It was around 6 A.M. and I had the worst headache of my life, it seemed. I arrived at Rhoda's home that night, introduced myself and immediately dozed off. I woke up the next day and it was almost 12 noon and I was late for my shift and had not called in. This was the second time that I had been homeless while working at this job. I knew my position as the head cashier was a thing of the past, it was only a matter of time before I would be let go. I had worked so hard to get this position as head cashier and now I could see it slipping right from up under me. When I arrived to work the following Monday, the manager called me in and told me I was one of his best employees, but he had to let me go. I was fired. The question of what I could have done differently with my living arrangements to keep my job kept plaguing me. It seemed to me that I used every opportunity I had to succeed but it was not enough. I should have thrown in the towel and packed up what little possessions I had left and returned home; but going back home as a failure in my eyes was not an option. I had to try again. I could not give up yet.

Rhoda allowed me to stay with her and she was excited that I had a car because most of the females I had met used public transportation. Rhoda lived in a low-income area and wanted to move into a better neighborhood but could not afford to do that on her own. After a few weeks, I got another job through a temporary agency and was hired at a Workman's Compensation Agency. Rhoda and I seemed to be getting along fine; so, we rented an apartment together and things appeared to start looking up. I had a new job, my own room, and personal space; and believed there was a ray of hope. However, during my first week at my new residence, someone tried to break into my car and steal it. They had drilled a hole right below the key entrance on the driver side door panel and all they had to do was open the door to gain entry, but they were unsuccessful. A couple of weeks later, a second attempt was made to break into my car. They broke out my passenger window. However, the steering wheel was equipped with an anti-steering wheel lock after the first attempt was made. I was relieved that they had not stolen my car but frustrated because now I had to pay for a broken window. I barely had enough money for rent, food, and gas. These thieves were relentless; it seemed nothing would deter them from the 1988 white Mustang GT.

When I walked out of my apartment one morning, my car was sitting on four center blocks. In their third attempt, they gave up on stealing the car and set their aspirations on the tires and rims. Tears came rushing down my face, but I absolutely did not make a sound. I felt like I was an open target for disaster to hit me at any moment again. How was I going to afford four new tires and rims? I barely had enough money for my bare essentials. I was determined not to give up. I had to come up with a plan. I just could not face going back home as a disappointment. A few days later, I contacted my landlord and explained my situation. He allowed me to put off a portion of the rent for the next month so I could purchase new tires and rims for my car.

When I did not think things could get worse, I found out I was pregnant for Benjamin. One night of unprotected sex, now I was pregnant. I thought I was going to lose my mind. I was twenty-three years old and I knew better. Later, I found out my roommate, Rhoda was pregnant also. I knew I only had one choice and that was to get an abortion. I could barely take care of myself and bringing a child into my mess was not an option. I asked Benjamin for part of the money and he refused, he advised me to have the baby. It was not that he wanted me to have the baby; he was too cheap to give me the money for the procedure. But he knew I was resilient enough to do it on my own. He could barely afford to take care of the son he already had. Over the next couple of weeks, I had no extra money and time was running out to have the procedure. By this time, Michal had called my mother and informed her I was pregnant, also spreading vindictive lies about me that were totally untrue. My mom asked me about the pregnancy, and I denied it because I had planned to have an abortion before anyone found out. A few weeks later, after my conversation with my mother, a perfect opportunity came up to disguise my lie. An associate was going to my state to visit his family and he offered for me to ride home with him. I decided to go home for a visit just to get out of the city for a while and to prove that I was not pregnant. During my visit, I was only a few weeks pregnant, my stomach was completely flat, so my pregnancy was not obvious at least that was my thinking.

I returned to the city with a sigh of relief believing I had covered up my lie. Once I arrived back at my apartment, I immediately went to my room, so I could drop my luggage. As I looked around my room, I noticed my phone was missing and some items too. The only thing that I had in my room was a mattress, phone, clothes, shoes, and personal papers. Each one of us slept on the floor on top of our mattress in our rooms because we did not have bedrails or box spring to lie on. I called out for Rhoda to see if she was home, at which time she and her cousin, Rizpah, came out of her bedroom with frowns on their faces as if they were waiting on my return. I immediately confronted Rhoda about my possessions; she only rained insults on me and said nothing that made sense. I did not recognize this person I was dealing with now. Rhoda, whom for the past few months seemed to be caring and considerate had completely changed. I had no idea what caused her to act this way towards me. All the bills had been paid in the apartment so, other than that she had no reason to even be upset with me. What happened next still perplexes me today. I was not accustomed to what would happen next, but the country girl instincts came into action. The heated argument escalated to a fistfight and then a wrestling match with both of us gasping for air. Picture this: two pregnant women fighting, and one sneaky cousin observing from a close distance, watching and waiting for her opportunity to jump in and help her cousin with my demise. Once Rhoda realized she was losing the battle she yelled for Rizpah to grab the knife. At that split second, I recalled how my brother, Ishmael, used to put me in the headlock and how I was incapable of getting out of it. I knew exactly what to do. I grabbed my roommate by the neck and put her in the headlock that Ishmael had done so many times to me. I yelled at Rizpah and said, if she walked any closer, I would snap Rhoda's neck. The closer Rizpah would get the more pressure I would apply until finally, Rhoda screamed for Rizpah to put the knife down. I dragged her over to the door, still with a tight grip on her neck so I could have a clear exit out of the apartment. Once my back was up against the back door of the apartment, I released the grip from her neck and pushed her away from me, giving me room to exit the door. I immediately ran out the door. I rushed to the landlord's house and explained to him of everything that had occurred. I told him I had to leave the apartment because my roommate and her cousin tried to physically attack me. Later, it was revealed that Rhoda had been jealous of me the entire time because I had a car and an office job. She only befriended me to move into a better apartment and neighborhood, along with access to my vehicle. Now, of course, Rizpah, who I had never met until that day, had a different motive. She was Benjamin's other girlfriend, another woman who was jealous of me over a man that I did not even want in my life anymore. I should have known that if Jairus had two girlfriends so did Benjamin.

Homeless again, I was at a crossroad. My life had come close to death three times in this state at the hand of jealous women. I was still terrified about returning home. While contemplating what to do, I heard a voice speak to me. It was God. He let me know that he had been protecting me the entire time but now it is time for me to return home. I knew it was God because as he spoke to me a peace came over me about making the decision to return home. These evil spirits had tried to keep my mind in such a state of chaos to keep me from discerning God's voice. God is God, all-powerful, and omniscient. God was able to penetrate my heart and bypass all the evil spirits and to let me know that he loved me. I knew it was God speaking to me because all the other voices before him told me that I was not important, no one loved me and would be better off dead.

Reflecting on the words that God had spoken to me, I had put my life in danger so many times. At the time, I just wanted to disappear from my life. I realized that my situations could have turned out completely different. I could have been beaten up, paralyzed, kidnapped and even killed. Deep down in my spirit, I knew God was protecting me. There is no way I came out of all those situations unharmed, so I made the decision to return home no matter how I felt inwardly about myself. However, now in my eyes, not only would I be returning home as a failure, but as a failure with disgrace. I wanted to continue to hide the fact that I was pregnant until I could get the abortion. I figured I would still be within the time period to get the abortion and keep my secret safe. At that moment, I still had more pressing things to deal with, because I was homeless again with nowhere to go. Jairus always had an ace in the hole. Jairus got permission for me to stay with his, girlfriend number three, Julia. I was totally amazed at these men and all the relationships that they were involved in. I was also mystified by these women that I had dealt with and all the envy and jealousy that surrounded them. I knew if Jairus had girlfriend number three surely Benjamin did also. At that point, I did not care who Benjamin was having relations with all I wanted to do was the get out of this state. My experience in this state was awful from beginning to end except for me getting the position as head cashier. I will never forget these events that occurred while I was there, but there I have no desire to ever return to this state. Once I got to girlfriend number three's home, Julia, I surrendered. I contacted my uncle who lived one state over with plans to stay with his family for a few days until I could arrange for my return to North Carolina. Julia offered for me to stay with her for a while, but I told her, thank you, but no thanks. Most people strike out on three and I had made it, so I had no desire to tempt fate and try for number four. It was amazing how I attracted the same type of associates in every situation during this ordeal. This experience is a good example of how we attract what we think. I focused on all the negative experiences and people in my life along with why I was deserving of this treatment. This is a perfect example of why a person needs a change of mindset. However, a lot of times when we are under distress it become hard to change our thoughts during the experience because of the adrenaline of our emotions. It is imperative that we find a way during the situation to focus on any glimmer of good if we want to change our circumstances for the better. As for then, I just needed a place to get some rest until so I could get on the road and travel to my uncle's home. After I got some rest, I left the state and headed to my uncle to live in a safe environment until I left for home. I stayed with my family for a couple of days and tried to enjoy myself, but it was hard. All I could think about was the fact that I was still pregnant, and no one can find out. So, after a couple of days, I left for a 13-hour trip to return home to North Carolina.

I was so focused on running to conceal my narrative as a failure from my family that I never considered if where I was running was a better or healthier place. I left my family, whom I perceived did not have my best interest at heart to people who could take my life without a second thought. Each one of these people that I allowed in my life had their own personal motive, agenda, and I was just the individual they would use to try and get it. When I arrived this state, I allowed people in my circle that under normal circumstances, I would have thought twice about before connecting with them. I had no history with or on them, but I accepted them in my life with all their flaws. The people I did have a history with, I closed them out of my life and refused to accept them for who they were because they were a direct cause of what I perceived as some of my most hurtful experiences. However, with all the negative experiences I had with my family, I never felt like my life was in danger. They may not have known how to show me through their actions that they loved me, but I do not believe for one moment that they would have intentionally inflicted any physical pain on me.

Sometimes in life, we run away from the one place we need to be running to. I allowed Satan to plant negative thoughts in my mind about me and my family members that were all lies. Despite all the issues I had with my family, they would have been totally devastated if something would have happened to me. Every member of my family has issues that they were all dealing with and sometimes we hurt each other. A lot of the time a family member may not even realize that they hurt the other person and sometimes they might. In those cases, hurt people hurt people which is not an excuse just something to think about. With family, we may have to constantly forgive each other and love each other despite how we are treated. My family is not perfect but with my family at least I know who I am dealing with.

Most important we must all recognize who has our best interest at heart. "The thief (Satan) cometh not, but for to steal, and to kill, and to destroy: I (God) am come that they might have life and that they might have it more abundantly" (John 10:10, New International Version). I listened to the thoughts Satan planted in my mind and he tried to kill me. I had turned away from God, but he still came and rescued me. We may go astray and turn our backs on God, but He will never turn his backs on us. God loves us more than anyone. There is nothing that can separate us from the love of God. Although I had not been communicating with God on my journey to destruction, he still watched over me every moment. *"Though I walk in the midst of trouble, you preserve my life; you stretch out your hand against the wrath of my enemies, and your right hand delivers me"* **(Psalms 138:7, English Standard Version).** In three different attempts, my life was threatened, but I never received one scratch. In three different attempts, thieves tried to steal my vehicle, but I still own it. "And the Lord, it is He that doth go before thee; he will be with thee, he will not fail thee, neither forsake thee: fear not, neither be dismayed" (Deuteronomy 31:8, King James Version).

My perception then:	Living with strangers was better than returning home as a failure. My life had little meaning.
Message:	Family members must learn to treat each other like family instead of enemies. Home should be the one place a person can feel comfortable returning to, and not the place they are running from. Do not allow the assembly of a funeral to be the occasion you discover regret and remorse.
How this experience affected my future:	I put this experience behind me and believed that after this ordeal I was strong enough to make it through anything.
My perception now:	Family may not be perfect but at least I know who I am dealing with. I must accept them for who they are no more and no less. I realize that I am favored by God and I was never alone during this period in my life. God had angels watching over me the entire time ensuring that not one hair on my head was harmed. His angels protected my life, well-being and my property.

CHAPTER

Nine
The Gift of Life

When I returned to North Carolina, I moved in with my mother and stepfather, Nathan. I was 23 years old, single, pregnant and receiving unemployment benefits. By the time I arrived home, I was about 16 weeks pregnant. I had not gained a lot of weight, therefore, I continued to deny the existence of the pregnancy. I was running out of time, because the state I resided had a 20-week limit to perform an abortion. I could not even afford the abortion much less

pay to go out of state. Over the next couple of weeks, I walked around trying to fool everyone, waiting until I could obtain the rest of the funds for the procedure. Every day made it harder for me to go through with it. I felt so ashamed, trapped, and lonely, I did not know what to do next. At night, I would toss and turn in my bed. The lie I had tried to protect so long may be exposed if I did not follow through. What was I to do? Over and over I kept

wondering how I could take good care of me and my baby if I decided to keep him or her? An innocent baby was coming into my mess, with farces of failure and disgrace. How could I risk my child seeing what I saw when

I looked in the mirror, a failure? I wanted my baby to have the love of both parents and opportunities to excel in life. I felt there was no way to give this to my child and I wanted him or her to have the best.

I finally saved enough money to go through with the procedure. But over the next couple of weeks, I picked up the phone several times and attempted to make the appointment. With all the guilt I was feeling, I just could not bring myself to follow through with it. The baby had become a part of me. I could feel its presence and I become emotionally attached. I could not help but love my baby as he or she grew inside me. This precious unborn baby had caused me to bring down barriers that had surrounded my heart for years. I realized I had allowed myself to love again. After all these months, I would have to admit that I was pregnant as if they were not already aware. At least now, half of the pressure would be gone and there would be no more lying. Of course, when I admitted it to everyone that I was pregnant, they already knew. I was the only one walking around in denial. My family did not respond the way I had expected them to. No one criticized me about getting pregnant out of wedlock; at least not in my presence. This was a first for me to not be put down by family members. Most of my family and friends were excited about me having the baby. They were all ranting and raving over who was going to get to spoil and babysit.

Now, that I am five months pregnant, it was now time for me to start prenatal care. My first appointment for prenatal care was in the sixth month. During my check-up, the doctor said everything looked great and the baby appeared to be in good health. I had begun preparing as most new mothers do, buying baby clothes, furniture, and supplies. It was such a relief that the truth was out and that I could celebrate having my baby instead of denying his or her existence. I did not know how I was going to do it, but I was even more determined to become a success now for my baby's sake. My baby had melted my heart and has become the most important being in my life. The seventh month, I got the same report. The baby was developing according to schedule. It was this month that I found out I was having a baby boy. It never really mattered whether it was a girl or boy just if he or she was healthy. When it was confirmed it was a boy, I knew his name would be Samuel. I was so excited that things that used to matter to me did not matter anymore. The most important thing to me was being the best mother understanding my work is cut out for me. I had just made up in my mind that I was going to be a good provider, mother and nothing was going to stop me. For the first time in my life since I was a teenager, I had a reason to excel again. I finally had a purpose for being here. I planned to finish my last year in college and find a good job so I could provide a good quality of life for my son. Finally, I would have someone to love me unconditionally and would never stop loving me. Well, the eighth month, I missed my appointment, I cannot even remember why. In the last month of my pregnancy, it was Thanksgiving Day and I was eating dinner at my uncle Haman and Aunt Naomi's house, which is where I grew up. There were family members from both sides at the dinner along with both my Grandmother and great-Aunt Sophia. My anxiety level was high because anytime I was in the presence of both my grandmother and great-Aunt, I felt a lot of tension. My great-Aunt Sophia was my grandmother's sister from out of state. She would usually come home for the holidays and summer, but for some reason I was not one of her favorite persons. And when they were together, they had a way of making me feel like I was a "Mistake." During our Thanksgiving dinner, I only ate a small amount of food. My stomach was feeling queasy and my back was hurting so bad. It felt as if someone was using a stun gun to shock me. So afterward I went into the family room and sat in the recliner to relieve some of the stress off my back. Then the unbearable pain came, they were worse than any cramps I had ever experienced. I tried to conceal my pain. Here I was again living behind a mask. I felt like I was only a few moments from meeting my maker and instead of worrying about me and my baby, I was worried about how Deborah and Sophia perceived me. I was not sure how much longer I could hold on. I prayed that my mother would hurry up and arrive, so she could take me home. The pains were so sharp that I literary felt like I was going to die but I had to stay strong. I could not allow myself to show any weakness in front of Deborah and Sophia, or they would try to humiliate me. So, with every ounce of strength that I had within me, I tried to bear the pain.

My uncle's wife, Naomi, caught a glimpse of me bending over and holding my stomach. She asked if I was feeling OK. I respond that I was alright. Then either Deborah or Sophia said its probably just Braxton Hick's pains. Naomi responded to them it is too close to her due date to be Braxton Hick's. From that point on Naomi was observant of my every move. She kept asking me what seemed like every two minutes if I was OK. I could see the frowns on Deborah and Sophia's faces. I was hurting so bad, but I would not cry I just held it in and told her I was doing fine. Deborah and Sophia were washing dishes in the kitchen sink. From the view of the sink, they could look directly at the right-side view of my face. I could see them in my peripheral vision hunch each other and scrunch up their faces each time my aunt Naomi spoke to me. Naomi continued to question me on how I was doing. I just wanted her to stop asking so Deborah and Sophia would stop making those faces, but she was genuinely concerned. Each time Naomi inquired about my well-being, Deborah and Sophia would whisper something to each other while looking directly at me with smirks on their faces. The pain I felt was consuming me, I thought I was going to pass out. I used every bit of the strength I had in my mind and body to hold on. Naomi asked again, how I was doing and demanded that I let her know if I was hurting. As soon as she could get it out of her mouth, Deborah said, she is faking, just lazy do not want to get up and do anything. How could they say this? I was nine months pregnant. Both knew there was not a lazy bone in my body, but honestly, I did not expect any more from them I was used to it. I had heard this from them most of my childhood. I thought to myself I guess they had not condemned me enough when I was a child that they have a need to continue in my adulthood. The severe pain had only been going on for less than a half hour, but it seemed like eternity. Now, not only was I physically battling the labor pains, but also fighting this mental torture from my blood relatives. I had to remain strong no matter what until my mother arrived, refusing to let them see me hurt or get upset.

My mother finally arrived to pick me up and take me home. I just wanted to lie down and see if the pain would go away before I decided whether to go to the hospital. On the way home, I told my mom what had happened at dinner—a Thanksgiving's dinner that will never be forgotten. As I rode to my mom's house the ten-minute drive seemed like an hour. When we arrived at my mother's house for only a few minutes, I told my mom that the pain I was feeling seemed worse than just labor pains. We decided to go to the hospital immediately. My mother contacted Martha, to ask her to drive her because my car was a straight shift. The drive to the hospital was about 45 minutes away. I sat in the back seat of my Mustang scrunched over, feeling every bump on the highway. I did not think I was going to make it. I truly thought I would be dead before I arrived at the hospital. My pain was excruciating but during my few minutes of relief, all I could think about was why did my grandmother and great-aunt hate me so much. When I was no longer physically hurting, I was mentally suffering. I could not get a break from pain. I just wanted to give up right then. I had exhausted all the strength that was in me, thinking it was a matter of time before it would all be over.

When we arrived at the hospital, they immediately took me to the prep room. As soon as I was stretched out on the table, I told the nurse I was going to throw up. She put a bowl beside me, and I vomited the little dinner I had ingested. I could hear the nurses whispering to each other, but I could not make out what they were saying. I asked, is there anything wrong? They both answered no but pointed out that the baby's arm was just not in the right position. I did not believe them because their facial expressions said a whole lot more than what they were saying. Their expressions resembled concern and worry, but everything was going so fast, I did not have a lot of time to act on them. A few minutes later, I was pushed into the delivery room. My thoughts were about to overtake me. When the labor pains would come, I would think about that pain, when labor pains ceased, I would think about what Deborah and Sophia said about me. Rest evaded me, physical pain and mental anguish consumed me. I tried my best not to focus on their comments, but I was too weak to fight off the words replaying over and over in my mind. My last thought of them before the doctor came in was that Deborah and Sophia would not be satisfied until I was dead.

After a few minutes, which seemed like hours, the doctor came into the room. He approached my bed and I could tell by the expression on his face that something had gone terribly wrong. I could sense myself losing all control of my body not caring if I heard one word spoken out of his mouth. He spoke in a low and calm voice and said, "Ms. Hannah I am sorry to advise you, but your baby is stillborn." He expressed his sympathy but informed me that I would still have to deliver as if he was alive. Tears begin to roll down my face. I just did not understand. I laid on the bed for the next half hour unable to control any of my emotions. I felt like I was being punished for not wanting to be pregnant in the first place and lying about it for so long. I wanted it all to end right there. I wanted to go with my baby, the one thing that gave me a purpose for living was now gone and the agony that my relatives had put me through just made the decision even easier. The contractions started getting closer and closer. My cousin, Martha was putting ice in my mouth to help alleviate the dryness. The labor pain hit me so hard that I grabbed her hand and I began squeezing her hand as hard and I could. She tried to keep a candid face, but she politely grabbed my hand with her other hand and place my hand on the bed rail. I heard the doctor say push, I attempted but not with much effort. I told him I had no energy left in my body to even blow air. He told me I would have to push. I replied, "I am too weak." He then told me to pinch my nose with my two fingers, take a deep breath and push. I wanted everyone to just leave me alone. So, I followed his instructions, hoping that if I did it this one time correctly it would all be over. I did just as the doctor instructed.I pinched my nose and pushed as hard as I could and then I felt a big relief. It was done but there was no crying. I could hear the nurses, my mother, and Martha talking quietly. They asked me if I wanted to see my baby, but I refused. I knew I would not be able to handle seeing him dead. I figured that by not seeing him I would not miss him as much. But I was wrong. I felt the emptiness inside and part of me that was once there was gone. They asked me if I had a name for my baby and I said, yes. I named my little angel, Samuel. It was not long before I fell asleep. It seemed like it had been months since I had a good night's sleep. When I woke up, I thought it was just a nightmare but then reality hit, and it was all true. The doctor came in and apologized for my loss. He told me that the baby had been dead inside me for a while and that I was on the verge of death. My baby was poisoning my system, and time was of the essence due to life threatening complications. At that moment in time, I welcomed the outcome of the situation. After hearing from the doctor, the emotions I was dealing with were about to consume me. I asked him to please give me some medication to help me rest because I did not want to be awake another moment to have to deal with this.

After I returned home from the hospital, I was so depressed and filled with guilt I felt so empty on the inside now that he was no longer a part of me. I was dealing with so much grief even though I never saw my baby's face or held his little body. I did not think the pain would ever end and often questioned why I lived. Why God had not taken me too? My mom knew I was dealing with the loss of my baby, but she also knew I was dealing with the comments made by Deborah and Sophia. So, my mom mentioned to me that Sophia had called upset and had apologized for what she had said about me on Thanksgiving. I acknowledged it, but I really did not care much about her apology, I was dealing with having to bury my dead baby boy. A few days later we had a graveside burial for him. It was short and sweet. During and after the service, I was just numb. I could not imagine the pain I would have endured if Samuel would have come home and then died. I thought that not seeing him would make it easier, but the heartache was still so painful. Everyone wanted to know but was afraid to ask the question, when I noticed that the baby stopped moving. I did not know when the baby stopped kicking. I was in so much pain every day and night that I was unable to remember when I was not feeling pain. When I asked people about the pain associated with being pregnant, they would say, you are going to be in pain that is a part of being pregnant. So, I just endured it and did not complain, I did not want to be a burden to anyone. I thought it was normal to feel that way when you are pregnant. Afterward, I blamed myself for not realizing something was wrong with my baby. Now, I had to deal with whether I could have done something different to save his life. Now, I had just another thing to feel guilty about. If I had told someone sooner about my pain, maybe Samuel would have lived. Before I became pregnant, I had felt dead on the inside and then Samuel caused me to feel alive again. A part of me felt I deserved punishment for lying about my pregnancy and considering an abortion. So, I just accepted my fate and responsibility.

This grief continued for the next couple of months. However, I decided that I could not allow myself to be defeated. A strong desire arose in me to get up. I had a second chance at life and if there was any chance of me succeeding, I had to change my surroundings. I realized that to get the type of opportunities I desired in life that I would have to return to the city. Four months after the death of my baby, I relocated to Richmond and moved in with my cousin and a couple of friends. A few weeks later, I started as a correctional officer at a women's correctional facility. Eventually, the pain eased, and I felt some relief knowing that he had made it to heaven and believing that he would be watching over me. However, it was not until years later that I had the courage to visit his grave again. When I finally arrived, I was disappointed with myself for allowing my baby's grave to go so unkempt. I cleaned off his little grave and then contacted the local funeral home and purchased a headstone for my sweet baby, Samuel's grave.

Samuel was conceived during one of the most dreadful times of my life. But who knew this little boy would have such a positive impact on my future? It was not until years later that I discovered Samuel's purpose in my life. After all the pain and hurt had diminished from his death I was able to see more clearly. Samuel never had the opportunity to experience life outside my body, but he was a gift to my life. Samuel was only here on earth a short time in my womb, but he left me two special gifts. He gave me the gift to feel love again and the gift to excel again. I had built up walls so high and thick around my heart to ensure that no one could penetrate it. But, this little boy in a matter of a few months tore down all my walls and captured my heart. He had taught me to feel love again and I remembered how I felt when I believed I was going to have the opportunity to be Samuel's mom. I wanted nothing more than to give 110 percent and be the best mom for him. I liked how that felt and I could still feel that desire even after he was gone. My little angel was sent here to help his mom get her life back on track.

A woman during pregnancy, endures a lot of changes both physically and mentally. She may experience some great memories as well as some bad ones. Some days physically, she will be strong and some days she will be weak. Some days mentally, she will be inspired and some days she will be discouraged. Some days visions of expectations will be apparent, and some days visions of her expectations may be uncertain. She will need a lot of support, encouragement, and understanding throughout the entire ordeal. It is like the contrast of what we go through in life. There will be some dark days and we cannot see what is ahead of us and we do not know the outcome. But if we have a relationship with God, then we must trust that he is leading us during these times of uncertainty. God speaks to our heart and Satan speaks to our minds. So, Satan will do everything within his power to distract us from focusing on the words God speak to our heart. Satan uses our senses to manipulate and control us. We tend to believe what we hear with our ears, see with our eyes and feel with our emotions. Therefore, it is impossible for us to beat Satan on his turf, this earthly world. If we have any chance of defeating him, we must fight him from the spirit world where God has given us all the authority. When God speaks to our hearts we must listen and not cast his words aside. We must focus on his word and continue moving forward despite what we see, hear or feel. We must completely ignore our senses. Satan will also use our fear of walking in the darkness without sight to keep us from obtaining the blessings that have been stored up for us. God wants you to know that in your darkest days when it seems impossible for you to see anything good in your life, when it seems like there is no way out of your situation, and when it seems like death is the only option that He is right there with you holding your hands leading you to your blessings. He asked that you do not let go of His hand because He can only act on your behalf if you have the faith to hold on and trust Him.

During those seasons of difficult times when people are involved, we tend to focus more on the individuals that are seeking to cause us harm than, the individuals that are intending to do us good. I should have focused on my family and friends that were excited about my pregnancy, like my aunt Naomi who was genuinely concerned about my health, my mother who had been supportive throughout my pregnancy, my cousin

Martha who drove me to the hospital and stayed with me the entire time. In life, we will face challenging times and we will need all our strength to stand against the wickedness of this world. "For we wrestle not against flesh and blood, but against principalities, against powers, against the rulers of the darkness of this world, against spiritual wickedness in high places" (Ephesians 6:12, King James Version). In order to do that, we need to focus all our energies on the positives and rebuke the negatives. If we allow negativity to consume us, then we will be too weak to fight but if we allow positivity to consume us, then we will have the mental forte to use the authority God has given us to defeat our enemy.

I had several people that showed they cared about me, but I allowed the opinions of two to almost determine my fate because they had played an intricate part in my life. Other people's opinion should never have had that much power over me if I hadn't valued myself based on their approval. If there are people in your life (regardless of the affiliations) seeking to harm you, separate yourself from them. My mother had decided that she would not prepare Thanksgiving dinner as usual because she had been invited to eat with a friend. I had the choice to go with my mother at her friends' or to go eat with my immediate family. I made the decision to eat with my family because I loved them and wanted to be with them. However, once I was aware that my grandmother and great-aunt would be attending the dinner because of my health condition I should have chosen the alternative. I knew from past experiences that being with them made me feel uneasy. I should never have exposed myself to such a toxic environment just because they were family. Sometimes, you must learn to love some family members from a distance. In the meantime, continue to pray for them and respect their titles. God can replace those family members with people who will uplift, encourage and support you when you need it the most.

My grandmother and great-aunt's lack of empathy towards me is a mirror reflection of the insensitive environment we all grew up in. However, we do not have to be subjective to the negative exposures of our surroundings. We all have a choice. There comes a time in life when we must stop expecting so much from certain family members. They cannot give us what they do not have. We expect them to show us love, compassion, empathy, encouragement and so on when they have not recovered from their traumatic past. Instead of them expressing love, they express the effects of their trauma. As an adult now looking back on this experience, I believe it may have saved my life. "You intended to harm me, but God intended it for good to accomplish what is now being done, the saving of many lives."(Genesis 50:20, New International Version) I had endured so much pain in the last few weeks of my pregnancy that I had built a high level of tolerance for pain. I could have died from trying so hard to endure, even before getting any medical attention. However, the combination of both the physical and mental agony precipitated by Deborah and Sophia overwhelmed me and caused me to make the decision to go to the hospital. Those insensitive, slanderous, and judgmental comments and gestures made by them about me was a blessing to me. My response to their actions saved my life.

In life, we all make choices some good and some bad. However, there are just some things we have no control over. "The secret things belong unto the LORD our God: but those things which are revealed belong unto us and to our children forever, that we may do all the words of this law" (Deuteronomy 29:29, King James Version). God spared my life for a reason. I may not have considered my life to be important, but God did, and He had a purpose for me despite what I believed or how I felt. I discovered what was important. It is important that I work out my salvation and align myself with the word of God to fulfill and operate in my purpose. Once I started operating in my purpose, the activities to achieve my goals seemed effortless and fulfilling. "Therefore, my dear friends, as you have always obeyed not only in my presence, but now much more in my absence continue to work out your salvation with fear and trembling, 13 for it is God who works in you to will and to act in order to fulfill his good purpose"(Philippians 2:12-13, New International Version).

My perception then:	Initially, I wanted an abortion because I felt I would be unable to provide my baby with a good life. Later, my desire to strive for greatness again was a direct result of me wanting to be a good mother and provide the best quality of life for my baby. My grandmother and great-aunt had no concern about my physical or emotional well-being. I wanted to die along with my baby.
Message:	In life we will endure pain, however, we have the choice to carry the residual effects of the experience or not. When we must go through these life experiences, it is imperative to identify and focus on the positivity in it. Gifts can be found in every experience you have even the ones you have deemed as detrimental.
How this experience affected my future:	It catapulted my ambition.
My perception now:	Samuel was my angel sent here on earth to get me back on course for my destiny. My grandmother and great-aunt were imprisoned in their minds by their traumatic experiences and unaware how much I desired their love and validation at the time. I have learned to accept and love them right where they are. It is not what you go through it is what you grow to.

CHAPTER

Ten
Discovery

Now almost ten years later since my angel Samuel passed on to heaven and I had to relocate to the city. A lot had happened over the past ten years. I have encountered some challenges as we all do, but most importantly I had been highly favored and blessed. However, all those blessings have not been able to replace this feeling of emptiness in me. I created a façade just to help me function day to day leaving others to judge me from behind my mask. At this point in my life, I had been separated from my spouse, Canaan of six years and I was feeling like a complete failure again. I just recently left my new home of three months and moved into a luxury one-bedroom apartment. I felt that the separation was vital to my mental survival. At home, I was dealing with the lack of respect from Canaan and stepsons; and Canaan's inability to be an authoritative figure in the home. I was now facing all the emotions that came from my earlier experiences of feeling abandoned, rejected, and unworthy and it was almost driving me to go into a state of depression. No one could sense all the misery that I encompassed daily. It was like déjà  vu being surrounded by people that showed me little or no affection, regard, or appreciation. I felt like I was reliving my childhood all over again, feeling rejected leaving me with the illusion that I was not enough.

I recalled one night I was heading back home to the city from Freetown. It was about an hour and a half drive between the two locations. It was raining hard and it was pitch dark this particular night, more so than normal. I was driving distraught in my Lexus sports car. I had no business driving this night because my emotional state could have been compared to a person who was three times over the legally intoxicated level. I was in a state of frantic; my eyes were filled with tears and I could barely see past my windshield. My vision of the road was obscured, the road was being repaved and there was complete darkness, yet I continued to drive in that dreadful condition. I started out driving at a slow pace and did my best to drive as safely as I could, but I thought to myself maybe tonight is the night. I had no intentions of stopping to avoid the hazardous road conditions. I had decided that if a car accident was the cause of my death then that would be how God had decided to take me. I had no intentions of interfering or contributing to it, so I exonerated myself completely from the outcome of the situation. I continued to drive in the horrible weather, road and mental conditions as if everything was perfectly fine. The last thing I remember before falling into a trance was crying ferociously, being blinded by my tears, dark pavement and the heavy rain. My body became numb and weightless, almost as if I fell asleep. That night I was incoherent, and unaware of anything that was going on around me. I had driven this route many times in the past, however, this night I had no mental recollection of the trip at all. All I can remember is opening my eyes and my car was parked in the parking space in front of my apartment. Between the dark road, the heavy pour of rain, flushing tears from my eyes, my emotional state, and my partial loss of memory my only explanation for making it home safely that night was that God had taken over the steering wheel.

Most people in my surrounding thought I had a good life and perceived me as being a success and a pillar of strength. Some people judge me more harshly and called me high and mighty just because I appeared confident, well-groomed and owned a few nice possessions. But here I was feeling so unworthy on the inside and others perceived me as being uppity. What I find most bizarre was that when I was in the presence of these same people, I tried to shrink around them, so I would not make them feel insecure. As if I didn't already have my own share of insecurity to deal with. It is so funny how other people can see you in a totally different manner than you see yourself. You should never judge a book by its cover. The view from outside the picture does look rather fabulous. But it is the inside that is alarming where you can see the rips and tears. Most people in life take care of themselves like Canaan took care of his vehicles. He would clean, dry, and wax the exterior of the vehicle leaving it with a lustrous and glistening finish. The interior of the vehicle would go untouched left messy and unclean on the inside. People are often so focused on making their outside appearance look good to impress others, yet they give little attention to the internal wounds that need repairing. We as human beings have been conditioned to look at the outward appearance and judge based solely on the surface instead of taking time to explore the inside and discover the heart within. It is time for more loving and less judging.

Our Greatest Fear

It is our light, not our darkness that most frightens us
Our deepest fear is not that we are inadequate.
Our deepest fear is that we are powerful beyond measure.
It is our light, not our darkness that most frightens us.
We ask ourselves, who am I to be brilliant, gorgeous,
talented and fabulous?
Actually, who are you not to be?

You are a child of God.
Your playing small does not serve the world.
There's nothing enlightened about shrinking so that other
People won't feel insecure around you.
We were born to make manifest the glory of
God that is within us.

It's not just in some of us; it's in everyone.
And as we let our own light shine,
we unconsciously give other people
permission to do the same.
As we are liberated from our own fear,
Our presence automatically liberates others.

—Marianne Williamson

As for me, it may have appeared like I had everything together, but I was falling apart. All I could envision was the gloom in whatever situation or endeavor I was a part of at this time. It was as if I had been blinded from the truth. My friends would tell me that whatever I touched was blessed, and that it was obvious that I had the favor of God in my life. But I had an entirely different view of my life. I could easily identify every negative aspect of myself and found it very hard to focus on any of the good qualities that I possessed. None of my achievements thus far had brought me any comfort or satisfaction, leaving me even more hollowed inside. I felt alone, rejected, purposeless, and held a poor self-image of myself. Remnants of my childhood experiences had emerged from the past and surfaced into my present-day events. Canaan and stepsons not being appreciative triggered my illusion of rejection. My inability to find fulfillment created my illusion of purposelessness. The years of adverse opinions and lack of validation supported my poor self-image. At this point in my life, after years of disappointment, I did not believe that life would get any better for me, only worse. So many times, I prayed for God to take me like He did Enoch. "Enoch walked faithfully with God; then he was no more because God took him away" (Genesis 5:24, New International Version). I had no intention of committing suicide or harming myself physically because of my beliefs but believing that if God took me, I still had a possibility of making it into heaven.

As I stated earlier, I left my marriage, home and moved into an apartment because I thought I would lose my sanity if I continued to stay. I walked away from it all, my home, my marriage, and my stepchildren. The material possessions and social status I had obtained meant absolutely nothing to me. I had no problem trading it in for what I thought would be a life of peace. I was now in my apartment all alone hoping to finally find the peace I so longed for, but it did not take long before I realized I was still miserable. The only peace I got was quietness which was not the type of peace I was looking for. The move, the separation, the privacy, had no effect on how I was feeling on the inside. But do not get that confused with me moving out. I was elated to be away from Canaan. Communicating with Canaan was as difficult as two individuals who spoke different languages trying to converse. However, the separation gave me the opportunity to focus more on me and I did not like what I saw. I had been so focused on caring for others that I had not been attentive to my own needs. I realized that the wounds from my past had never healed or been addressed and had since festered over the years. Instead of focusing on the real issues including my traumas, I focused on the observable problems that were right in front of me dealing with Canaan and my stepsons. The pain that I endured from dealing with the problems between Canaan my stepsons only added salt to my wound but were not the root of my problem or the cause of my inner pain. It was so easy to blame my unhappiness on Canaan and my stepsons because it was those matters that I dealt with daily. However, they were not the blame for my unhappiness, I was the proprietor.

If the action of someone else gets an emotional reaction out of you then this is an area in your life that requires attention and needs healing. There is a high probability that if I had addressed my hurt from the past before meeting Canaan there would have been no marriage. It was years later that God revealed this lesson and I absorbed it. I had a poor self-image of myself and I attracted a man with a poor self-image. My perception of myself guaranteed that I would get involved in an unhealthy relationship. Self-confidence is an essential component for creating and maintaining a healthy relationship and I was lacking in this area. The only way I could have obtained self-confidence was to have addressed my childhood traumas and go through the healing and restoration process. I was not physically sick, but I was emotionally ill, and I made a lot of poor decisions while in this condition. A lot of times in life we focus on developing ourselves physically because we can visualize it but, we overlook our emotional development because we cannot see it. If I had been in a hospital bed or home in the bed ill, it is likely I would have made no major decisions because I was physically ill. It is the same thing as being emotionally sick. I should have not pursued a relationship with a man having custody of his two sons with me being emotionally damaged and bruised. I made the decision to get into this relationship in belief that I would have someone(s) I could faithfully love and that maybe I could finally feel appreciated, happy and secure, but instead I received the extreme opposite. So, my advice to anyone making a lifetime commitment make sure you have attended to your emotional wounds if not, it is likely that you will end up with adverse and undesirable results. Therefore, if you have experienced some of these then it is likely because of a trauma in your life that you have suffered. This trauma may leave you with insecurity or fear and when faced with it you may relive the same adverse emotions caused by the trauma. My traumas had to be faced and dealt with for me to take back my power to restore the peace and joy within.

During my separation, I continued to face the same sadness,

depression and meaninglessness almost every day of my life. I had concluded that my life was a complete waste. No accomplishment or achievement gave me any sense of value or worth, so I accepted that the only way I would find happiness and fulfillment was with God in heaven. I tried to take the easy way out by pleading my case to God why he should take me. I explained to him that I really had no purpose to be here and that my absence would barely be noticed on Earth. I had no kids of my own, my two stepsons did not appreciate my concern for them, Canaan had no comprehension of who or what a good wife was, and my family members wouldn't care if I was gone. As I talked and pleaded with God, trying to explain why he should take me, the tears would not stop. My heart was so heavy and overwhelmed with grief that I could barely speak; my words were such a slur. I felt like I could not go on living like this, this was not living; it was Hell here on Earth. My body had become so weak and my mind was in chaos that words no longer came out of my mouth, so my heart began to communicate with God. I then heard the voice of God speak to my spirit. He said, "Hannah, I have always been with you even when you thought you were all alone." He then carried me down memory lane reminding me of several important events that had occurred in my life that He enlighten me of his presence. As he spoke to my spirit, it was if he had removed a blindfold from off my eyes. God said when you were a child, I showed you favor in all you did. God said, no one may have come to your games, but I made you the Most Valuable Player. God said, no one may have taken pictures of you at your graduation, but I made you stand out being Class President all four years. God said, no one may have applauded your grades, but I sent you to a prestigious college. God said, when you started at your first career job and a head cashier would be selected, I set you above 29 women on the job. God said, when you worked at women's prison, I assigned you to an all-male P.E.R.T. (prison emergency response team) before you completed the probation period. God said when you worked at the men's prison, you were the first female officer assigned to the transportation unit. God said, when the prison administration needed an intermediate personal supervisor, I placed you in that position which you had no prior experience. Tears of joy and sadness ran down my face as God revealed the truths that had been staring at me all the while. Those same life events the devil had blinded me and swarmed my mind with all the negative responses that had surrounded each of these accomplishments. It was during this night in my apartment that I rededicated my life to the Lord.

The greatest revelation for me that night was that God had always been there with me even when I felt like I was all alone. It gave me such an overwhelming pouring of affection that I was not able to remain on my knees, so I prostrated on the floor. The aura of love consumed my body, mind, and spirit, leaving my body weak but my spirit overflowing with joy and peace. It was the greatest sensation I had ever experienced to date knowing that God was with me through my darkest times when I thought no one loved me. It felt so good to feel that I was cared about so much that I did not want to let go of that awareness of warmth and closeness. You have never experienced true intimacy until you have felt it with God. God became the most important being in my life that night. I had finally found someone I could trust to be there for me unconditionally and to have my back even when I refused to love myself. My greatest desire was to make God proud of me. I was a baby in Christ, so I did not have the understanding to realize that God was already proud of me. It was I who had to find self-assurance within. I returned to church, so I could decipher his word and have a closer relationship with him. I still had a long journey ahead to rid myself of all the childhood experiences that held me in bondage. I was just at the first stage of identifying and acknowledging the strongholds in my life. These strongholds held me in bondage for over thirty years and had become a part of me and they had no intentions of letting go without a fight. Beware! Even though I had this experience with God these strongholds have a way of making you question everything you experience expecting you to conclude that it was all in your head.

When I moved into my apartment, I wanted a fresh start and to leave my past behind me. I did not realize that when I packed my bags with all my provisions and loaded up my vehicle that I forgot to unpack my feelings of abandonment, rejection, and a sense of unworthiness to make room for my new resurgence. These emotional needs had never been identified or addressed much less fulfilled, so they concealed themselves until the craving was too much for them to bear. As an adult, the desire for these basic emotional needs that I was lacking: the need to love and be loved by someone, the need to belong, the need to have a purpose and the need to have a positive self-image had grown even stronger. I could not get those basic emotional needs fulfilled by my family members, so I looked for it from Canaan. Canaan at the time already had his own emotional deficiency therefore, he was not able to satisfy mine. During our marriage Canaan did not show me true love, make me feel like part of the family or important, leaving me to presume that I was insignificant once again. When Canaan failed to fulfill my emotional needs it almost destroyed my self-esteem completely. It was as if I had given this man and this relationship complete dominance over my existence. The same man that, if I had valued my worth, I would have never married. Do not go into any relationship expecting others to make you happy. No one can control your happiness but you. If you are miserable going into a relationship, then you are putting a lot of responsibility on the other person to give you validation. Believing that someone else can make you feel complete or whole is unfair and setting yourself up and the relationship for failure. "Cursed is the one who trusts in man, who draws strength from mere flesh and whose heart turns away from the Lord" (Jeremiah 17:5, New International Version)."But my God shall supply all your need according to his riches in glory by Christ Jesus" (Philippians 4:19, King James Version). "Be not ye, therefore, like unto them: for your, Father knoweth what things ye have need of before ye ask him." (Matthew 6:8, King James Version) The first step is to make you a priority and; love and cherish yourself.

Achievements, accomplishments, and material possessions will not fulfill you if you are lacking these emotional needs. No matter what I achieved it was never good enough. I always felt I could have done better. I gave little value or worth to my achievements and accomplishments, dismissing them as meaningless and insignificant. Canaan and I had just purchased and moved into a beautiful, spacious new home and within three months I gave it up. I left my house and moved into a one-bedroom apartment. The material possessions did not give me any peace or joy on the inside or fulfill my emotional needs. Material possessions will only bring short-term happiness and after a while, you become bored with it. True fulfillment and self-worth must be found from within. My self-worth was discovered through my relationship with God. It did not happen overnight instead it took years building a trusting relationship with God to allow Him to fulfill my basic emotional needs. It was not until I finally trusted God completely that I was able to truly receive His love for me. Once I did, God fulfilled every one of my emotional needs. I love Him, and he loves me. He made me realize that I was a part of Him. He gave me the purpose which was to encourage and inspire others.

Yes, Canaan and my stepsons exposed me to a lot of distress. However, I also contributed to my own suffering. I devoted so much time focusing on helping others with their issues that it left little time to focus on the real issue which was me and my open wounds. I was so busy trying to satisfy other people's needs to receive their approval and validation that I overlooked the person who needed me the most, Hannah. I was just as guilty as all the others that had caused me any type of heartache. I had abandoned, rejected and made myself feel worse than anyone else was capable of. It was apparent at the time that Canaan and my stepsons were not appreciative of my help, therefore, instead focusing entirely on them I should have focused more on my needs. I wanted the best for my stepsons, however, I had to learn the hard way that you cannot force someone to accept you. Looking back now, once the boys made it clear of their intentions and aspirations in life, I should have refocused on me. It was the perfect time for me to discover me. Who I am, why am I here, what is my purpose, what inspires me and what gives me pleasure? However, I fell into self-pity, "Oh no one loves me or cares about me." Why should I expect someone else to love and care about me when it was obvious that I did not love and care about myself to continue in this vicious cycle. Doing the same thing repeatedly expecting a different result is the definition of insanity. We all must accept that there are consequences for our actions we either make a change or stay the same. One of the most important changes I needed to make in my life was to allow me to define who I was and not others. However, before I was able to define me, I had to rediscover me. For me to do that, I had to go on a long journey of discovery and get to know Hannah, so I could find the true person that inhabited within. I can't blame others for my shortcomings or happiness. It is a mission I must undertake and solve on my own. My first step was to forgive anyone that had wronged me, so my heart would be pure, free of any form of anger, bitterness or hatred. If we do not forgive others for their wrongs against us, then our mission will be over even before it starts.

My perception then:	I had no purpose in life and my current relationships only depicted a vicious cycle of the lack of approval and validation that I had already experienced my whole life.
Message:	No one is responsible for your happiness but you. If other people opinions of you upset or offend you it only uncovers symptoms of traumas that still require healing and restoration. Before you focus so much time and energy on resolving other external issues make sure your internal wounds have been mended and healed.
How this experience affected my future:	I sought a closer relationship with God and looked for my true purpose. It propelled me to gain insight into self-discovery.
My perception now:	Through this experience, I discovered that I am the Proprietor of my happiness and that whatever I desire must be initiated and validated internally eliminating external opinions and judgments.

CHAPTER

Eleven
Obedience

*D*uring my marriage, I had excelled in every position in my career. First, I was working in the prisons, next the insurance industry and then telecommunications. In every assigned position, before telecommunications, I was promoted or elevated to the next level. It was during my job at the telecommunications that I started experiencing unusual happenings, urges and desires to open my own business. The

truth is I had never thought about self-employment, so I was puzzled by these thoughts. I was accustomed to getting promoted so I looked forward to that type of advancement. With my work ethic, it was only a matter of time before I would get promoted. I had mastered my current job in telecommunications so well that all my tasks were completed before noon every day. No matter what was going on, my objective was to

get my tasks completed. On the days that had rumors of layoffs, my co-workers would be huddled around wondering if this would be their last day, but not me. My co-workers would ask if I was worried about the layoff and my response would be, "if they lay me off, I hope they allow me to finish these orders before I leave." Due to my strong focus and drive, I never stopped working until everything was completed and this was my daily routine.

While I was sitting at work one day with all my work completed and after assisting my co-workers, an overwhelming urge came over me to have a mobile concession trailer constructed. I thought to myself, "Wow where did that come from?" It was if something had uploaded the thoughts into me, I had never thought about doing this before this moment. Without even a second thought, the goal was established to open a concession trailer and, on the weekends, sell food at the racetrack and at other events. So, after lunch each day on my job, I began researching information on how to get the concession trailer. I envisioned in my mind what my mobile concession would look like and how to arrange all the commercial appliances inside for serving convenience. I never thought about the fact that I had no money or previous experience on how to get this done. This overwhelming force instructed me on what to do next and gave me such a peace that I never questioned why I was pursuing this endeavor. I just continued to be obedient and follow its instructions.

In my initial research, I found the cost of having a mobile concession licensed. Then, being continually led by this force after a few days of searching, I found a business that sold bare trailers that would allow me to have commercial equipment installed. My next task was finding a company that would install the commercial appliances, which was accomplished within a few days. The cost included the licensing fees, cost of the trailer and the cost of commercial equipment. My last mission was to acquire the funds to pay for all of this. I never considered for one moment where I was going to get funds from. This force driving me had no fear or worry and this caused me to be in complete alignment. One morning on my way to work the force instructed me to go to the bank and apply for the loan. So, during my lunch period that afternoon, I decided to go to the bank and inquire about a loan. I went into the bank and spoke with one of the loan officers regarding getting a loan for my new business adventure. She told me that a business plan was needed to get a business loan. I walked out of the bank pondering in thoughts but not disheartened. I had never written a business plan and writing was not one of my best attributes, but that did not mean I could not do it. Even after the loan officer's response, I left the bank with no worries as if I already had the loan. This overwhelming force only presented me with two options which were to believe and expect. So, when I returned to work, I continued to research about mobile concessions, such as locations to set up and advertising ideas.

About a week later, Canaan went into the bank where I had met with the loan officer. We patronized the bank frequently, so the loan officer was very familiar with us. The loan officer asked Canaan, "Why did Hannah not come to get the loan?" He told her the business plan was the holdup. The loan officer then stated Hannah can get approved without a business plan. She had only suggested the business plan to provide a better interest rate. After hearing that news, I walked into the bank the next day and walked out with an unsecured amount of funds to pay for my concession trailer and equipment. I was overjoyed with excitement. An idea that had come through this overwhelming force was now only a few steps from coming into fruition. Everything had come together so smoothly and effortlessly and now it was just a matter of time before the mobile concession business was up and running. The final step was to get my it inspected before I could start serving food. Once the city health inspector inspected my concession trailer, he stated, that "it was the nicest mobile concession trailer that he had licensed." This meant a lot since my health inspector worked for the capital city in my state. After the inspector signed off, my 8 by 18-foot mobile concession trailer with stainless steel commercial equipment was ready for business. Within a few months of having an overwhelming force imparted as an idea into my inner self from out of the blue, became reality.

> *Delight thyself also in the Lord: and*
> *he shall give thee the desires of thine heart*
> *(Psalms 37:4, King James Version)*

Of course, I did not realize or even comprehend at the time that this overwhelming force was God speaking to my spirit. I had not rededicated my life to God at this point but that did not stop him from communicating with me. However, what was clear was that I trusted this force that came over me. I felt its omnipotence and it conveyed such aura of peace and assurance that it moved me to complete submission. It was this force that initiated the business idea and directed the plan until its completion. This would be the first of several businesses that I would open after the encounter with this force. Unknowingly at the time, God had given me the Faith Blueprint to Opening a Business but due to my lack of faith and confidence, it would take time before I was able to accept and internalize what God had given me. It would not be revealed to me until years later that I was following the same plan he had given me on this endeavor with my mobile concession trailer to use on all my future businesses. More detailed instructions will have to be illustrated in another book, however, listed below is a diagram of the steps which were given by God obediently followed.

Faith Blueprint to Opening a Business

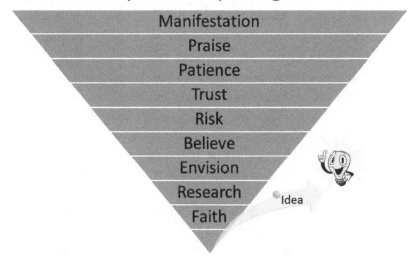

After almost a year, I realized the mobile concession business was not compatible with my current aspirations. I sold the mobile concession trailer and paid off my loan. The mobile concession business was now a thing of the past. However, it would later be revealed that it was not about me sustaining the business, but God teaching me to trust through obedience. Through my obedience, he would build my faith in him and confidence in myself. He wanted me to see that I could do anything that I set my mind to if I was obedient and trusted in him. God taught me these lessons to give me the strength to overcome the challenges I would have in the future to ensure my destiny would be fulfilled. He understood that due to my low self-esteem, lack of confidence, and trust issues that he would have to allow me to experience other situations to build my faith and confidence. So, another overwhelming force came over me to start creating Bible lessons and teach them. By this time, I had rededicated my life to the Lord and was fully aware that it is God speaking to my spirit. However, this request would force me to step out of my comfort zone because writing was not my best attribute. In my opinion, my vocabulary was inadequate. Now, God was calling me to create and teach Bible lessons but without hesitation, I started reading and studying the bible. The conviction was so strong that I trusted the voice of God more than my own inabilities.

So, God gave me my first lesson to teach and it was titled "What in Your Life Needs to Be Cleaned Up" and it came from the following scriptures; Genesis 17: 12-14; Exodus 4: 1, 10, and 13; Exodus 4:21-26. Initially, I had no confidence in myself that I could write the first lesson, but with God in the midst, my writing was remarkable. The lessons were so simple for me to write that it was as if someone else had taken over my body as I began typing out each lesson every week. This would go on for over a year, God would give me lessons to write out with specific instructions on what scriptures to reference and what life situations examples to use. I would type out the Bible lesson, email it out to several family members, friends and associates and then drive an hour and a half on Friday nights to teach it at my home church. It was amazing how God would give me the lessons. Sometimes, He would give me the lesson a couple of days in advance and some days a couple hours before it was time to teach it. Weekly, I would receive emails from my readers asking me how I knew what they were going through and others commenting that the message was especially for them. I would immediately respond; it was God not me.

I wish I could say everyone had favorable compliments for my lessons, but the envious ones gave credit to the internet for my lessons. My co-workers that witnessed me write them weekly were appalled at the naysayers. I did not allow that to hinder me because one thing was for sure, I knew every lesson came from God because I was aware of my weaknesses and my strengths. I recognized that God was the only one that could turn one of my weaknesses into strength. But most of all I was so proud, ecstatic and amazed that God had used my weaknesses to give me confidence in an area of my life that I felt so inadequate. As time went on, I continued to do the Bible lessons but then I heard another voice say, "Hannah, open a group home for girls." Where did this come from? I wondered because I had never thought about a group home, never worked in a group home, and really did not know anyone that had. At the time, when I was dealing with this experience, I did not initially relate it to God speaking to my spirit. This thought had just come from nowhere and then consumed me and my yearning to fulfill it was relentless. The overwhelming desire for me to open this girls group home was as if it was a lifetime dream, however, it was a newly instilled thought. I did not think twice because I was full of excitement. I began to immediately research my new project giving it my full attention. I had not identified that God was creating a pattern of events in my life even though I had these prior experiences until I wrote it in a journal for my book.

I had no prior experience in this field, so I had to start from scratch. I did not even know how much it would cost to start up the business, or the income I could profit from this new business endeavor. I just listened to the small voice speaking to me and followed it. After some research, I discovered I would have to have a sustainable amount of income to pull off opening this business, which I did not have. I would have to write policies and procedures, get certifications, get licenses and locate a property for the home just a few of the requirements. Then, I would have to pay for the vacant property for months while it was in the licensing process. I had no idea how I was going to get this done with my limited funds and knowledge, but then I recognized that this was the same situation as with the mobile concession unit. The group home had originated from an overwhelming desire the same as the concession trailer. So finally, it clicked, and the light bulb came on in my head; it was God speaking to me again. He was the one that ministered the idea into my spirit and was orchestrating my footsteps. This is the same scenario as the mobile concession trailer as there was no prior experience or funds. The only difference between the two was that it would require more money, more effort and more time before the group home would come into fruition than it did with the mobile concession unit.

So, over the next few months, I continued to believe that the group home would be licensed and ready to provide services for young girls. Some days I felt like I lacked the knowledge to get the job done, but I continued to trust God with supplying me with the needed information. There were several times when the project required additional funds and I had no idea where the finances would come from, but I chose to trust that God would provide. The licensing process was somewhat lengthy and stressful at times, but it was then that I learned how to be more patient and focus on my faith. Throughout the entire process, I continued to believe in and praise God, even when things did not go as planned. Within less than a year the girl's group home was opened and ready for occupancy. I had been given an idea of a business opportunity and successfully opened it all because of this small voice that spoke to my spirit. With no prior experience, no funds, and feelings of inadequacy, what seemed impossible became a reality.

I decided that I would hire someone to run my group home while I continued to work at my fulltime job. But in this situation, I would learn that God's plans and my plans were not the same. I can remember just like it was yesterday. I had received a call in the month of October from the Area Administrator stating they had a young female that they wanted to place in my group home. They were expecting her to be placed around the third week in November. I was so excited at the thought of getting my first client. I had already hired a young lady that was to oversee the group home for me while I continued to work at my job, so everything seemed to be going as planned. In a few weeks I would be getting my first client and I could continue to receive my current income without interruption. The first week in November, our group had been assigned a new manager at the telecommunications company and she called a meeting. I attended the meeting and sat at the back of the room making out my group home schedule not paying a whole a lot of attention. I was half listening to the conversations going on in the meeting. I had completed the most orders in my group and maintained the lowest number of orders, so I could not imagine that they would have any complaints about my work. The new manager stated that there was an imbalance in the number of orders between associates, so all the orders would have to be redistributed throughout all the team members again. Most of my co-workers had about 100 to 250 orders to be worked on their desk and I only had about 40. I did not think it was right because I put in extra effort to keep my orders low, but I thought to myself, I will process all my new orders and do whatever I have to do to get them completed even if it meant working overtime.

I was motivated by results and closure, so I work fervently to control my volume of orders to ensure I got that feeling. I was very organized and structured. I had become accustomed to always being a step ahead. However, the next comment would change all my previous plans, my desire, my performance, and my intentions. My manager gave this example during the meeting: if Mary closes one order, she would be assigned one more order and if John closes five orders, he would be assigned five more orders. I immediately stood up and pulled my chair towards the front of the room and asked the manager to please repeat what you just said. She cheerfully repeated the same thing. I was in total disagreement and I explained to her why I did not feel that it was fair for the co-workers that work the most diligent would be punished the most. I then made the statement, "the more orders I close the more I will get, and the fewer orders another person closes the less they will get!" To which she replied, "You are not looking at it the right way," and said that I was not being a team player. Not a team player I thought to myself. My first two weeks at the company my first manager would not allow me to work solo, so I developed a training curriculum for new and old associates. I wrote step by step procedures on how to setup up folders, files, and email address books and how to complete the orders from start to finish. I walked out of that meeting feeling some kind of way. I knew things would never be the same. One of my co-workers jokingly said to me after the meeting, "Don't worry Hannah I will not close any orders, so you can close mine", with a grin on his face. I walked back to my desk and the desire to work on another order had completely diminished. I sat at my desk for the next few hours contemplating what I was going to do because my longings to thrive here at this job was gone. The next day I gave my two-week notice because I couldn't bear not giving a 100 percent to my job. It was not in my nature to perform below standards. The buzz got around the office that I was going to leave and manage my own business. However, they knew after the meeting, that the new job requirements did not sit right with me and were not surprised by my decision. So, they congratulated me on the opening of my new business and wished me the best.

Before the meeting, I was afraid to step out on faith. My intentions were to remain in my stable job with my guaranteed salary until the group home had begun to show some profits. It is amazing how my manager's comments changed my heart regarding a position that I found so much gratification and turned it into mere loathing in a matter of minutes. I did a one-eighty. I went from working fervently on orders from the time it was initiated and completed to not being able to open and view one order. All desire had completely left me. God was the only one that could bring about such an immediate change of emotion in my life. Therefore, I believe God directed my manager's comments to ensure I managed my own business. God knows my heart and what drives me and impedes me. Those comments gave me the ambition and courage to walk away from financial stability and trust God with my financial well-being. I had no idea what it would be like not having a steady income, but I believed God purposely changed my plans, so I stepped out in faith not knowing if the group home would be a success or not. Well, it ended up being the best decision I ever made. I opened the group home and I never struggled financially after walking away from my job. Within a few months, I had almost tripled my salary from my previous job. Again because of the small voice, God's voice, I had successfully opened another business by being obedient.

We all have talents within us, some we are aware of and others we are not. I had no idea that I had the ability to be an entrepreneur or a bible study teacher. I have always felt inadequate in several areas of my life two to be specific; one is my ability to communicate well and the other my lack of education. I have always feared to speak in front of others due to my perceived lack of vocabulary. I can recall my 11th grade English teacher saying that our class vocabulary was poverty-stricken; I believed it because I always kept in mind her statement and never did anything to change it. And I was also disappointed with myself for the lack of reading accomplished over my lifetime and I regret not furthering my education which I felt could have expanded my knowledge a great deal. However, God sees our weakness as strengths. By listening to God's voice and being obedient to his directions, I discovered that I had the spiritual gifts of administration, teaching, and faith. It is very important that we slowdown in this fast pace world and listen for God's voice. God speaks to our spirits quite often, but it is usually drowned out by the chaos of this world in our minds. It may be difficult to hear God if we do not understand how God communicates with us and we get it confused with how Satan communicates with us. God speaks to our heart (spirit) and Satan speaks to our mind. Though our human body, our mind believes what it sees in the natural, and it is distracted by our feelings and causes us to doubt. Through our spiritual man, our spirit believes God's word and disregards our feelings and have confidence that God's word will come to past. So sometimes when we hear God's voice, we tend to dismiss it because it does not correspond with what we see from in the natural. It is very important that daily we talk with God and listen for his small voice and then be obedient to His instructions. "If you are willing and obedient, you will eat the good things of the land" (Isaiah, 1:19 New International Version).

While writing this book, I discovered the most important lesson for me was through my acts of obedience in the areas I felt the weakest

God gave me strength. But, He said to me, "My grace is sufficient for you, for my power is made perfect in weakness." "Therefore, I will boast all the more gladly about my weaknesses, so that Christ's power may rest on me" (2 Corinthians 12:9, King James Version). This was a major turning point for me because so many times in life I allowed my inadequacies to hinder me from pursuing a lot of other opportunities. God made it clear to me that there was only one thing required of me in these experiences which was my obedience. He proved to me that if I was obedient to him and followed his word that regardless of my inadequacies, experience, or finances that he would equip me and supply my every need.

It is very easy to second guess yourself when you hear the voice of God and believe that you misunderstood what you heard. However, we tend to believe everything the satan says. When you have a call or an assignment from God, it tends to consume you and you find it hard to put it out of your mind. If you refuse to acknowledge it, you find yourself lacking peace and begin questioning why you feel like doing something else. Then, once you accept the voice of the Lord, you begin questioning why you would be given this task because you feel totally unqualified. You then create a list in your mind of why you are not capable of performing this request or making it happen. If you have experienced these signs, then it is likely that God has called you for His purpose. If you hear that small voice, do not just dismiss it out of fear of the call or assignment. Acknowledge it and know that God who called you will equip you. God wanted me to make it clear that you do not need experience, skills, degree, people's approval, connection or money, obedience is the Key that will unlock every door for you.

My perception then:	In the areas that I felt inadequate, I would have never attempted to try. It is best to have financial stability than to leave your job for self-employment.
Message:	If God calls you to an assignment, He will equip you with all you need to be a success. God only requires obedience. Regardless of your inadequacies, experience, skills, degree, people's approval, connection or money you can be a success. All you need is God; He will supply all your needs.
How this experience affected my future:	When I heard that small voice instructs me to leave my home and open a business in another state with limited funds and the unknown, I was obedient and did not hesitate. I recognized it as the voice of God.
My perception now:	God's purpose is not limited by my weakness; He will turn my weakness into strengths to carry out his mission. If I am obedient to his instructions, then I can reach new levels of greatest.

CHAPTER

Twelve
Humility

*I*n September of 2002, after five and a half years of marriage, Canaan, my stepsons and I move into our second home. It was very spacious: four bedrooms, two and a half baths, living room, dining room, loft, office/exercise room, a large den and a two-car garage. It was almost 3400 square feet and every room was furnished and decorated beautifully. To the outside world I had a great life. However, by December of 2002, less than three months after moving into our brand-new home, I had moved out due to a life of complete misery. Some of these events of this move also reference in the chapter Discovery. Canaan's actions and his lack of discipline towards my stepsons was unbearable for me. My stepsons acted as though they were the adults in the home and did whatever they wanted to do in and outside the home. However, I did not expect much from my stepsons because their father acted as if he was their friend instead of their father. There were physical altercations on several occasions more than I care to recall. However, this one particular  occasion both boys had jumped on their father and he demanded I go and get my gun. My response to him was that they were not fighting me, why do you need my gun? I continued to watch them fight, saying to myself no one would believe me if I told them what goes on here because I am living it and I can barely conceive it. Less than an hour after the altercation, Canaan asked if I wanted to go to the movies with them. I said, "Go to the movies with who?" I asked out of shock because I knew he better not be talking about with him and the boys. He replied with him and the boys. I said, "Absolutely not! You just finished fighting each other and now you want to reward them for their bad behavior. I want no part in it." And this pattern of behavior with the boys continued throughout most of our marriage. The reason I refused to get involved during the incident I just discussed was due to the fact that on many occasions prior I would recommend that Canaan discipline the boys for their actions but he refused and told me not to worry about how they behaved. And just the same as this incident he would reward them for their negative behaviors. I had many turbulent days and sleepless nights worrying about my stepsons and their future. However, after years of no improvement, I could no longer cope with the total disrespect from Canaan and my stepsons towards each other and Canaan's lack of respect for me as his wife and their unruly behavior. So, I moved out into my new apartment.

Now I have been living in my apartment for a few months. I knew Canaan was seeing someone, but I did not care because I knew once I left it gave him freedom and permission to date. And you cannot hold someone accountable if they get involved with another while you are separated. I tried dating for a while, but I realized I needed time alone to get myself together. Anyway, seven months after moving out and into my new apartment, I rededicated my life to God. Then, a few weeks later, God told me to return home to my husband. I could not believe what I was hearing. But I knew it had to be the voice of God because my desire to return home was non-existent. All I could think about was all the negative emotions I felt over the years and I did not want to relive those experiences again. So, I had to be sure that it was God speaking to my spirit. I questioned why God would want me to return home and live with three males who had not appreciated my presence or had shown any type of real love towards me over the last five years. Tears rolled down with the thought of having to go back for the next couple of days hoping that God would change his mind and give me another option, but he did not. As much as I hated to return, I was afraid to disobey God. God has never directed me down the wrong path before, so I made the decision to talk with Canaan about what God had told me to do. Now, I would have to humble myself and ask Canaan if I could return home because I was the one who had left. My flesh was in total disagreement with this, especially with the resentment I had towards him for his parenting skills and maintaining relationships with his female friends that I was not privy to meet. This was not an easy task for me. I felt like I was admitting that I was wrong for leaving him and my returning gave him permission to continue with those behaviors, actions, and tricks. But God said I must go back home, so I was obedient. I spoke to Canaan about it and he responded, "You can come back, but I am not going to change." A part of me was happy with Canaan's response and a part of me felt like he stuck a knife in my already wounded heart. Why would any sane person want to expose themselves to this man's insensitivity? At least now I felt like I now had some evidence to take to God to show why I should not have to return. During my conversation with God, I relayed to him what Canaan had said, and his response was still the same: go back home. Tears began to run down my face. Fear, frustration, despair, and anger all consumed me, coupled with agony my head was going to explode. I was so confused, hurt, and afraid. I just could not understand why God would require me to go back into the same situation I had left. God knew better than anyone how I felt during the marriage and everything that I had to deal with when I was there, so I could not even begin to comprehend why he would choose this path for me. I cried and battled for the next couple of days with the instructions God had given me, but then one day I just stopped crying and wiped away the tears and took a stand. I realized that God was not going to change his mind, so I accepted his decision for me, and I prayed and asked him to please help me through it.

God spoke to my spirit again and I heard clearly what he expected me to do next. God expected me to forgive Canaan and treat him with kindness and humility. "Humble yourselves in the sight of the Lord, and he shall lift you up" (James, 4:10). He was requiring me to put aside my pride and reach out to Canaan. This was a lot for me to swallow. I did not even believe in my marriage anymore, but I had to obey God regardless of my personal feelings. But I could not help but feel like Canaan had wronged me and God was punishing me. Regardless of my feelings, I trusted God. I did as God instructed me and reached out to Canaan to make amends. In the beginning, it was hard, but I continued to pray and ask God to give me the strength to deal with this man. For the next few months, Canaan and I started dating again. Without notice, one day I realized my feelings had changed for Canaan and that God had supernaturally rekindled my affection for him. I have no idea how that happened. So now I am vulnerable, and my heart is in it, I will now be faced with my first test. A few weeks before it was time for me to return home, Canaan was supposed to come over to my apartment, but he never showed up. I called him several times and he did not answer the phone. All the fear, anxiety and worry within me emerged. I knew he was back up to his old tricks. But I was more upset with myself for allowing myself to be hurt again. I was furious. Why would God ask me to put myself through this knowing what Canaan was up to? I will never forget that night as long as I live. I cried uncontrollably. I thought I was going to lose my mind. It was like I lost all control of my mind, body, and soul. The tears would not stop, and my heart was so heavy it felt like it was going to plunge out of my body, gasping for breath, I asked God, why do I have to go through this? I was like an infant needing my mother to hold and squeeze me, so I would not feel like I was falling apart. I cried continuously for several hours, with no sleep in sight. I understood at that very moment why it was good that I had never taken any illegal drugs because if I had been accustomed to it, I am not sure if I would have been alive to tell this story. All I wanted to do was to be relieved of this pain. Then suddenly, I felt my body being caressed and held so gently a feeling I had never felt before in my life. My tears stopped, and I felt an amazing peace come over me and I felt so safe, warm and comforted. There was never a question of who it was. I recognized God's presence and he had come personally to comfort me. The next moments were surreal. I could feel Him rocking me as His arms held me close while His hands caressed me until I fell asleep. The next morning, when I woke up, I was in complete awe of this experience. My God came and rescued me. Canaan was the least of my concern. I yearned for God's presence and his touch to return but somehow, I knew he was only there for that night when I needed him the most. God personally came to rescue me when I was at my darkest and lowest point.

Later during my ordeals, when I would be going through tough times, I would always desire for God to return and hold me like He did that night, but He never did. God came when I needed him the most. God knew I credited him for opening my heart to Canaan and blamed Him for the betrayal. It was unclear why He would purposely put me in harm's way of this man again and allow him to hurt me. If I could not trust God, who could I trust? God knew every emotion that night and the fact that I felt helpless. People have often asked me; how do you know your God is real? My response has always been, "one night when my degree of anguish was so intense and my soul was in so much despair that I was clinging to life, my God personally came and rescued me and held me through the night." No human being has ever made me feel the love, security, warmth, and peace that I felt that night in God's arms. I often think about it now and ask God, "Can you just stop by and hold me every now and then like that night"?

After nine months of leaving my new house, I returned home and nothing or no one had changed except me. God had warned me to hold my peace and allow him to fight my battle. Again, I prayed to God to please help me keep my mouth shut because dealing with their absurdity in the past was a sure way to get me screaming and yelling. Over the next few years, God allowed me to blossom during the chaos. God restored the love that I had so longed for under the same roof with three males who did not have the ability to show it for their own personal reasons. I finally realized why God had sent me back home with all the disorder in that house. No human being would be able to get credit for my love being restored. God would get it all. God was true to his word. I kept my mouth shut and things were a lot better for me. My living arrangement was extremely peaceful, but as for Canaan, he was not as fortunate. I prayed for God to help him. My stepsons were showing him Hell on Earth. They were staying out all night, using drugs, stealing, missing school, fighting and having physical altercations with him, and so on. Amazingly, their actions no longer affected me anymore. We were all living under the same roof and I witnessed all of this going on. However, it was as if I was in a glass room looking out at them. It was during this period that I opened my businesses and the dysfunction in my relationships at home did not hinder me. I had accomplished and excelled in ways I never believed was possible for me considering my history. However, God still had higher expectations for me but there were still some strongholds that were deterring me from reaching my true potential and God's purpose for my life.

December 2004 Canaan and I had just returned from a Carnival cruise. We arrived home around 6 pm that evening. Once we arrived, we discovered that my youngest stepson was not home after calling in sick from school. By this time, my older stepson had dropped out of school, received the remainder of his trust fund account, and moved out into his own apartment. Canaan was really concerned because he kept calling both my stepsons and received no answer. After a long day of traveling, I was extremely tired, and I went to bed around 11 pm. My stepson had still not returned home. Around 1:00 am following the instructions of the police, Canaan came upstairs and tried to wake me up. I was in a deep sleep, so I turned over and looked at him but went right back to sleep. Canaan then went back downstairs and told the police that he tried to wake me up, but I would not get up. The police told him you need to go and tell her that the police are downstairs, and she needs to get up. A few minutes later he came again to wake me, and this time when he woke me up, he said, "Hannah the police said you have to come downstairs." "Police?" I responded. Every ounce of sleep left my body when I heard the word police. I immediately got up and went downstairs and two police officers were standing in our living room. I invited them into the kitchen, so I could sit down before I passed out. I already felt it had something to do with my stepsons, the day I had feared. At that point, I did not know if they were living or dead. Their first statement was that my vehicle had been involved in a homicide. It was my Mustang that I had just recently sold to my stepson, but the paperwork had not changed at DMV yet. I knew what homicide meant, but that morning I felt as if the meaning was incorrect because this could not possibly be happening. We did not know who was dead, alive or who was involved, and the police did not have a lot of information either. They were sent to our residence thinking we were drug dealers, actually Drug Kingpins. At the time, Canaan and I had a few properties; we owned several vehicles a Jaguar, Lexus, Escalade, F150, and the Mustang that was still in my name. In addition to the vehicles Canaan had for his side car business. Later, it was established that my two stepsons along with three other young men had been involved in a murder. They went to a drug dealer's home in pretense of buying drugs, but instead, they robbed the drug dealer and three other guys. In the commission of the robbery, the drug dealer was shot and killed. Being found guilty, both my stepsons were sentenced to ten years in prison for second-degree murder and armed robbery. They were both 17 and 19 respectively when they committed the crime. This really took a toll on me because it was my worst nightmare coming true. I tried so hard to convince Canaan to hold them accountable for their actions, but for reasons best known to him, he just did not have the heart to do it. The boys had lost their mother at a young age and I believe Canaan could not bear to cause them any more pain. He made sure they had the best of everything. I expressed my concern that giving them so much might affect them in the future. Canaan lived under the premise that they were boys being boys, and that one day they would grow out of it. He also referred to me as a drill sergeant, being too strict expecting too much from them, all the while he was out on the road every evening and night leaving them under my supervision. Well, I guess if expecting them to come home at night, do homework, keep grades up, do their chores and reframe from indulging in alcohol or drugs defines me as being a drill sergeant, then I am guilty. I even made arrangements for my stepsons to get a tour in the male prison that I worked. I had the inmates talk to my stepsons about their experiences, mistakes, regrets in hopes it would help change their course in life. But that did not do any good. Structure is required at home first. After years of fighting with Canaan about me disagreeing with his parenting skills, I no longer had the energy or perseverance to fight anymore so I allowed him to do it his way. The outcome of my stepson's future is what I was trying to prevent.

Life went on as years passed. It was around the middle of the year in 2008, I had just forgiven Canaan about a newly discovered indiscretion, yet he was still reluctant to change. Initially, I refused to walk out on my marriage again because of my relationship with God. I persuaded Canaan to attend marriage counseling classes to save our marriage. During one of the first meetings, Canaan told the counselor that I needed to stop arguing all the time about the incident. The counselor responded, because of your actions she might argue with you for the next five years, ten years, or even 15 years. It is what you are willing to deal with. He said, "There is a lot of internal damage that you have done to Hannah." The counselor further stated, "If you hit a car from behind and from looking at it there could be no external damage, but if you get on your knees and look under the car, you could see a lot of internal damage. This is what you have done to her, caused her 11 years of internal damage." Canaan just looked at him with a blank expression on his face. During another session, I explained to the marriage counselor about all the female friends that Canaan associated with and how he refused to introduce me to them and refuse to talk with them on the phone in my presence. The counselor asked Canaan, "How can Hannah feel like the Queen in her home when you have all these other female friends?" Canaan responded, "That is how people get killed when you give up all your friends and then your wife leaves you." I knew before he finished the sentence that I was out! God had opened the door for me to leave this marriage. The reason I knew it for sure as if the word "killed" was not enough. Two days after that counseling session a friend called me out of the blue unaware of my circumstances with an attorney's name and phone number. For months, I had been looking for an affordable attorney regarding my situation and had been unsuccessful.

I contacted the attorney the following day. After speaking with the attorney, she advised me that we would have to live in separate residences for a year before I could get a divorce. I thought about it, and since I was more financially stable, I decided to move into one of our smaller homes. We had properties that needed to be divided and I had all intentions on being fair about the division. However, I did not know how I was going to move without him interfering or how I would get the furniture out without him catching me in the process. So, I just talked with God about my situation and waited for an answer. In less than a week after meeting the attorney I received a phone call from Canaan. I was at the hair salon on a Thursday afternoon when Canaan informed me, he was going to Vegas for the weekend with a male friend and he was leaving the next day. I just sniggered and shook my head thinking to myself, yes, this is a man trying to work out his marriage. I then asked how long he would be gone. He stated that he would be back that following Tuesday. As soon as I hit the end button on my cell phone, I quickly strolled down the contact list to the owner of a moving company I had used previously and asked him if he could be at my house on Saturday. He informed me that he could. I then called five of my girlfriends simultaneously and advised them that I needed their assistance at my house on Friday evening. They all showed up ready to work. I had instructed my girlfriends what I was going to leave and what I was going to take. However, one of my girlfriends decided to pack items I had previously informed I was leaving for Canaan. She decided on her own that I should have these certain items. I reminded her that God was looking at me and I had to be fair or I would lose out in another way. So, far the move was going smoothly with no conflict. Then, on Saturday one of my neighbors saw the moving truck in our yard and he called Canaan. The neighbor told Canaan that a moving truck was backed up to his house. Canaan then called me. I informed him I was moving out, but I would be fair about furniture and vehicles. There was nothing he could do to interfere with the move because he was over 2500 miles away and was not due back until Tuesday. Once he returned, he continued to live in the marital home for two years rent-free. For those two years, back and forth to court, he was trying to sue me for alimony and equitable distribution. I just could not wait for it to end. Spending money that I really did not have to spare, I was already paying for the marital home where he was living. The home was deeded in both our names, but the loan was financed in my name only and I could not afford to allow my credit to go bad, so I paid it.

After the divorce was finally over and some time had passed, I was able to see things clearer once some of the pain had diminished. I realized Canaan had a wounded heart when we got together however that did not minimize the anguish for me at the time. He had been hurt by his first wife. He really loved her, and I believe he was faithful to her, but after a few years of marriage, she joined the military with a promise to send back for him and the boys. However, she only kept half of her promise and she sent for her sons only. She divorced Canaan and then married someone else in the military. I believe this experience really crushed his self-esteem. When she left him, he told me he had no real friends to comfort him after the separation. I imagined he never wanted to expose himself to that kind of feelings again. So, when he married me, I am sure it was in his subconscious that I might do the same thing, so he took precautions. I, who was already broken, would be punished for someone else's wrongdoings. It took me years to understand why Canaan treated me the way he did, but I forgave him a long time ago. Hurt people, hurt people. Now I believe he later realized where he went wrong, and he is remorseful, but it has come just a little too late. I hope this situation will help someone look at how they are treating their significant other. Are you holding them accountable for what they did to you or what someone else did to you? Please change before it is too late, and you lose a good person out of fear!

When God first directed me to go home, there was nothing good that I could see coming out of this situation, especially when Canaan had already made it clear to me that he was going to continue to do the same thing and had no intentions of changing. But for God, it was not about Canaan's actions. It was all about mine. God knew my heart had become dark in this area. I was never going to let anyone hurt me again, nor put up with any mess. God would just use Canaan to humble me. Because of my past, I refused to yield to anyone I knew was intentionally hurting me. God knew about this protective barrier. The wall I had built around myself would hinder me from becoming the person that he destined me to be. My heart would have to be free from all the negative baggage that I was carrying before I could truly see myself how God saw me.

This experience was so crucial in my life. I trusted God and he showed me regardless of my situation or surroundings with him in the midst nothing or no one could hinder me except me. God sent me back home to a place there was initially no peace and instructed me to hold my peace. Amid that situation, he gave me peace. Instead of the environment getting better it got worse. But because I was obedient and held my peace the chaos that surrounded me was unable to impinge on my spirit. God had given me so much peace in the circumstances it was as if I had been sedated with a drug, I was so relaxed. As if that was not enough, he allowed me to start up new businesses that I had no prior knowledge before running. He proved to me that with Him I could still flourish and prosper amid turmoil if I continued to focus on Him and not on my surroundings and follow His path for me.

Sometimes in life, we run away from the place we need to be running to. God knows our beginning and our ending. We have no idea what is going to happen any day thus it is imperative that we listen to God when he speaks to our spirits. What he directs us to do a lot of times in life is totally out of our comfort zone, but it is when we are uncomfortable that our growth comes. By being obedient and humbling myself as God instructed, it took my faith to a new level. I was in complete awe of how God had protected me from all the negativity that surrounded me during this experience. I knew God only had the power to keep my mouth closed with what I witnessed going on around me. He gave me a peace that surpassed all understanding, what once bothered me did not even bother me anymore.

My perception then:	I felt that God asking me to return home meant I was giving in, admitting wrong and condoning my husband behavior.
Message:	When God gives us instructions that put us in uncomfortable positions, we must press through regardless of our emotions or past hurts. God will use that situation to give you growth. I can promise you that the reward at the end will be well worth the sacrifice.
How this experience affected my future:	Whenever I go through situations that cause me discomfort, I focus on the changes that I need to make within myself and expect growth.
My perception now:	Whatever God calls me to do, he will bring me through. If you are obedient to his word no matter how difficult a situation may look, he will give you peace during the storm.

CHAPTER

Thirteen
Kindness

We are going back in time to when Canaan and I first got married. It was my first day of work at the male prison and it was a welcome change. Leaving the women's prison was like a breath of fresh air as if a weight had been lifted off me. Working in a women's prison, you will experience things that you would never have imagined. I recall this one incident while I was working on death row, which was part of the segregation unit that I had been assigned to work. The building itself was old with cement floors; cold, creepy and needed to be torn down. In the meantime, the correctional facility was undergoing renovations to build a new segregation unit to house the female inmates on death row and inmates that had committed offenses while at the correctional unit. However, our current condition on death row where the females would congregate daily was an old drafty sitting room with brick walls. The room was about 300 square feet with a few windows that were looking out to the walls of other building. Inside the room,  there was a television, chairs, and tables lined up against the wall for the ladies to sit, talk, sew or do whatever hobby of their choice while being supervised by one officer. In this setting, officers can sit down on this post. On this day, it was around the holidays and volunteers could bring in special treats for the death row inmates. The volunteers gave each lady a styrofoam plate which contained a couple of pieces of baked chicken, two vegetables, rolls, and dessert. I was sitting next to one of the inmates. I will keep her name confidential. However, I will refer to her as Gomer. Gomer was convicted for murdering her boyfriend by slipping arsenic in his food and suspected of killing three more people. Gomer was an attractive older lady with lovely hair, stunning facial features, and a charming smile. While in prison I found her to be a very pleasant lady, she never caused any trouble and appeared to get along with everyone but of course in prison no one can be trusted. However, on this day, as she was eating her baked chicken and she offered me some, I responded, "thanks but no thanks." Taking anything from an inmate was a no, no. And, if you accepted it, you would be putting yourself in a compromising position. She further stated, "I have some barbecue sauce that I have saved, and it tastes a lot better with the sauce on it." The moment I opened my mouth to say no thank you, she put a piece of that baked chicken with the barbecue sauce on it in my mouth and I swallowed it. There is truth to the power of thought. Once I realized I had swallowed the piece of chicken, I called for one of the other officers to come and relieve me. While I was waiting, I felt nauseated, weak as if powerful waves of pain rumbling through my stomach. As soon as the officer arrived, I rushed into the restroom and threw up. I had less than an hour left on my shift and I remained in the restroom vomiting until it was time to go. Once I was relieved from my shift, I ran to my car with the intentions of getting home as fast as possible to get medication and lie down. I left the parking lot driving like a maniac skidding wheels in my 5.0 Mustang GT. In less than a mile from the facility, I had to stop the car, get out and vomit again. My thoughts were spiraling out of control. I got back into the car wiped my mouth and stopped at the first convenient store I saw. I did not like beer but this day I went into that store and purchased a beer and drank it straight down. I had to calm my nerves, and why I chose a beer I do not know to this day. I just knew ginger ale was not going to do it for me today. The mind is a powerful thing.

The power of thought is one of the most powerful and beneficial powers we have been given. I was aware of the circumstances that surrounded Gomer's high profiled case as it had been made into a movie which I had watched several times. The thought of Gomer's conviction presented in this scenario created a belief in me that she had poisoned me.

Once the belief had been established it manifested on my psychological state of mind which triggered my physical state into uneasiness. The truth of the matter was that I was not sick. My thoughts made my body produce symptoms of sickness. My body reacted to my false interpretation of an acquired belief. "For as he thinketh in his heart so is he" (Proverbs 23:7, King James Version). This system of thinking, feeling, and manifesting can also hold true from a positive perspective in one's fulfilling their own desires. The late Napoleon Hill states "Whatever the mind can conceive and believe it can achieve."

Well enough about my experience at the women's prison, after about a year and some months, I transferred to a male prison. Most of my first day at the male's prison would be spent in the administration office where all the required documents for employment would have to be signed. After I had completed all my paperwork, I was getting ready to go tour the facility when I saw a young lady waiting outside the office. It would have been hard for me to just speak and keep on walking, so I introduced myself and she introduced herself to me as Officer Sapphira. We chatted for a few minutes and I encouraged her to contact me if she ever needed help with anything. I had really enjoyed our conversation those few minutes. I could sense that she was a pretty smart, intelligent young lady. This was her first day working at a prison and by this time I had over a year and a half experience from the women's prison. I was assigned to the first shift and she was assigned to the third shift. As time went on, I would meet her during shift change. She was tall, skinny with the most beautiful blue eyes along with a strong presence. I would observe her interacting with the inmates and she was one to be reckoned with. Even though her physique was not large in statute once she opened her mouth it was like the roaring of a lion and the inmates conceded to it. She reminded me of myself and I instantly took a liking to her. Every opportunity I got during shift changes, I observed her interact with the inmates. I enjoyed watching her in action. Hardworking, strong women truly intrigue me, and she fits the bill. One day during shift changes, I asked her if she was going to take the Sergeant's exam. She said no because she was not eligible. By that time, I had already been promoted to sergeant. I informed her that she was eligible because she met the two-year requirement. I was confident about her eligibility date because we had started on the same day. I encouraged her to investigate it. A few days later, she informed me that she had signed up to take the sergeant's exam. I knew without a doubt that she would pass. And, of course, Officer Sapphira took the exam and

I wasn't surprised that she passed with flying colors.

Originally, after being promoted to sergeant, I was assigned to second shift then a few months later reassigned to first shift. The state representatives had decided to close the current prison and open a new one about an hour away. This would require the superintendent to staff both prisons. The superintendent asked me to become the acting personnel supervisor at the current facility. I was thrilled to take this opportunity, but I did not have one day of administration experience. At the time, I wondered why he had considered me. I thought to myself, I can barely type, and he is asking me to supervise the personnel office. Later, I found out that I had made an impression on the Superintendent and Captain because of a work project I had completed prior to that time.

One week while serving in the position as an officer, I was assigned the post of the Captain's office. I have always found it difficult to work in an area that is not clean and organized. And this is what I was faced within the Captain's office. The Captain's office was in an old building. It had a couple of desks with books and files spread over them with lots of file cabinets that contained files with a limited filing system, to say the least. Not to even discuss all the excess items that was in the office that caused even more clutter. I knew it would be impossible for me to effectively do my officer duties under that condition. So, I looked around and envisioned how the office should be set up for efficiency and then proceeded to make it happened. I started out by throwing away all unnecessary items and trash. Then I decided I would need the muscle of a few inmates to help get the furniture moved. So, I went on the yard to select a few inmates to come and assist me. This would be one of the hardest tasks of all because the inmates had a habit of going in the opposite direction when they saw me coming and putting their heads down on the picnic tables pretending that they were sleeping. This was all because I had the reputation of working hard. And when I first started working at the prison, inmates would flirtatiously whistle at me and I would ask an inmate to identify who had done it. They would say, Officer Hannah, I do not know. And my response would be that is ok, I will just have you do what I needed him to do. After a few months of consistency, the inmates started scattering when they saw me approaching, doing their best to avoid me. So, no more whistles for me after that. Only occasional "E", "E," implying I looked like Michael Jackson. Anyway, after I finally recruited my help, the inmates moved the desks and cabinets in the designated spaces. Once all the furniture was in place, I began to organize the clutter on top of the desks and then desk drawers. Next, I started organizing the filing system in the office. As I reorganized, I swept, dusted and cleaned throughout the entire process. In less than a few days, I had cleaned and reorganized the entire office. Everyone was amazed when they saw all the changes that I had made, and the Captain's staff was really impressed with the new setup. I had made my mark without even realizing it. In my mind, I was just making the working conditions better, so I could work without having an anxiety attack from looking at all that clutter.

When I was offered the position to temporarily take over the personnel office, I had absolutely no administrative training. But what I did have was excellent organization skills thanks to my grandmother, Deborah. I accepted the challenge, because I knew this would be a great learning opportunity for me. A part of me was intimidated while another part of me believed I could do it if I just tried. So, I decided to abide by the saying, "Fake it until you make it." My first day, I dressed the part in my blue skirt, white shirt, blue blazer, and blue heels. There was comfort in knowing that I would be free of that uniform for at least a few months. My first day as a personnel supervisor, I walked in not knowing the first thing to do. My mind was on overdrive and emotions were in an uproar, but you could not tell by looking at me. I did a great job controlling my emotions to disguise my anxiety. I was thinking to myself can these ladies tell that I am clueless about overseeing this position! But then that thought was overshadowed by the thought telling me, "You are very capable of handling this job." I stepped forward, introduced myself, and conveyed to my new personnel staff how much I looked forward to working with them. I advised the ladies that the first week I would familiarize myself with the day to day operations and observe their specific tasks before I would make any suggestions or changes. What they did not know was that I had no clue, so I really had to observe and learn their duties and how to perform them.

However, there was one staff that was not excited about my arrival and I could not help but feel the tension in the air. The tension was so thick that you would need a chain saw to cut through it. She made it very clear by her attitude towards me. She refused to even acknowledge my presence, to say the least. I immediately realized that her dislike for me was not personal. I had visited the administration office on several occasions as an officer and sergeant, and she was very polite to me. She had never displayed any animosity towards me before I had the position that she had expected to get. It was obvious that she felt she had been robbed of this promotion that she was qualified and deserved. I was glad she was not capable of reading my mind to know how unqualified I felt. I refused to allow my negative thoughts to the show. She had seniority over all the current personnel staff and with the knowledge she possessed she assumed the supervisor position was hers to take. However, instead of getting the promotion, she was asked to train the new temporary personnel supervisor. It must have been humiliating for her that the administration brought in an outsider for the position and then expected her to share her knowledge with them. I imagine that it would be a hard pill for anyone to swallow. I am sure she could not help but think, "If my knowledge is not good enough to get me promoted, why then is it good enough for me to train?

It was evident to me that she was the most knowledgeable of all the personnel staff and I could really use her knowledge. Now the challenge of getting a woman who cannot stand me to help me was something I didn't know how to go about. How would I change her opinion of me even though I had never personally wronged her? Every day for a week I would greet her, treat her with kindness, and allow her to do her work without interference or pressure from me. Some days were harder than others for me to keep up this attitude of kindness, but I knew I had to be consistent for things to change. Dr. Martin Luther King's so eloquently stated, "Darkness cannot drive out darkness: only light can do that. Hate cannot drive out hate: only love can do that." So, I continued with my mission to use kindness to draw out the resentment she had towards me. The second week, I called her into my office and told her how much I appreciated her opinion. I commended her on the job I had witnessed her do so far and assured her that her hard work and dedication would not go unnoticed. I also emphasized that we were a team and she was a vital component to the success of our team.

Every day I continued to pay close attention to all three personnel staff members and absorbed as much knowledge as I could. I was a quick learner and usually only needed to see something once before I got it. After about a couple of weeks, I had pretty much caught on to how the office functions, the required tasks, and how to perform them without question. However, daily I continued to treat that staff member that was opposing me, with kindness and empathy regardless of her reaction to me. I praised her for her work and continued to reassure her that she was valuable to the team. Within a few weeks, she came around and she began collaborating with me little by little. It was truly a welcoming change to finally have some unity in the office. A great deal of pressure was removed off me once the tension had disintegrated.

Now that we were all working as a team, the only issue now was organization, structure and that was my area of expertise. With my obsessive-compulsive behavior, I had issues working where there was no order, so I knew it would be only a matter of time before I would have everything organized. And within a couple of months, the personnel office was reorganized and functioning in a way that I could do my best. I reflected on how unfamiliarity had me question my capabilities prior to accepting the position and look at me now. I had been exalted to a position in which I had no prior training or experience and had excelled in it. I remained in this position until we successfully opened the new facility and closed the old one. "For those who exalt themselves will be humbled, and those who humble themselves will be exalted" (Matthew 23:12, King James Version).

When I made the decision to reorganize and clean up the Captain's office, I had no idea that this one gesture would materialize into such a valuable experience that would be utilized in my future. My intention was not to show off my skills or even impress anyone. I did it because I felt it would make the working conditions better for us all. It was likely that it would be months before I would ever be reassigned to that position again because we were on a rotation schedule. My act of kindness got noticed and opened a door for me that I had never even considered. So sometimes in life, it may seem like you are being overlooked and unnoticed but never stop being who you truly are because, one day, an opportunity will present itself that you will be the benefactor. Being given the opportunity to work in the personnel office was a big deal to me. And working at this capacity as a personnel supervisor and excelling gave me a lot of confidence. It showed that things I thought were impossible for me to do were possible if I believed in myself. It made me realize that I had abilities within me that I was not even aware of or capable of doing.

However, the greatest lesson I learned was to be careful about how I treat people. The staff member that had given me the opposition became my best supporter and my greatest cheerleader. And she would eventually confide in me about her physical and mental abuse as well as her financial crisis. Her spouse was an officer on the police force whom she stated was controlling, manipulative, and used his authoritative status to threaten her and use their child as a pawn to instill fear. She had held onto the hope that she would get promoted and get a raise which would allow her to escape this dominating relationship. I had no idea what my staff member had been going through such an ordeal, but I am so glad that I treated her with kindness regardless of how she had treated me. I know if I had responded differently, I would have regretted it to this today. Who knows if I had allowed my negative actions to prevail, I could have been a contributor to her torture and forced her into a quicker downward spiral. Now, I consciously try to always treat people good regardless of how I am treated because you never know what a person is dealing with mentally, physically, or financially.

My perception then:	Making working conditions better for us all. Treat people with kindness regardless of how they treat you.
Message:	Never allow situations to divert you from who you truly are, always do your best and be your best you never know who is watching. Always treat people with kindness regardless of how they treat you because you never know the hurt, they may be encountering. Your light may be the only good that they see in their darkness and misery.
How this experience affected my future:	I always put forth my best effort in everything I do no matter how big or small. People that negatively respond to me I always try to show them compassion.
My perception now:	My experiences have taught me that my act of kindness has a way of coming full circle and frees me from remorse. I find that I have fewer regrets by not intentionally inflicting harm or causing discomfort to others.

CHAPTER

Forteen
What the Eyes Cannot See

O nce the new correctional facility was opened and the old one had been closed, I was offered the position of fiscal sergeant. In this position, I would oversee the mailroom and the eight canteens in the facility. This was a great opportunity for me. I would remain on first shift and have holidays and weekends off. My main responsibilities were to supervise the officers in the mailroom and the inmates who worked in the canteens. When I had my first opportunity to select an additional officer to work for me, I knew exactly who I wanted to fill that position: Officer Sapphira. We both seem to have the same work ethic and I wanted her to have the weekday schedule also. She had two young daughters and working on third shift was difficult at times. I wanted this position for her probably more than she wanted it for herself. So, after talking with the superintendent, he accepted my request to have Officer Sapphira reassign to work with me. Officer Sapphira did a great job, as expected, but I knew she would not remain in this position for too  long. With her intelligence and work ethic, I knew it was a matter of time before she was promoted. And just as I expected, within a few months she was promoted to sergeant and assigned to the third shift.

Prior to my promotion to fiscal sergeant, I was well respected by the inmates. I had a reputation for being firm but fair. But, of course, when I became the sergeant over their mail, money, food, and cigarettes the respect reached a whole new level. However, amongst the staff, I was respected, but of course, not necessarily liked. I was a sergeant that followed the rules and some staff members did not take kindly to authority figures, especially females. But I had gotten used to people judging me. However, I had made an impression on the superintendent with my hard work and dedication. I had found favor in his sight. I was always coming up with ideas to make it better for inmates and staff, which really impressed him. Almost any request I made the superintendent would say yes. The staff and supervisors started making remarks like "Sergeant Hannah has more power than the assistant superintendent." However, the requests I would make would require more work on my behalf. It's not like I was making more money. And, of course, the next gossip was that I was having an affair with him. However, he was more like a father figure to me, so when Sergeant Sapphira was assigned to third shift I immediately spoke to him on her behalf. I pleaded her case to him and gave him reasons why she needed to be reassigned to first shift. While I was pleading to him, he asked me a question, why do I feel the need to always put myself on the line for someone else? I really did not have an answer at the time, but it is evident to me now what he was trying to show me. However, he told me that he would consider my request. Within a few weeks, she was assigned to the first shift. It was obvious that I had grown quite fond of Sergeant Sapphira and we became close friends, at least, so I thought.

Sergeant Sapphira and I were both shy of one year of credits from finishing our bachelor's degrees. Not sure if it was me or her that found out about the evening program where we could complete our degree, but we both took all the necessary steps to apply for the program. We were accepted. We would go to class one night in a week, but we had a lot of reading and paperwork to complete. It was a long, hard journey. After having to work all day at the prison and then deal with Canaan and my rebellious stepsons, some days I wanted to quit. But because of Sergeant Sapphira's dedication, I was inspired not to give up. I kept in mind that if she could do it with two small daughters, surely, I could do it also. So, we pressed through and completed the program together. A little over a year, we both had our bachelor's degrees and were ready to lookout for new career opportunities.

We both left the prison within a week of each other to pursue other careers. There was another Sergeant that I had befriended, and she was leaving at the same time as Sergeant Sapphira and me. The superintendent was losing three sergeants at the same time. Sergeant Sapphira and I both had going away parties scheduled but on two different occasions. Sergeant Sapphira's going away party was first, and the superintendent attended it, but he did not attend mine. I was really hurt and disappointed. I could not understand why he did not attend my party considering we had a good relationship. I honestly thought that he would say goodbye. He was like a father figure to me and his approval meant a lot. I really enjoyed the praise and accolades that I would receive from him once I finished a project. So, when he did not show up to my going away party, it was like opening an old fresh wound and someone jabbing a knife in my heart. The emotions of rejection and disapproval consumed me yet again. I thought to myself, would I ever be able to trust anyone? This man that I admired, trusted and respected treated me with so much admiration and respect turned his back on me. I saw his action as abandonment and rejection the same thing my stepfather did to me.

Years later, the superintendent and I would meet again. Immediately I saw him, my first thoughts were of his absence from my going away party. On the surface, the wound was healed, but the moment I saw him, it brought back all those old memories. I guess it must have been heavy on his mind also because he gave me an explanation why he did what he did. He explained to me that it was not that he had lost three sergeants, but he had lost his best. He was disappointed with me because I had never discussed that I planned on leaving. He felt out of respect for our relationship that I should have been more upfront with him and communicated with him before I made my final decision to leave. Instead, he found out when I handed in my resignation letter. I thought about what he said, and he was correct. I was immature about how I handled the situation. I should have talked to him about my decision before I made it. Of course, by this time the damage had already been done. The feelings of abandonment, rejection, and disapproval had already penetrated my heart and left another scar. However, it did give me some comfort and closure to know why he acted the way he did.

It had been over two years now since I had communicated with Sapphira. We had both moved on with different careers and lost track of each other. I had just closed my group home in December of 2005. I had no idea what I was going to do next, so daily I walked in my subdivision talking to God asking him for direction. Then one day God sent a friend with an answer, Esther. Esther and I had grown close. We both went to the same high school, but I was about eight years older, we had moved to the same city not knowing each other but would later become acquainted because we both had group homes. While we were talking, Esther suggested I should consider opening a community support agency. She gave me a few more details regarding the program, and I did not look back. I went full speed ahead into my new venture. However, I wanted a business partner this time for my new business venture and Sapphira was the first person to come to mind.

By that time, I did not have Sapphira contact information. Her last known address was in a city about an hour away and I recall someone stating she was a claims adjuster now. So, I had to use my detective skills to locate her. I found a website that listed licensed claims adjuster in that county and found hers. I sent an email with all my contact information. Within a short period, she contacted me. I told her that I was starting a company and I wanted her to partner with me. We met in the month of April and started all the necessary paperwork to get the company up and running. We would both work long hours on the weekends to get the paperwork done. She was still working claims full time and I was collecting unemployment. Thank God I had the insight to pay unemployment insurance as a self-employed person because it helped in the down times.

God had proven to me in prior endeavors that I did not need experience or money, all I needed was to be obedient and trust him. And in this new venture, I had a lot more than I had when I started my first two businesses. With the community support agency, I at least had some experience in the field and some capital so why did I need a business partner? Even though I closed my group home by choice, the feeling of failure still would not leave me. My insecurities of not feeling good enough lead me to presume that my success was predicated on another person's involvement. I justified it by believing I needed someone with the same work ethic as me and an invested interest to help grow and protect the business. Instead of seeking God first, I left him out of the equation, and I allowed my insecurities to direct me. However, I would have to pay for my actions in the long run.

Prior to the start of the company there were some signs that signaled that the partnership would not work. But I was blinded by my fear and self-worth and I rejected the signs that God was giving me. Within the first couple of months, I was warned in my spirit to get rid of Sapphira, but I dismissed the warning. Later, I heard a voice saying, "this partner is not for you," but I dismissed that voice again. From the beginning, once we rented the office, I was the one at the office early in the morning every day completing most of the work because Sapphira still had a full-time job. She would come in some evenings when she had an opportunity. I talked with her concerning the workload and she did her best to try and do better. I had all the experience of how to open the business, but I was ignorant about the division of the business. I gave an individual with no experience in this field 50 percent share in my company. But hindsight is always twenty-twenty. By August, less than four months after our first meeting, our company was up and running. By the following year, we were both making six-figure incomes.

In 2009, things would change with my personal life and business. I left Canaan in 2009 for good and the state began changing all the rules and regulations with the community support services. The state came in and changed many things to minimize the number of providers. This was due to other provider taking advantage of the lucrative funds and making it bad for all of us. They required us to get accreditation, add licensed therapists and medical doctors into our staff; this would assure the demise of several providers. So, after three years, we could no longer deal with the on-going changes, so we closed the agency. We had plans on starting a new venture together, opening family care homes.

We rented a family care home with intentions of opening a chain of homes but that would never come into fruition. We started work on the new home in preparation for licensing it. In order to get the home licensed we had to have electrical work, plumbing work, construction, fire-retardant paint, and several other things done. Policies and procedures had to be written, classes had to be taken and certifications had to be received. Everything was completed except for the plumbing work and turning in the paperwork. But during that time, Sapphira started distancing herself from me. I could not understand why because at this point in our relationship, I thought we had become more than just business partners. We hung out at each other's homes for events; we had been on trips together, and we went shopping together. But the thing I remember most was how we had each other's backs when our spouses were up to no good. She was like a sister that I had come to love.

Later she would tell me that she decided to pursue a partnership with her spouse who had just recently opened family care homes. By that time, I was not surprised. I could tell by her attitude. The once sweet and humble business partner had now become condescending. I had always treated her as an equal partner. That was my nature. But now that she appeared to be doing financially better than me, so she showed me an entirely different side of her. After closing our offices, there were some bills that still required payment—an electric bill and old tax bill. I sent Sapphira, a copy of the bills and advised her to please just send her half directly to the company and I would do the same. Well, once she got the bills, I received a text message from Sapphira.

> Received correspondence referencing public works and county taxes. Unfortunately, at this time I will not be able to personally contribute to these business expenses. I am an unemployed full-time student with one child in college and three others entering college next year. On another note please provide me with the name of the accountant that completed the business taxes for 2010. I have not been provided with this info. It's July 1, 2011. This information was needed in April in order to file my 2010 taxes.

My response:

> Sorry about your current situation however I have to step in and make the best decision for the company and finalize the closing. Fortunately, I can pay the $xxx water bill and $xxx county tax, my half and your half. Currently, I am out of state and unable to pick up taxes. Contact Ms. Pearson at 919-555-1212 at Pearson's Financial Group.

Sapphira's 2nd response: Great
Sapphira's 3rd response: (24 hours later)

> Two Things,
>
> I believe u misunderstood my message or maybe me. There is no need for apologies, God continues to bless me and my family, fortunately, my husband is able to allow us to continue to live a good quality of life while I pursue my academic endeavors. Nothing has changed, (vacations, new cars, private school, and college). His business continues to grow. In fact, tomorrow he is opening his 5th pizza restaurant. My children are doing extremely well, Anna, Candace, and Julia are all seniors. Anna is working, has her own car, scored high on SAT, and still playing soccer. Julia continues to Excel n school and

music. The beautiful thing about it is that we all r active n community outreach activities. So there truly is nothing to apologize about.

The second thing is that one of the benefits about having Ur business incorporated is that if something happens and the entity is no longer able to operate then the shareholders aren't personally held liable. I would have loved to close the agency owing no one, Unfortunately, it's not the case, I know that the agency has an outstanding balance with HP as well in excess of $xxxxx. Therefore, it is going to be impossible to satisfy all creditors. I am happy to hear that Ur situation isn't what has been reported to me. As small as Freetown is I am always hearing news about Ur situation (turned Jaguar n, owe Jaguar money, unable to pay utility deposit for a house in Freetown, utilities n Canaan name and many more). I am glad to hear from u that Ur doing well and the rumors r false. I truly wish the best for u.

Once I received this text, I never responded. "Bless them that curse you, and pray for them which despitefully use you" (Luke 6:28, King James Version). This was someone that I brought into the business and into my heart. I cared for Sapphira like a sister. It felt like someone had stuck a knife in my back and twisted it a million times. My first thought was that if she thought I was doing that bad, why did she not reach out to help me? I would have done it for her without hesitation. But then God reminded me of the warnings he had given to me and how I had dismissed them. Yes, the way she treated me really penetrated my heart and caused me sorrow, but I had no one else to blame but myself. God had forewarned me and now I was reaping the consequences of my actions. Regardless of Sapphira actions God told me to pray for her and to forgive her. At the time I was in so much pain dealing with everything else falling apart and now God was expecting for me to be the better person. I wondered how He could expect so much from me when I was just barely holding onto my sanity. Anyway, I knew I had to pray for her, so I told God I am going to pray for her but right now I do not mean one word that I am saying. Each day in obedience I prayed for her and each day it got a little easier. Then one day, I realized my heart had truly forgiven her. It seemed mystic because I have no idea when the pain left. God had supernaturally intervened and freed me from the hurt and just like that I felt free about the relationship. Therefore, my advice to all when deciding on a partnership I highly recommend you fast and pray before going into any partnership.

For me, friendship is portrayed as affection, loyalty, respect, and trust. The dictionary defines friendship as a relationship of mutual affection between two or more people and a stronger form of interpersonal bond than an association. The words the dictionary uses to describe friendships are closeness, devotion, friendliness, goodwill, harmony, mutual esteem, and understanding. But friendships mean different things to different people. To some it is unconditional and to some, it's a thing of convenience. But the truth of the matter is that the word friend has become a cliché. Most people are not in friendships but in relationships with associates, not friends. Associates are connected or related through work, church, school, college, social events, other friends, and so on. Yet we pal around with these people a few times, feel a common connection, they smile, and agreed to our opinion, they seem to have our backs in a few situations and then we give them the title friend! A title that they have not even earned. True friendship is determined only when it survives the test of adversity and remains true. An example of true friendship is the friendship between David and Saul's son, Jonathan, in the Bible. Even though Saul was in pursuit and trying to kill David, Jonathan warned David of his father's intentions. This story can be found in 1 Samuel chapters 18-20. "If you haven't learned the meaning of friendship, you really haven't learned anything." This is a notable quote by the great Muhammed Ali.

What's missing in most relationships is what the Eyes cannot see. But God sees and knows the heart of everyone. He knew I did not have the heart to break up the partnership with Sapphira out of affection and loyalty. But God had other plans for me. He had plans for me to relocate to another state away from family and friends, so I could find myself, my purpose, and complete this book. First and foremost, he had to remove my business partner out of my life. God was aware that my business partner did not have my best interest at heart, He even warned me several times. But through her new-found financial stability, she would be exposed, and I would see her for who she truly was all the time. "Enemies disguise themselves with their lips, but in their hearts, they harbor deceit. 25 Though their speech is charming, do not believe them, for seven abominations fill their hearts 26 Their malice may be concealed by deception, but their wickedness will be exposed in the assembly" (Proverbs, 26:24-26 New International Version).

This all occurred during an extremely difficult and stressful time in my life. I was subjected to an exasperating divorce, closed my company, my business partner decided to pursue a new venture with her husband, and some of my family members gloated in what they thought was my downfall. "You should not gloat over your brother in the day of his misfortune, nor rejoice over the people of Judah in the day of their destruction, nor boast so much in the day of their trouble" (Obadiah 1:12, New International Version). The worst part about this experience was that the people I thought would be supportive were betting against me in hopes of seeing me fail. What we all did not realize was that God was just repositioning me. He had something greater in store. Now I am grateful for the actions of my business partner. "Delight thyself also in the LORD; and he shall give thee the desires of thine heart" (Psalms 37:4, King James Version). I have always desired to live in the Sunshine State, but I had two homes and new business potential in my home state, so relocating made no sense to me at the time. Who knows? If my business partner had not done what she did, I might not be living in this state. Being in Sunshine state separated from everyone with limited distractions allowed me to find myself, my purpose, and write this book. "And we know that all things work together for good to them that love God, to them who are the called according to *his* purpose" (Romans 8:28, King James Version).

My perception then:	I wanted the best for my friend and had every intention of helping her acquire it.
Message:	We must seek God first in everything we do. Only God knows the true heart of a man because it cannot be seen with the naked eye. And be cautious who you bring into your circle and label them as a friend. It's not your known enemy that will do you the most harm, it is the adversary that you call a friend that will cause the greatest hurt.
How this experience affected my future:	All new business partnerships will have to be approved by God. The title friend would have to be earned.
My perception now:	This experience taught me one of my greatest lessons and through this lesson, I would receive some of my greatest blessings.

CHAPTER

Fifteen
Expectancy

$\mathcal{E}$xpectancy is the feeling of hope that something exciting, interesting, or good is about to happen. I remember when I was three years old, up until I was age eight, every day I expected something good to happen. "Now to him who is able to do immeasurably more than all we ask or imagine, according to his power that is at work within us" (Ephesians 3:20, New International Version). I so wish I could experience those times again when life was so innocent and filled with so much expectancy.

Believing that nothing was impossible for me to do. Now, I allowed my undesirable life experiences to diminish the hopes and dreams of a young vibrate girl who believed all things were possible. I allowed myself to be conditioned to the world's view to think negatively and expect the worst and accept it as my truth. However, God has given me experiences as an adult that has given me hope again. Despite what we see in the natural, it's important that we still live a life with expectancy in our hearts.

Motorcade

During the summer and fall of 2008, Sapphira and I volunteered to help with the Obama campaign. We had duties such as making phone calls, talking to people in the community, handing out flyers, registering people to vote, and so on. No matter what I did I abide under the principle to always do my best regardless of whether I am rewarded or not. However, my favorite job was going out into the community talking with people and registering them to vote. I was very successful at registering voters and that was due to the fact I would go in areas that others were afraid of entering. My co-volunteers would often ask how are you not afraid of getting robbed or shot? And to top it all, you are driving a new convertible Jaguar. I always told them I wasn't afraid because they are people like me, why should I be afraid? I just talk with them like I would anyone else with no judgment and they all seem comfortable around me. As a matter of fact, when I pull up in neighborhoods known for criminal activities, I talk with the first person I see that is in a stationary position. I introduce myself, tell them what I am doing, chat with them for a few minutes, then I ask them to please watch out for my car while I out walking around the neighborhood. One hundred percent of the time, when I returned, they would usually say, Mrs. Hannah, I watched out for your car and made sure no one touched it. But most importantly, I knew they were watching out for me if I did not return by an expected time, they would come looking for me. Most of my business clientele are residents of these types of neighborhood, so I have experienced that by making them feel important and trusted, you could trust them for their help and support.

Well, my dedication and resilience to the campaign did not go unnoticed. The unexpected happened. I was asked to drive in the motorcade for the upcoming President Obama during his campaign in my home state in a neighboring county. He was scheduled to arrive in the month of October in 2008. You cannot imagine the excitement I felt knowing I would get to meet the soon to be elected President in person. Only three people were selected to drive in the motorcade in our area of the state and I was one of them. I was certain this would be an experience I would always remember and treasure. Being given this opportunity I believed I had the favor of God on my side. An opportunity that I had never dreamed of or expected was before me.

The day prior to driving in the motorcade, we had to be trained on what to do and what was expected of us. This was the first time I would also meet the two men that had been selected also. They appeared even more excited than me about meeting the soon to be elected President. We all discussed how blessed we felt to have been selected for such an appointment. We became acquainted with each other quick. So, after our training, we stayed around a few minutes and discussed what we expected to happen in the next two days. Our main conversation was how we would act when we finally had the opportunity to meet the president aspirant face to face. The consensus was that we would be professional, remain calm, but not star struck. Now when I think back on this conversation, I cannot help but smile and chuckle. We all have a habit of saying how we will react when presented with a situation, the truth is that you never know until it happens.

The big day was here, it is evening time and we are waiting at the airport for the soon to be elected President to arrive. The Boeing 757 jet with the word Change had landed on the airstrip. President aspirant and his team had finally arrived. My excitement knew no bound. I was dressed to impress, in an all-black pants suit, white blouse with black angle platform boots. I oversaw driving one of the vans while one volunteer also drove a van and the other an SUV. I was the sixth vehicle in the motorcade line. Directly in front of me was an SUV and then two black SUVs in front of it. Because of the location of my vehicle, I could not see the President aspirant when he got off the plane, but I could see the fifty or more campaign staff members flying along with him. My vehicle was inhabited by three of his advisors. Once everyone had settled in their vehicles our destination was the hotel.

We drove approximately 35 to 40 minutes before we arrived at the hotel. Once we arrived at the hotel, the advisor got out, and then I parked the van. As I approached the hotel, I observed as security tried to keep the people back until the Presidential candidate could get settled. As expected, there was chaos because some were excited about the President aspirant's arrival and others were upset. People had reservations, and others were there because of the news of the President aspirant's stay. I looked around the hotel and felt uncomfortable with the President aspirant staying there due to the openness of the hotel. The hotel had a medium size structure that appeared to be out in the middle of nowhere. While I was standing outside the hotel, apparently, I looked like real security. The mayor and several other politicians were asking me to help them get in and see the soon to be President. I thought to myself I am yet to see him myself. I then informed them that I was not able to get them an appointment with the President aspirant. The mayor and the other politicians kept insisting so I called them to the side and told them I was a volunteer, but it was like talking to a wall. They were relentless and maintained that with my position I could still get close enough to him and ask. I just shook my head and continued to watch in amazement the reactions of these grown men on seeing the President aspirant. He was truly their idol, a representation of change; you could see it in their facial expressions and in their eyes.

The next morning, we arrived at the hotel to escort the President aspirant and drive his advisory team to the campaign's destination. Again, I was dressed in another black pant suit. People were still thinking I was one of the security personnel which made me feel some kind of way but in a good way. However, when we arrived at the hotel, the scene was much different from the night before. Apparently, during the night, they brought in several buses to surround the hotel providing a barricade to protect the President aspirant. There was something else also different from the night before. It seems like everyone in the town knew that the President aspirant was at this hotel. People were lined up in multitudes waiting just to get a glimpse of him. I was not sure if I would get to see the President aspirant until we arrived at the Coliseum because I had to remain close to my vehicle ready to move in a moment's notice.

Then I heard the loud voices hollering and screaming President Obama, President Obama. The moment the crowd had been waiting for had arrived. Against his security's advice, the President aspirant decided to come out of the hotel and talk with the people waiting to meet him. He greeted the crowd with comments and shaking of hands for about ten minutes before finally departing. I could not see the President aspirant, but I could see the tears on the faces of people in the crowd as he thanked them for all their help. One of the volunteers who had an opportunity to see the President aspirant called me. He said "Hannah, I saw him. You know I am not gay, but he is beautiful. Hannah, you will have to just see for yourself." It was not just the words he spoke but the tone he used when describing him. His tone was that of a star-stricken man. I was in amazement at the way this heterosexual man's demeanor had been melted at the presence of President aspirant.

On the way to the Coliseum, President aspirant decided to take a pit stop at a local Barbecue restaurant. The motorcade lined up outside the restaurant as he went inside and spoke with and shook the hands of the people there. Secret service surrounded the President aspirant with every step. This was the first time I had a clear sight of the soon to be President. While I was sitting in the vehicle, a guy I grew up with named Gideon was walking towards the restaurant to meet the President aspirant. I called him on the cell phone and told him to turn around. He approached my vehicle and asked me how I got the opportunity to drive for Mr. Obama. I just smiled. Gideon and I were only one year apart in school. We grew up in each other's backyards. Our houses backyards faced each other. People considered Gideon to be a pretty hardcore man. After a few minutes of talking, Gideon left in pursuit of meeting the President aspirant. A few minutes later he came out with a glow and a smile on his face that I had never seen before. I asked him if he was OK. He stated, "Hannah I touched him," in such a low tone as he grinned from ear to ear. He appeared to be in a daze. It was as if Mr. Obama had cast a spell over him. Then I saw a young lady crossing the 4-way highway, the same lady I just observe servicing customers at the Burger King drive-through window. She left everything to come see the President aspirant. I could not help but laugh, because it looked like these people were losing their minds with pure delight.

Now the fun part for me, we were heading towards the highway on our way to the Coliseum. This was a four-lane divided highway. However, the oncoming traffic on the other side was halted. I could see the secret service men and the high-powered weapons that were positioned in the back of the SUV that was guarding the President aspirant. I thought to myself, the President aspirant is well protected. I hate to see anyone try anything. We got to drive at maximum speed which was right up my alley. I loved driving fast and now I had permission to do it. It gave me such a rush. Once we finally arrived at the Coliseum I saw Sapphira, sitting on the front row. I stood at the back of the Coliseum and watched as President aspirant gave his speech. The crowd was enthralled with the Mr. Obama's words and displayed it with the loud cheers so loud you could not hear yourself think. Then once the speech was over, he shook hands and gave hugs to anyone that was in close proximity. I watched as he hugged Sapphira from a distance and I could see the expression on her face. She called me on my cell phone and told me how good it felt to hug the President aspirant. Again, I smiled. I loved the Mr. Obama, too, but I was just in astonished at the reactions from everyone. I said to myself, I'm not going to act star struck like them when I meet him.

The event was over, and we were on our way back to the airport. The President aspirant and his team were scheduled to leave as soon as we got them there. We drove onto the airstrip, so everyone would be near the airplane. There were about sixty plus people volunteering on different details who wanted to get a chance to speak with the President aspirant. His security advisor suggested to the President aspirant that since he was going to take pictures, to take them in groups. But the President aspirant said no. He took individual pictures with every person. Needless to say, it took a while. As he was talking to the volunteers in front of me, I was practicing what to say in our conversation. At the same time, I was reflecting on how all the others had been mesmerized but confident that I could control my emotions. The time had finally arrived. Mr. Obama walked up and the first thing I noticed was that caramel colored, smooth, flawless skin and I was in complete awe. He asked my name and for a moment I couldn't remember it. A few seconds later, I finally responded, Hannah. He was talking and telling me how much he appreciated my service, and so on. But the truth: after the first few words, I did not hear anything he said. It was if I had become tone dead. I could see his lips moving but I heard nothing. His presence had captivated me. I wanted to hug him so bad, but I kept my distance. I could see the reporters on the side taking pictures and I did not want them to have anything else to use against him, so I just shook his hand. His aura was so intoxicating that when I was back at my vehicle, I had to sit a moment to compose myself. Now I could relate and understand how the other volunteer, Gideon, and Sapphira felt. It was truly an incredible and memorable experience.

Day in Court

One afternoon Sapphira, and I were on our way to work, riding the hour-long drive. I was discussing with her about paying the full mortgage and how Canaan was not holding up to his end of the deal. Canaan and I had a separation agreement in place, and we were to split the mortgage 50-50, but he reneged. So Sapphira came up with the idea that I should go on the Judge Matthis show to settle the case. Sapphira had excellent writing skills and within a matter of hours Sapphira had written a brief summation of my life with Canaan and issue regarding mortgage and submitted it to the show. I figured she was just wasting her time. I did not expect them to call me. And the most important concern: I did not like speaking in front of large groups of people, much less a television show, so I really did not think much of it. Well three days later, the unexpected happened. I received a call from the Judge Ferris show. The representative from the show stated that the Judge Matthis show was booked but they had an opening in November on the Judge Ferris show. I was truly in shock that I had received the call, but I informed her that I was not interested.

She told me that she would pay my airfare, my witness, and hotel expenses. I told her again, no thank you. But she would not take no for an answer. She then said if I won, they would pay for the mortgages that I am suing him for. I then said no again, I am going on a cruise that week. She then told me they would fly me to the port of my choice. Something inside of me would not allow me to say no and that was confusing to me because I dreaded talking in front of large audiences. So instead, I said, "call Canaan and if he says yes, then I will go." I was sure Canaan would say no, but I was wrong. He said yes.

A few months later, Esther and I flew out to Chicago for the show. Notice I said Esther and not Sapphira who had set this all up from the beginning. When it was time to make travel arrangements for the show, she told me her spouse said she could not go as a witness for me. The writing was on the wall and I was already starting to realize things were not what they seem. However, Esther and I arrived in Chicago and checked into the hotel the evening before the show. It puzzled me why I had even agreed to go on the show knowing I felt inadequate with my vocabulary and speaking in public forums. Well, it was too late now. There I was and I was going to have to make the best of it. So, for the next few hours I practice speaking in the hotel room until I decided to go to sleep.

The following day we were picked up by a shuttle and taken to the studio. Once we arrived, we were offered some refreshments and then taken to a small private room. The studio representative came in and provided me with a script that I was supposed to follow. I did not expect to have to learn a script I had just planned to tell the truth. The script consisted of highlights that Sapphira had mentioned in the summation. They wanted it spoken in the order they found to have the most impact. When the producer representative came into the room, she advised me that there were about thirteen cases in front of ours, advising me that I had enough time to memorize it. She left Esther and me in the room for a few minutes. Then she returned to go over the script with me. I could not recite the first line and I had good memorization skills. My anxiety skyrocketed. It was only a matter of time before they would be calling my name and I felt so unprepared. The representative left again and told me to just relax. My adrenaline was pumping so fast it was almost impossible for me to calm down. I could not even concentrate on the words in the script, because I was so nervous. All I could think about was my inadequacy being exposed in front of millions of people. The representative returned and told me only four cases were left before my case would be called. And

I was yet to recite the first line. I was shaking all over and, when I looked at Esther's face, I could see the concern in her eyes. And through her eyes, it mirrored the panic and fear in me. My heart was palpitating, my hands were sweating, my mouth was dry, and I felt as if I was going to pass out. I went into the restroom that was inside our small room because I was overcome by a strong feeling of nausea. I vomited, but only a little. I knew I had to get myself together, but how? It would take at least an hour just to slow my heart beat down. I had to think and think fast. There was a closet in the room, I immediately rushed towards it and closed myself up in it. I began praying to God. I asked God to please help me. I said, God in a few minutes I am going on national television in front of millions and I do not want to make a fool out of myself. God, at this rate I am going to pass out in front of the cameras. Lord, I need you to show up now, please!

The door opened to our small room and they advised me that is was time to go on. I walked down the dark, drafty hallway until I reach a wall with backdrops hanging from it. In the middle of that wall was a double door. I stood in front of the door still praying in my heart asking God to help me get through this. The representative then opened the door and directed me to enter. I walked into the staged courtroom up to the podium. I noticed Canaan and his brother, Asher, standing at the other podium on the left side. Less than a minute later, Judge Ferris walked up to the bench and everyone in the audience stood until they were instructed to sit. Esther was in the audience behind my podium. She later informed me that she thought I was going to pass out when they opened the doors. And I told her I also thought that I would.   Then the unexpected happened. Judge Ferris said, "Mrs. Hannah plead your case." I opened my mouth the words came out with such confidence. It felt as if someone had taken over my body. I spoke with such poise, passion, and eloquence that I even surprised myself. It was as if I had been doing this as a profession all my life. I responded to questions, provided my evidence and defended my case. Fear escaped me, I forgot I was on national television. "He gives strength to the weary and increases the power of the weak" (Isaiah 40:29, New International Version). It was obvious to me that God had heard my prayer. I will never forget this day God showed up in the courtroom for me and gave me confidence and strength. For all those interested in the outcome of the case, I had proven my case, but because we had a separation agreement already in place, they did not pay me for the back mortgages. Instead, the judge instructed me to adhere to the separation agreement which meant I should immediately initiate the eviction for

Canaan.

It would later be revealed to me why it was important for me to go on the show. It was not about winning the case instead it was to serve as a reminder of my demeanor before and during the show. A few years later I recall telling someone that I feel I'm called to be a spiritual motivator but, I do not like speaking in front of large crowds so I do not understand why God would expect me to. I also said, "I fear I would sound ignorant and not say the appropriate thing when I'm asked to respond on the spot." At the moment these words came out of my mouth, I heard that small voice say you did not know what you were going to say on the judge show, but you spoke with poise and confidence then. I knew it was the voice of God reminding me of that experience and showing me why I had no reason to fear anymore. The fear was all in my head for years and had no merit.

Prison Sentence

I had decided to sell my portion of the office furniture from the division of the partnership between Sapphira and me. It was still located at the residence that we had rented for the adult care home and I wanted the furniture out before the end of the month. So, over the next several weeks, I would sell off as much of the office furniture that I could. My friend, Ariel, who was an angel, would help me. She would go up to the home wait on potential buyers to show up when I could not make it. However, this one day a lady named Peninnah that I knew from my out of state came to browse the items I had for sale. She had a daycare for children with special needs. She drove up in her luxury vehicle with her long blonde hair all dolled up, long nails, alluring make-up, and gorgeous outfit. She appeared to be soft spoken, but she did it with such elegance. While she was deciding on what items she would buy, she was telling me how well her company was doing. I commented that it was great to hear and that I was happy for her. But then I thought about my own company and I asked God why he did not allow my company to be a success also. I had just compared my business to someone else's, whom I really knew nothing about except for what I had seen on the outside. I immediately felt convicted after the statement and asked God for forgiveness.

About two years later after incident, that I would receive an unexpected phone call. By that time, I had already relocated to Florida and opened my new business. An associate of Peninnah called me and asked me if had heard. My response was, heard what? Peninnah had been convicted and was sentenced to a year in prison. After getting over the shock I asked, for what? I was informed it was for tax evasion. While I was still in disbelief God would bring me back to my thoughts on the day, I encountered her. I had no idea the things she was doing while managing her business, but I had judged her solely on her outward appearance. What we see is not always a true representation. This is a perfect example of why we should never envy or compare ourselves to anyone else.

God has a plan for each one of us. Just because you may be at a low point in your life today does not mean you will be there forever. In my life, I have discovered that during my darkest days my greatest lessons were learned which in turn propelled me into my next blessing. We should never feel that we must compare ourselves to anyone. The only image we should aspire to is that of Jesus Christ. We were all made uniquely different for our own designated purpose that's why no two persons on earth have the same fingerprint. Acceptance of one's own individuality is the beginning of one's creativity. Look within yourselves and find the talents that have never been revealed. It's important that we discover our true selves, so we can achieve our highest potential. Trying to imitate another person will make it impossible for you to ever be the best you that you were destined to be. No one can be better at being you than you.

My perception then:	Do the best job regardless of whether there is a reward or not. I dreaded speaking in presence of large groups for fear of being or sounding incompetent. I was a failure again in business.
Message:	Every day of our lives we should be hopeful and expect positive outcomes. We should also treat everyone the way we would like to be treated and not judge them based on outward appearances. And we should never compare ourselves to anyone else because we do not know the price of their journey or the direction they are headed.
How this experience affected my future:	I opened myself to believe for the unexpected. I trust God to show up when I needed him. I'm hesitant to compare myself to others.
My perception now:	Live my life with a daily expectancy.

CHAPTER

Sixteen
Doubting Hannah

I came face to face with the second fear that I had of God, which of course, had been misdirected. I feared that God was going to take everything away from me and now it appeared that my worst fear was upon me. I had closed my business and I no longer had the six-figure income and I had no idea how I was going to make it financially. I still had a mortgage payment, my jaguar payment, credit cards, insurances and all other household bills that had to be paid. And as if that was not enough, I was dealing with new arising health conditions, going through a divorce, being mocked by my ex-business partner, was betrayed by a friend, talked about by relatives, and they all gloated in what they deemed as my downfall. I felt like I had nowhere to turn; it seemed the people I had helped the most were the same people that hurt  me the most. I was clueless on the next step to take, but I was determined not to give them the satisfaction of remaining in my current state.

I was living back and forth between my two homes the one in my hometown and the one in the city. No matter which home I was living in, I would have the same daily routine. I stayed at home a lot trying to figure out what I would do next. I felt like my life had come to an end. I was going to lose everything I had worked so hard for and then I would have to deal with my relative's criticism. In the morning, it would take everything I had within me to drag myself out of bed. I just wanted to sleep my life away. When I did get up, I did not feel like getting dressed or fixing myself up. I would put on sweatpants and a tee shirt and just lay around until I got hungry. Some days I would try to find enough energy to read the Bible. Some days I was successful, and others not so successful. My negative thoughts about my situation were consuming me because in my mind I could not see a way out. I felt like it was only a matter of time before I would be homeless and living on the streets, even though one of my houses was paid for. I could not seek help from the people I had helped and cared about, because now they were working against me and I felt I had nowhere to turn. It was as if the walls were closing in on me and it was only a matter of time before I would be squashed. With obstacles hitting me on every side, I had become so fragile and so weak that I did not feel I had the strength to fight back.

This particular month, I stayed in the city the entire month. Most days when I felt the spirit of depression coming over me, I would walk in my subdivision and talk to the Lord because I did not want to sink further into depression. I found myself one day pleading again with God to supernaturally take me because I was exhausted, tired and weak and I told him I could not deal with anything else. He responded, "No I have something for you to do." I just broke down crying. I thought to myself he just does not know how terrible it is for me. I could not understand how he could expect me to do anything when I was so weak, and I was barely holding on. It took everything I had not to just lay in my bed and die. What could I possibly do when it takes everything I have just to get up out of bed in the morning? I questioned God, "Why God, why me, I have no purpose here just take me please?"

As I arrived back to the cul-de-sac, I really wanted to talk to a human being so bad and just explain how I was feeling. So, I decided to stop by my neighbor's house. They were both ministers, Mr. Malachi and Mrs. Rebekah. But before I got to my neighbor's front door, I heard a voice say you are not to speak a word of it. Then this voice said you are going to learn to deal with your problems alone with the Lord. And fix your face. My flesh so wanted to have a pity party, but I was fearful to disobey the instructions of the small voice. So, I fixed my face by wiping away my tears from it so no one would detect that I had been crying or upset.

I rang the doorbell and Mr. Malachi came to the door and announced to Mrs. Rebekah that I was there. She was upstairs at the time. Mr. Malachi and I approached the kitchen and I spoke to Mrs. Rebekah's sister who was down visiting from upstate. As I waited for Mrs. Rebekah to come down, I tried to keep my composure I did not want them to realize I had been crying or to see me bust out in tears. While waiting Mr. Malachi asked, "How was your day?" I responded that everything was fine and that I just wanted to stop by and have a chat after my walk before I went home. The pressure to blurt it out was pressing, but I held it back and put on a phony smile instead. After a while, Mr. Malachi said, you better go up to her; does not look like she is coming down. I think I was trying to get myself together before I faced her because it was common practice that I would just go upstairs, but this particular time I went and sat in the kitchen for a while.

Finally, I walked upstairs, and she was eating and watching a movie. We greeted each other and did some small talk and then I sat down and started watching the movie that was showing. I did not say much. I just focused on the movie and tried not to show my emotions on my face. I wanted to talk with her and get her advice, but I had been forbidden from doing so. I just had to hold it all inside and it took everything I had within me not to tear up. A few minutes later, Mr. Malachi came in and began talking and at the same time, he changed the video to a sermon. He said that he wanted us to hear the sermon being preached. I was up to hearing any motivation that I could get, especially since God had instructed me not to speak about my situation. I listened throughout the sermon as the minister preached but it was not until the end that he caught my undivided attention. The sermon had originally aired five years early from the night we were viewing it so what he said next had a great impact on me. He said God told him, "There will be a person in this service tonight, just like Paul wrote when I would do good evil is present. They have a great desire to do what is good but struggle consistently and go through a period of freedom and then bondage tries to come back. Learn to discipline your mind and put on the helmet of salvation, discipline yourself in life and you will be free from some of these things. The reason this person keeps going through this is because they are bored with their life. No challenges. They have prayed to God to take them out of their misery, but they have people they would miss them and that's what is keeping them here. They would have taken their life a long time ago if they were not afraid of being missed. This person is highly motivated by challenges it has always been a big thing in their life. Instead of allowing the enemy to use the fact that your life appears to be boring, start giving your life to people that are in need. Begin to take your gifts and abilities and all God has given you or shown you and start helping the needy, one on one. Concentrate on others and concentrate on what you can do to help others then life will cease to be boring. God is going to bring your deliverance. God is going to bring the freedom and joy that you want in life."

I knew immediately that he was speaking to me because everything that he said was how I was feeling and what I had said to God. The Mrs. Rebekah turned around and looked at me as the tears flowed down my cheeks and said, "He was talking about you, right?" as she nodded her head. I responded by nodding my head as the tears continued flowing down my face. I thought to myself God really does hear me. He used a sermon that had been recorded years ago to address what I was dealing with in the present. God is so wonderful and knows every thought of His children. In the past, when ministers had prophesized over me, and because their prophecy was only partially true, I would not receive it. That night, God made sure the minister directly spoke to me in every aspect with no mistake. Even though this sermon was preached years earlier God knew I would need this message at this place and at this moment in my life. That night I went to bed feeling elated. I was jubilant, like a child on Christmas morning, believing my God had heard my cry.

The next morning, I woke up like a doubting Thomas. Now Thomas (also known as Didymus), one of the Twelve, was not with the disciples when Jesus came.[25] So the other disciples told him, "We have seen the Lord!" But he said to them, "Unless I see the nail marks in his hands and put my finger where the nails were, and put my hand into his side, I will not believe."[26] A week later his disciples were in the house again, and Thomas was with them. Though the doors were locked, Jesus came and stood among them and said, "Peace be with you!"[27] Then he said to Thomas, "Put your finger here; see my hands. Reach out your hand and put it into my side. Stop doubting and believe."[28] Thomas said to him, "My Lord and my God!"[29] Then Jesus told him, "Because you have seen me, you have believed; blessed are those who have not seen and yet have believed." This was the fourth unwarranted fear I had of God. I feared that the words in the Bible did not apply to me, but only to others (John 20:24-31, New International Version).

After thinking about the sermon, the following morning, I wished God had only mentioned my name in the sermon somehow so I could know it was truly for me. I did not even know how I expected him to do that. I just wanted some type of proof and the only thing I could come up with was to have heard my name. The feeling of joy from the previous night had suddenly left me and I was left with pure skepticism. I would only allow myself to have a few minutes of gratification then I would go back to disbelief. I would always revert to these same misguided beliefs that the word is for someone else that is not me. I just could not believe I was worthy enough to matter. Thank God he looked over all my shortcomings and faults and he knew what my reaction would be that following day. My curiosity was too strong, so the following day I borrowed the video from my neighbors and watched it all over again. Originally, I had missed the beginning because my neighbors had resumed it from their last clip. Terry Jones was the host of the show and the message was titled Jagged Sword. He introduced his longtime friends, Samuel and Toni Stevens, and then acknowledged that his wife's name was, Hannah Stone. He further stated that Samuel and he had preached together for 17 or 18 years. I could hardly believe what I was hearing, and I was truly shocked. Why was this even significant for me? Because the people associated with this sermon had my name, Hannah, my late son's name, Samuel. And on the night, I watched the show, if my son, Samuel, were to be alive he would have been 17 years old. God left nothing out for doubting Thomas—no, doubting Hannah. He covered them all. I could no longer doubt that the word was for me. So, I did as God directed, I started ministering to people one on one as God had instructed me.

Satan was not pleased with me ministering to others, so whenever he saw an opening to attack my mind he did. On this particular occasion, I woke up thinking about all my past mistakes and what had gotten me to this point. I decided to take a walk to clear my mind. While walking in my yard in my hometown, I had all intentions of talking to God as I normally did, but instead, I started talking to myself. I guess it was Bash Hannah Day because that is what I was doing. I started out saying things like, I cannot believe how stupid you were with some of the decisions that you have made. You were so dumb to do the things you did and trust the people you did. Now look at yourself, you have exhausted your bank account, you have no money, no career and everyone has turned their backs against you. I bet you really feel stupid and crazy now. I kept bashing and putting myself down as if I was being paid to do it. Then suddenly I heard a voice say, "Stop talking about my daughter like that," I was immediately startled and afraid. I was afraid because the voice was small but sterner than I had ever heard before. I knew it was God and that he was not pleased with what I was saying. I was on a rampage criticizing myself and to hear the stern voice defend me stopped me in my tracks. I knew it was the voice of the Lord because everything I had spoken about myself, I deeply believed and embodied it. He further said, "Stop defining yourself by your bank account and define yourself in me." It would be years later before I understood and started to live that statement. However, after His comments, the tears just flowed down my face and I was ashamed. God was not pleased with my actions or my words. I knew I had to make a change because God was the only one that I could depend on at this point in my life and I did not want him to turn his back on me also.

I felt like this test was a pinnacle point in my life, it was going to make me or break me. I realized I needed to be equipped with more than what I currently had on the inside. My faith was not where it needed to be to deal with the satanic spirits that had been sent to take my life. So, I had to figure out how I could increase my faith and do it fast. I thought about Daniel and the three Hebrew boys. It had always amazed me how much faith Daniel had when he was thrown in the lion's den and the Hebrew boys when they were thrown in a fiery furnace. I felt like the only way I could overcome my situation was to have their kind of faith. So, I begin studying the book of Daniel. I decided that if I wanted the kind of faith, they had I must do what they did but with some modern-day modifications. The first thing I did was I started praying three times a day. I set my alarm at 6 am 12 pm, and 6 pm as reminders. The second thing I did was that I gave up eating all meat with exception of seafood. I felt I had to make a sacrifice because I needed God more than ever and I wanted Him to know I meant business and that I was determined not to allow Satan to defeat me.

I began praying every day, but it seemed like the more I prayed, the more obstacles came my way. I was committed to following through even if nothing seemed to be changing with my circumstances. I tried to stay positive with all I was facing but the spirit of depression was equally trying to overtake me. I did not want anyone to know how much I was suffering on the inside. When I would go out in public, I would try to keep up a façade that I was happy. I would keep my head up and with a smile on my face. I felt like I was carrying two full sacks of rocks on both of my shoulders. My throat would feel dry and breathing which occurs without human intervention even became a chore. Sometimes I felt like bursting out into tears, but I would take deep breathes and hold it in. But as soon as I would get out of sight, I would put on my shades because I knew it was only a matter of time before I would break down in tears. I would grab pieces of tissue to wipe away my tears, but the tissues could not contain the flood of tears that would stream down my face.

During these times, I could not help but reflect on all the times that God had delivered me in the past. However, when new issues arouse, initially I did not draw strength from the blessings of the past to assist me with the present troubles. Those blessings tended to fade in my memory. God had delivered me several times and I started feeling guilty for not trusting him to get me out of this situation. So, I devised a strategic plan to overcome this obstacle, my memory. I purchased a tape recorder and started recording my daily challenges and prayers. Whatever issues I was facing at the time, I would record and later when God would resolve it, I would record that also. Over time when new issues arouse, I would listen to older recordings of previous concerns and reflect on how they had worked out. By doing this, my faith began to grow stronger through each new obstacle I would face because the recordings supplied me with a vivid memory of how God showed up every time.

As time went on, things got better. Some days were better than others. I found myself still having to fight off the spirit of depression and crying but I just kept praying to God to help me make it through. Then one day it all changed. I had to go and meet the lady that was going to assume the lease for the family care home that Sapphira and I had rented. Sapphira had found someone interested in investing in an adult care home. I had the keys to the home, so I agreed to meet with her and turnover the keys. Having agreed to this meeting, I had to get up, get dressed, style my hair and put on my make-up. These actions alone made me feel a lot better because some days it took everything I had just to bathe and put on some clothes. My spirit was still heavy, but I was determined not to allow anyone else to see me down. I met with the lady and I talked for a few minutes and she informed that Sapphira was going to do the policies and procedures for her adult home. I reassured her that Sapphira was very capable of handling the paperwork. We said our goodbyes and I left. A few days later, out of the blue, she called me. She said, "Are you willing to write the policies and procedures for me?" And further stated how much she was willing to pay me to do it. I then asked her what happened to Sapphira writing them. She said, "There is just something about you that

I like that I cannot explain." She then asked if I would consider being her partner. I told her I could write the policies for her, but I would have to think about the partnership.

I was elated after receiving that phone call about the job because now I had something else to focus on instead of my situation. God had thrown me a lifeline. I now had a reason to get out of bed. I had a job to do and I was excited about getting it done. It's funny sometimes how things work out. The lady that Sapphira discovered was the same lady that was used to motivate me. I started working immediately. My idle mind was no longer vacant for the negative thoughts to consume me on a constant basis. The same week I started working on the policies and procedures, the small voice said, call your previous business landlord about the deposit. It had been almost a year since we had vacated the office and we were yet to receive our deposit. The landlord was the only one that could approve it. However, during that time, he was out of his real estate office and was performing his duties within the government. He was a member of the House of Representatives. I called the landlord's office and the office manager answered the phone. She immediately recognized my voice and said, hello, Hannah, glad you called, Mr. Bartholomew just returned and signed your check today for the deposit and the tenant that moved in your old office just returned after months of being gone and I got his number for you yesterday. I said to myself, is this for real? Several months earlier, I had informed the office manager that I had telephones that went to the phone system in the office and I wanted to know if the new renter would like to purchase them. Our conversation ended with her confirming my address to mail the check and her providing me with the new renter's phone number. I thanked her for all that she had done for me.

The next phone call would change the total direction of my life. I immediately called the new renter of my old office to see if he was interested in the telephones after hanging up with the office manager. When the gentleman answered the phone, I introduced myself and I explained the purpose of my call. He said he would have to check with his business partner before buying the phones, but he was very much interested. He then inquired about the type of business we had previously run in the office. I informed him that it was a mental health agency and he pointed out that he wished he could have purchased our licenses before we closed. His agency was also a mental health agency but with different services. He was currently in the process of trying to get licensed for the services we previously had. I replied, "Yes that would have been great."

Then he said, I am going to Florida they have the same policies and rules we have here. And a friend of mine from here has already opened his mental health agency in Florida. I responded, why are you telling me this? He said, "There is enough money for all of us to make some. I can give you the website where to find the requirements tomorrow because I do not have it right now." I called him back the next day, but I was unable to contact him.

I immediately started searching for the Florida Medicaid requirements and it took only a few days before I found most of them. After gathering all the information, I went to God and shared my concerns and frustrations about Medicaid because I felt He had aligned every connection, meeting, phone call and response to get me to this point. When I closed my previous mental health agency, I told God I never wanted to be in this business again. I was fed up with all the rules, regulations and changes and the thought of working in this field again made me sick to my stomach. I wanted no part of it. God responded and told me that this time will be different because he would be the head. A peace came over me when He made it known that He would be in charge. This removed a lot of the stress off my shoulder knowing I would not have to carry the load all by myself when issues came up with Medicaid. It was now obvious that God had given me this outlet: an opportunity for new business in another state away from all the chaos. So, in order to help me overcome my fears and frustrations, I identified God as the CEO and I would now set up and work for this mental health agency. I was just the vessel he was using to establish it.

Initially, I had feared that God was going to take everything from me until it was revealed that it was my childhood experiences with my grandmother that had shaped that belief. My previous childhood experiences with my grandmother had conditioned my mind into believing that maintaining possessions for me had a limited time period. I constantly lived in fear that I was going to lose everything. I believed it and felt it. I later realized that it my belief and thoughts created these situations and brought my loss into reality. Now it appeared that what I feared the most had come upon me. "For the thing which I greatly feared is come upon me, and that which I was afraid of is come unto me." (Job 3:25, King James Version) Regardless of what we have been through in life, we all have the power to change our outcomes with the most powerful gift we have, our mind. If we can change our negative belief system and focus on what we want instead of what we fear, we can create the reality we desire. "Therefore, I say unto you, what things soever ye desire, when ye pray, believe that ye receive *them*, and ye shall have *them*" (Mark 11:24, King James Version).

From my perspective at the time, it seemed like all hope was lost and it was impossible to overcome my current situation with all the obstacles that surrounded me. These were some of the darkest days in my journey. I wanted to throw a pity party for myself! Did I lose my income? Yes! Was my health attacked? Yes! Did my relatives talk negatively about me? Yes! Did my friend betray me? Yes! Did my ex-business partner mock me? Yes! Did I have the right to self-pity? No! Self-pity and doubt are just a waste of time and distraction with no gains of progress or reward. Instead, you remain at the same state or digress to a downward spiral of more issues. "We all have the power within us to overcome our circumstances no matter how hopeless they may seem.8 We are hard pressed on every side, but not crushed; perplexed, but not in despair;9 persecuted, but not abandoned; struck down, but not destroyed.10 We always carry around in our body the death of Jesus, so that the life of Jesus may also be revealed in our body.11 For we who are alive are always being given over to death for Jesus' sake, so that his life may also be revealed in our mortal body.12 So then, death is at work in us, but life is at work in you" (2 Corinthians, 4:8-12 New International Version). No one can stop you from fulfilling your desires, your dreams, and your destiny, except, you! The moment I got up, got dressed, and took the first steps I activated my faith, God already had everything there waiting for me. So my advice to you is this, if you have the need to waste your valuable time attending your pity parties, crying boatloads of tears, consuming boxes of tissues, swallowing bottles of pills for the migraines, and so on, go ahead. However, if you value yourself and your time, focus on what is positive in your life and look for the good in the situation by starting to believe for a change to come. So, wipe away the tears, fix your face, get dressed, style your hair, hold your head up and walk in confidence as you know without a shadow of a doubt that your change is coming.

God will use whoever he sees fit to carry out his mission. "The steps of a *good* man are ordered by the LORD: and he delighteth in his way" (Psalms 37:23, King James Version). He used my current situation, my neighbors, my ex-business partner, the lady, the landlord, the office manager, and the new office renter to bring me to where I am today. Each person was a vital component in directing my path. "I make thine enemies thy footstool" (Luke 20:43, King James Version). My ex-business partner had the most influential position because she was the one that established contact with the lady. And the lady was used to give me hope and motivation during a very low point in my life. After meeting with the lady everything changed for me. I had a purpose to get out of bed, which led to me contacting the landlord. After contacting the landlord, I was given the phone number of the new office renter who ultimately God used to point me in the direction I should go. I was given a new business opportunity and it would be established in a state I secretly desired to live.

"If God is for you then who can be against you?" (Romans 8:31, King James Version). I spent so many days and nights crying. What a waste of time and energy I lost. Instead of shedding tears of pity, I should have been shedding tears of joy. God had moved toxic people out of my life and had revealed the hearts of others. It is said that if one door closes another one opens. I believe that to be true. However, what I have discovered is that you better make sure the other door is completely sealed shut in your mind before you step into another door. Carrying baggage from the past has no other option but to smell after a while. God cleaned up my surroundings completely before he opened the other door for me. I realized he did not want the shifty parasites to maneuver their way undetected into my new opportunity in attempts to continue to try and suck the life out of me. My life needed fumigation and I was given a clean slate with a new safe, irritate free environment to pursue my destiny.

My perception then:	My worst fears had come upon me and I would lose everything I had. And people I thought were for me were secretly conspiring against me.
Message:	There is no situation so hopeless that God cannot deliver you. We are all more than conquerors. The whole world can be against you but if God is with you who has the power to stand against you?
How this experience affected my future:	Through this experience, I developed a strategic plan to build my faith.
My perception now:	It was the pivotal point in my life that positioned me to receive my heart desires. This experience is also the reason for much of my growth and newly found wisdom.

CHAPTER

Seventeen
My Other God

I was not even aware that I had created another god in my life. This other god gave me such a feeling of freedom, confidence, and worth. And looking up to this god, I felt like I was accomplished, validated and approved. In my eyes, I had finally established some meaning and significance in my life. Now I find myself in a place of despair with the threat of losing something else so close and dear to my heart. I felt like I had already lost everything else and now if I lose this there is no way that I will be able to recover. I could not understand what I had done so wrong to deserve such a punishment at the time. I had done everything within my power to maintain this other god in my life. I made so many sacrifices just to keep this other god, but all my faithfulness didn't seem to be enough. This other god in my life was my credit. I had lost everything else regarding my financial security and it was the only thing I had left to hold onto. I did not want to let go of it.

My credit gave me so much power and pleasure. I could just walk into a bank, a store or car dealership with an expectancy of purchasing whatever I desired. And if that was not enough, I expected to pay zero interest on certain items. I remember the time we purchased our brand-new Ford Excursion. The day we signed the deal I was approved for a five percent interest rate on the vehicle and I felt satisfied with the deal. However, a few days later, while watching television I observed a Ford dealership commercial advertisement. The commercial was promoting the new zero percent interest rate with a qualifying credit score. Without hesitation, the following day, I drove back to the dealership and requested the zero percent interest rate. I explained to them that I had purchased the vehicle three days ago and received a five percent interest rate and I would like the zero percent interest rate that they are now advertising. They looked at my credit score and without delay revised the loan with the zero percent interest rate. I was really impressed with my accomplishment because during my college years all the credit cards I obtained destroyed my credit score.

It was during Memorial Day weekend 2012 that I realized I would have to let my credit go. I was traveling for the holidays from Florida to the Queen city in North Carolina to my sister's home. My eight-hour drive had been so pleasant and peaceful. During the trip, I had talked with many of my friends as I so often do on these long trips. I had been testifying about how good God had been to me even during my struggles. My mood was great, I was positive, and everyone I had talked to that day could tell it. They were happy to see that I was back to my old self, cheerful and encouraging others again. Within two hours of reaching my destination, the ball dropped. My tenants called and said they did not have the rent money to pay towards my mortgage for May. They were already late and had promised to have it before the end of May. I had previously prayed that they would have it before the thirty days was up so it would not affect my credit. They asked if they could get May deferred and just start paying in June on time.   I no longer had the income coming in to cover my mortgage, so I felt helpless. I was also furious, but what else could I do except take them to small claims court? But even that was not going to satisfy the pressing issue of my credit taking a hit.

The trip that had been so pleasant had been ruined in my mind. I was literally sick, the bottom of my stomach felt like it was dropping, and my chest felt like someone had just sucked the air out of me. I cried out to God and asked why. I said, God if you knew you were not going to allow me to keep my credit why did you not take it earlier so I wouldn't have lost all my savings and used my entire unemployment check to cover those mortgage payments these last three years. I told God I sacrificed everything to save my credit and now He was going to take it too! Especially after all the sacrifices I had made. I was infuriated.

I wondered why He would allow me to spend so much money on this house if He was not going to allow me to keep that one thing. I was so hot I felt like I could blow fire out of my mouth like a dragon. I just could not understand why God would allow this to happen to me along with everything else. God said to me, you no longer depend on me; you now rely on your credit. The moment God spoke those words to me I knew them to be true. You have made a God out of your credit. God said, "I will supply all of your needs and you will never go lacking." Despite how my flesh was feeling at the time, I agreed with God. I had put my faith in my credit and taken my eyes off my one and only true source, God.

After closing my company and losing my six-figure income, I had struggled for three years to maintain my credit. I spent every dollar I had to ensure that I kept that credit score rating. If it was a choice between paying my bills and eating, I would choose to pay my bills. During these three years, the only income I had was my unemployment and my savings. And after all was said and done, I had spent over $100,000 trying to maintain my material possessions and my credit. My credit score was just the beginning of the problems I would have to face over the next 25 days. If I would have known prior to leaving Florida the troubles that awaited me during that trip to North Carolina and then my return to Florida, I would have just given up. Sometimes it is great that we do not know the outcome of something ahead of time because our hearts may not be able to deal with the information. God will not give us more than we can bear. "He'll never let you be pushed past your limit; he'll always be there to help you come through it." (1 Corinthians 10:13, Message)

There was a few times which I stated earlier that I would sacrifice what I ate to ensure my bills were paid. One particular time, prior to relocating to the Sunshine State, my funds had gotten low. After paying all my bills that particular month I did not have much left to buy any groceries for myself or food for my puppy, Cocoa. So, the choice was to buy for me or my dog. I remember praying to God telling him how bad I felt for not having enough money to buy food for my puppy. I felt so guilty, it was my responsibility to take care of my puppy and I could not even do that. This was just another reason to feel like a failure again. My family had no idea that things were this bad for me and I refused to share it with them. I was aware that a few family members hoped I would lose everything and would be glad to see me in this situation. So, I did not reach out for any help. A couple of days after I talked with God my friend, Ariel invited me over to their cookout. I really did not feel like going. I had been feeling some kind of way about my current situation, but this person was special to me, so I decided to put aside my emotions and go anyway. When I arrived at their house, I tried to maintain my cheerful composure. I did not want them to know I was struggling with anything. We talked and had a good time, but I did not eat much because I had given up meat as a sacrifice and that's mostly what they had prepared. So, I was content eating a few chips and baked beans. Well, when it was time to leave, Ariel pointed to a large bag of dog food on the floor in another room. She asked, me, if my dog liked that brand of food and stated, her dog would not eat it. The bag of dog food was the same dog brand that I frequently purchase for my puppy and the bag was almost full. I told her yes. She said well please take it. I thanked her profusely to show I was appreciative. I know she didn't understand how thankful I really was and how bad I needed the dog food. I could not share with her what I was going through because I know she would have felt sorry for me and start worrying about me. That was just the kind of person she is. I soon as I left her house and got into my car, I could not hold back the tears any longer. I was overwhelmed with gratitude and I just began to praise God and could not stop. Tears were running down my face as if a dam had broken. They were not tears of sorrow but tears of joy and gratitude to God. This personal experience really touched my heart, knowing that God would not only provide for me but my dog also.

My finances and credit were linked to my greatest desire. To me the greatest loss I suffered was not having the financial resources to give anymore. The greatest joy I had ever found in life was giving. And I did as much as I possibly could; mostly financially but I gave some of my time also. It was the only time in my life that I really and truly felt at my best. The joy of giving was like a lifeline to me. When I would give, it gave me an instant high and when the feeling went away, I wanted to reach it again. Many times, in my life, I questioned my purpose wondering why I was even born. So, when I help others it felt like I had found a purpose. If I was buying or doing something for someone else, I could just get lost in time spending hours doing it. But if it was for me, spending fifteen minutes on me would seem like a lifetime. The satisfaction of giving was one of the things that helped me hold on when I would want to give up on life. And now I felt like I was going to lose it too. So, when I was not able to give any more financially, it almost destroyed me mentally.

When I had money and that small voice would say give, I would walk up and give to complete strangers. People I knew I often gave anonymously. If I saw that someone needed something, I would buy it, take it to them, or have it delivered to them. Relatives and friends that needed college tuitions paid and supplies brought, I would pay and buy them. For college students, I felt compelled to do what I could for them because I knew how it felt not having support while in college. I even purchased a house just so one of my friends could rent it and have a nice place to stay. Some decisions I made probably were not the best, but my heart was in the right place at the time. Whenever and whoever God told me to bless I did, and I never **questioned**. I was a **little** extreme, but I realize now I was trying to fill a void. When I would go out in public and had cash in my purse, I would give it all away. So, I stopped carrying cash in my wallet in hopes to slow down my giving. But then I would just write them a check and would leave the space for their name blank, fill out all the rest and give it to them. When I did favors or jobs for people and they tried to pay me, I would refuse it. I did not want or need their money; I wanted my reward from God. **"Take heed that ye do not your alms before men, to be seen of them: otherwise ye have no reward of your Father which is in heaven"** (Matthew 6:1, King James Version). I wanted God to fill that emptiness that I felt so deeply inside. I knew He was the only one that could help me.

The only thing I felt I had left that I could give was my time and knowledge, so I started giving more of it. I refused to let go of giving, the one thing that gave me inner joy and peace. So, I started giving people advice on opening their businesses. I did not stop there. For others, I have cleaned the inside of their homes and power washed the outside. I painted for them, installed ceiling fans, put together furniture, and baked cakes for many. I even purchased a portable shampoo bowl so I could wash and style the elderly women's hair in their own homes. Nathan had taught me a few things about mechanic work. He also showed me how to use the tractor to disk a garden, plant vegetables and smooth the gravel on the road. So, I also did this for people. I can recall one day while I was in Florida, all alone as usual. At the time, I could not understand why God had moved everyone out of my life and not replace them with anyone. I was in a store picking up a few items and feeling somewhat down. The pressure of waiting on my company to start making a profit, having less than $50 in my bank account, all alone and feeling worthless was about to consume me. When I think about how I felt that day, I often reflect on the scene in the movie 'The Color Purple' when Sofia was in the store picking up groceries and Celie helped her. Sofia said, "I's feelin' real down. I's feelin' mighty bad." That is how I was feeling that day. I just wanted to pay for my items and get out of the store so I could go home and cry. While I was standing in line to pay for the few items I had picked up, a tall, thick lady was standing a few people behind me. She was talking loudly, so she had everyone's attention. Then she asked in a manly tone for the time; for anyone to answer. I looked at my phone and turned towards her and gave her the time. She said, "Hey you are the lady that fixed my car." I looked at her for a moment because I was not sure who she was because I had done that for a few people since I had been in Florida. But after a few seconds, she told me the name of the complex we met at and then I remembered. I responded, yes it was me and I smiled. I walked out of the store feeling encouraged. A sense of pride washed over me believing God was giving me a sign that He had not forgotten about me.

One thing that I learned through all my acts of service is that most times it would cause a chain of reaction. One day an associate and I were out walking and pushing her baby in the stroller. As we approached a four-way intersection, I observed a white van come through the intersection and then stop in the middle of the three-lane highway. The man that was a passenger in the vehicle opened his door and jumped out, then started running towards the adjacent apartment complex. I thought to myself he must have a warrant for his arrest or something. He ran like a deer crossing a highway in less than a few seconds he was completely out of sight. I noticed a lady sitting in the van as if she had frozen. I immediately ran to assist the lady. She was so scared that she had jumped out of the driver's seat into the passenger seat and braced herself. I told her I was there to help her, and I asked her to get back into the driver seat. I instructed her to put the vehicle in neutral so I could push it. She got back into the driver seat, but she was shaking so bad that I had to steer the wheel and push at the same time. Then my associate grabbed her baby out of the stroller with her baby in one hand and one hand on the van she started pushing. The van was almost halfway off the road when a man stopped his vehicle behind us and helped us push it the rest of the way. I told the gentlemen how grateful I was for his help. The lady then secured her tow truck. She told me and my associate thank you, we left and continued with our walk.

Another thing I learned was that the less financially fortunate are more likely to help than the more financially fortunate. On another occasion, I was approaching the stop light and a lady's vehicle had broken down again, except for this time it was in rush hour traffic in a well-traveled area. Of course, there was a traffic build up due to the breakdown and it was agitating drivers who were delayed. Cars passed by and no one stopped to help the stranded lady with her truck. But a homeless man in a wheelchair did come to help. When my vehicle approached hers, I stopped directly behind her vehicle and put my flashers on. I approached the lady and asked what was wrong. She said she had run out of gas and the man in the wheelchair had given her four dollars for gas. I only had five one-dollar bills in cash on me, so I gave that to her. She asked if she could give the four of the five dollars back to the man in the wheelchair. I said, sure. So, she gave the man in the wheelchair four of the one-dollar bills and she said she would use the one left to put in her gas tank. The man in the wheelchair said, "I am so glad you stopped to help her because I am useless." I responded, "You are not useless, you were more helpful than all of the other able-bodied people that had driven past her." He nodded his head, smiled, and said thank you. She cranked up her truck—a gas station was near the intersection—so she pulled into the station, and I pulled in behind her. She pulled up to the gas tank unaware that I had also pulled into the station parking lot. She took the one dollar that she had left into the store to give to the store clerk. While she was in the store, I used my bank card to put some gas in her tank. She came out and saw me pumping gas in her tank. She was so thankful and grateful, and she said you did not have to do that. I just smiled. She asked if she could get my name and address, so she could send me the money back. I told her no, that was ok, but she was determined to get a pen so she could get my address. So, when she went into the store to get the pen and the one dollar back from the clerk, I left. I left that day expressing to God I wish I could have done more. I had witnessed a handicap homeless man in a wheelchair help a lady when others ignored, and an unselfish lady appreciate and did not take for granted the help of others.

Idolatry is the worship of an idol or a physical object as a representation of a god. Idolatry can be particularly dangerous because it creates a situation where we place material possessions, aspirations and works above God.

> *"You shall have no other gods before me"*
> *(Exodus, 20:3 New International Version).*

If we are not careful, we can find ourselves, serving money and things which might end up controlling us, instead of serving God. "No one can serve two masters. Either you will hate the one and love the other, or you will be devoted to the one and despise the other. You cannot serve both God and money" (Matthew 6:24, New International Version). In life, we get so caught up in our day to day activities that we tend to leave God out and give deception the opportunity to enter our life. Money is not the only idols people create. Some of us have made our spouse and children our gods. For others, it is their bank accounts, jobs, positions, houses, vehicles, clothing, jewelry, bodies, hair, drugs, and alcohol. The very thing that you make your idol is what you will be confronted with and if you choose not to give it up there will be consequences to your actions. This idol can never replace God so whatever your idol is let go of it right now, the satisfaction or pleasure that idol gives you, the one and only true living God can give you more.

I decided the day I received the dog food from my friend that no matter how small I may think an act of kindness is I am still going to do it. The friend that day probably assumed that what she did was not much but how she allowed God to use her was worth more than money to me. I once believed that I had to do something big, for someone, for it to really matter, so a lot of the times I would go to the extreme just to do something good. If someone said to me, I need to borrow $20 for lunch this week because I am a little short, my mind would just start turning. I would conclude in my mind that it would not be enough for them to eat for the whole week and so I would give them more. And if I could not help as much as I wanted, I would see my actions as not enough. But when my financial situation changed, I realized that five dollars to a person in need could mean just as much as $20 or $500 to another depending on their circumstances. It's not always about the amount which satisfies us externally, the gesture itself can sometimes go further and help us internally where we really need it. The greatest lesson for me is that it showed me that God would take care of everything associated with me and that was priceless. The other lesson was that if we sit around in misery, having pity parties refusing to get up, it's likely that we will miss out on the blessing that God has ordained for us.

For as long as I can remember I have always been a giver. I believe it is a gift from God because it comes just like breathing for me and it gives me my greatest joy. As an adult, I have been careful to share some of the good deeds that I have done because of the criticism and judgment that sometimes comes with it. The good deeds I am mainly referring to is when I have stopped and helped people on the highways. People have made comments such as "People are crazy now and you cannot help everyone." Yes, I do know that this is true to an extent, but when I am led to help someone in this type of situation, I am led by my spirit man not by my fleshly man. God has not given me a spirit of fear but of love, power, and a sound mind so I choose not to allow others to try and instill the fear of helping others in me. Fear is one of the greatest emotions that can paralyze us from carrying out God's commandment, love your neighbor as yourself. God has given me assurance that he will protect me from any danger when I am helping others. He is confident in knowing that I will do things others will not do and I will go places others may not go. Therefore, I will not allow fear to be imparted on me by earthly men where God has given me peace.

My perception then:	My credit was the last remnants of my false sense of financial security.
Message:	We cannot take our eyes off God and be persuaded by the world's values system. We must not put success, money, material possessions, people or anything before our relationship with God.
How this experience affected my future:	I started trusting more in God than my bank account and credit. I witness God as he used people as vessels to provide for me. I continue to go out of my way to help others and be a blessing.
My perception now:	There is nothing more important than my relationship with God. Wealth and power are meaningless without God and can only carry you so far.

CHAPTER

Eighteen
Not This Time

ikipedia defines fear as a feeling induced by perceived danger or threat that occurs in certain types of organisms, which causes a change in metabolic and organ functions and ultimately a change in behavior, such as fleeing, hiding or freezing from perceived traumatic events. Fear in human beings can be a response to a specific stimulus occurring in the present, or in anticipation or expectation of a future threat perceived as a risk to the body or life. The fear response arises from the perception of danger leading to a confrontation with or escape from/ avoiding the threat (also known as the fight-or-flight response), which in extreme cases of fear (horror and terror) can be a freeze response or paralysis. However, in my story, fear is defined as false evidence appearing to be real. I can hardly conceive how I was terrified to trust in myself yet found it so comfortable putting my trust in someone else. Fear has a way of impelling you to repeat the same old mistakes over and over again even when those situations have been found to be uncomfortable in the past.  Yet when the opportunity presents, we receive the similar package (with a few enhancements but containing the same menace inside) with open arms.

I almost allowed my fear and my lack of self-worth in my business to lead me down a road of deception again. God had already given me the talent and divine intuition to open and run my businesses, however, I was still so blinded by the worldly system. I did not get my knowledge through college, a training, or certification program, so internally I did not feel worthy or qualified. I often questioned myself and felt I was lacking important information that was vital to my success, therefore, I put little stock in my abilities. I never felt accomplished in one area. I had a lot of skills but not a specialty, so I often referred to myself as "a jack of all trades but a master of none." Honestly, I just wanted to feel like I was at least great at performing one thing. But our mind has a way of playing tricks on us. Sometimes we are so focused on ambition and what we do not have that we overlook what's right in front of us. I had—and still have—the capabilities of doing a lot of different things which makes me versatile and a more valuable asset, but I allowed the worldly system to marginalize my worth. So, what if I'm not a master of anything! I'm great at many things!

Prior to my relocation to Florida, while still residing in North Carolina, I had a male acquaintance, Lot, with whom I had some other business endeavors. His wife, Marie, and I were friends from college, and I met Lot through her about ten years later. Marie and I ended up working for the same company just in different departments. Once we reunited, Canaan and I went out on a few double dates with Lot and Marie. I found them to be a very loving couple and did not want to expose them to our miserable dispositions, so I deemed that Canaan and I were not good company for them at the time. Therefore, we lost contact again. However, a few years afterward Lot and I reconnected with a few business endeavors, but Marie and I had never reestablished our relationship. After the partnership with Sapphira, I started working on a project with Lot at the same time I was meeting with a lady about another partnership. Remember from the chapter Doubting Hannah, the lady is the lady that gave me hope and motivation. The businesses that Lot and I had researched were all starter projects and had not produced any income at the time. My options were still open, and I continued to meet with the lady to see how we could be beneficial to each other. But after a few visits with the lady, I realized that she had a lot on her plate, she owned couple group homes, a bar, and every week she was overwhelmed. I knew this was not going to be a good business partnership decision at the time. Initially, I believed that God had sent her to be my new business partner because of how everything occurred and the timing. At the time the lady came into my life, I was disheartened I had no idea how I would further my career and my funds were limited. However, I was wrong God only used her as the vessel to motivate me so I would stop feeling sorry for myself and move forward. Even though this lady was only in my life for a very short season, I am grateful that she came into my life. I thought she was there for one reason, but I found out later that she was there to rejuvenate me.

So, meanwhile, I continued working with my other associate partner, Lot, who proclaimed he was an Attorney. I also continued researching my information regarding my Florida venture and working on my other project with Lot. Around May 2011, I told him about the business opportunity I was pursing in Florida. Of course, he immediately wanted to become a part of it. I thought about it and believed this might be a resolution to my problem; the income to finance my business. I figured since I had all the knowledge, he could handle the financial portion. It seemed fair to me that I would do the research and he would invest the money. Lot agreed he would finance the business with no problem. However, as time went by, he was not able to produce the assets to fund the business and I was ready to get things rolling. I had a credit card that had a $10,000 limit with a zero balance. God spoke to me and told me to call the credit card company, so I did. Once I got the representative, I asked about a cash advance. She stated that they had a new program and she could put $9700 in my account that day and give me a zero percent interest for the next year. I was stunned, getting a zero percent interest rate on an existing card that was better than any bank business loan. Lot called me that evening and I informed him that I had obtained the funds. He said he would pay the loan monthly. When I got off the phone, I had a nagging feeling. What do I need him for? I have the knowledge and now the funds. The next time I talked with him I made him aware of my feelings. He started explaining to me about all the advertising and legal knowledge he had and all that he could bring to the table.

The following month in June, I made my first trip to Florida to look for an office space keeping Lot in the loop about everything that was going on. I found what I thought would be the perfect space, everything was included except phone and internet. I filled out the application and submitted it to the landlord. The receptionist said she saw no reason why I would not get the property. So, I left and headed back to North Carolina excited and waiting on the landlord's approval. A week went by and there was no response. Another week passed and I still heard nothing. I started to get a little concerned. My realtor and I had made several attempts to contact the landlord, but the receptionist kept saying that he was out of town. So finally, after a month, he replied and said he did not want another agency of our type in his building. His reason was that he had too many clients in that population and it was causing a ruckus. When I got his response, I was livid. My first question to God was, "why didn't you allow me to get that building? You know I do not have the funds to keep traveling back and forth to Florida!" I thought to myself, why does everything have to be so complicated why can't it just be simple? Can something please go right for me just this once? No, not this time! Once I got past my feelings, I knew God had my best interest at heart he had never led me astray before. So, I went into revenge mode refusing to give up. I knew God had ordained me to open this business in Florida, so I made up in my mind that I was going back, and I proclaimed that I was going to find me an even better office this time.

Now it is around the end of June and on this specific night something very unusual occurred. This is same evening that Sapphira had sent me the final text message, which is reference in the chapter, What the Eyes Can't See. That night I had fallen asleep on the couch. While I was sleeping, I felt an overwhelming presence over my body. Before I could get up it grabbed both my wrists and pinned me to the couch and began wrestling with me. My first thought was that Satan had come to kill me. I started tossing and turning trying to free myself from the hold, but I could not budge it. It had me in its grips and refused to let me go. No matter how hard I tried, I could not get it off me. I fought as hard as I could to get up, but after a while I became fatigued. All my energy had left my body and I had no choice but to quit. Yet, the moment I stopped fighting, it let me go. As soon as it let me go, I was awakened and startled by this unknown force. I had this pressing desire to go outside and shake it off as if the weight was still hovering over me. This all occurred around 4 o'clock in the morning. Once I gathered my thoughts it puzzled me what had just occurred. I had never had an encounter like this before and I had no idea what it was that had held me down. Whatever it was it had gained my full attention. While standing in my yard I raised both of my arms up to the sky, not saying a word just shaking my head in disbelief. I then heard the voice say to me, you have two options. "You get rid of that business partner or you do not open the business at all!" I was in awe because I recognized that voice. Initially, I thought it was Satan that had been wrestling with me, but it was the spirit of God. At that moment I was so afraid, I thought to myself if God is going to send a spirit to wrestle with me and give me such a clear directive, I knew he meant it. In the past, I have heard God speak to me but on this night his words appeared sharper and more precise than any time I had experienced before. I said, "God I hear You!" I stayed outside for a little while just trying to process all that had just happened. No, not this time! After I contained myself, I walked back into my home knowing there was one thing I was sure of and that was Lot had to go!

A few days later I contacted Lot and told him that I was not going to be able to pursue this venture with him. He wanted to know why, and I just told him I was unable to do so at this time. Over the next few weeks, Lot would call me about giving him directives on how to start the business. And my response to him was: how would this benefit me if I gave you my knowledge? I told him if I was going to do that, I should do the business myself. He said he would reimburse me on the end once the company was up and running. I let him know that it would only be worth my time and effort if I was paid upfront. He had already shown me that he did not have the funds to start the business, so I knew if I told him this, I would no longer have to worry about any more phone calls.

I returned to Florida that August to look for another office space. I had found a better office space with everything included as before and was now just waiting on my credit check to be completed. For the next couple of days, I remained in Florida, enjoying the beautiful sights. One afternoon I decided to go to the park. As I was sitting in the park, I was observing and appreciating all the amazing things God had made: the trees, flowers, grass, water, ducks, pelicans, birds and swans and just thanking Him for being so good to me. That same afternoon I received a phone call while sitting there on the park bench. An acquaintance that had done business with Lot called and indicated that Lot had lied about being an attorney. She said a friend of hers who was going to do some business with Lot, googled him and found nothing that proved he was an attorney. As she continued to speak all I could do was shake my head in disbelief. Once our conversation had ended, I immediately Googled him and confirmed it to be true. I could hardly believe that he had been so deceitful all these years, lying about being an attorney. I had no idea this man was a fraud. I immediately reflected on the night over a month ago that God sent the spirit to wrestle with me and giving me the two options about my business either to get rid of the business partner or not open the business at all. I immediately began to thank God and praise him for protecting me from making the same mistake twice. And then I thanked my ex-business partner, Sapphira, in my heart for sending me that "blessed" text. She had saved me from making the same mistake that I had made with her. The text that had been meant to do me harm was a blessing in disguise because it brought me awareness.

When I first met Lot, he seemed like a nice companion for Marie, her soon to be husband at the time. I was happy that she had found a nice partner because she had such a sweet aura about her. We also shared the same birthdate, however; I was two years older than her. I am not sure when it was that Lot informed me that he was an attorney, but I know it was around when we first met. I really had no reason to question him or Google him. I took him on his word. Really, at the time, his profession did not matter because it was none of my business. However, years later while I was in partnership with Sapphira, Lot asked to be our attorney and requested to be placed on a retainer for our company. He played his role very well. He was impressive and confident communicating using attorney's jargon to seal the deal. He enlightened us on all the benefits our company would have with him as our attorney. A few weeks later he asked us to meet him at his office. We met him at an attorney's office building, and he had reserved a conference room for us that day. He wrote up a contract proposing that we pay him around $500 or more a month so he could handle any arising issues with our company and in addition, giving us ideas, he had that could increase our company's revenue. Again, there was no reason for us to question him because, despite his best efforts, we did not agree with retaining him. However, in maintaining his impersonation, on another occasion, when my stepsons were charged with second-degree murder, he informed that one of his colleagues could handle their cases. After having a consultation with the criminal attorney, she was hired to represent one of my stepsons. With the charges my stepson was facing she arranged for a plea deal and we were satisfied with her services. He kept up his façade until the end never revealing the truth about his profession. One thing always perplexed me once Lot and I had reconnected I often wondered why he never suggested that we get together, Marie, Lot, and me. Well, I just assumed she did not want to hang out. It had been years since we had really communicated and I had a lot going on at the time, so I did not press the issue. Now I believe he did not want us to get together because it may have exposed his lie if it ever came up around Marie. Till today, I have no idea what his profession is and have made no attempts to find out.

If we are not careful fear will take us places, we have no business going. I had previously experienced a bad partnership in which God had previously warned me and now I was exposing myself to the same type of relationship again. I allowed my insecurities to direct my course of action which had me on a route headed for deceitfulness and lies. When I decided to reluctantly pursue this field again God informed me that He would be the CEO this time. Believing God required my assistance I sought out a partner that could finance my business not fully comprehending that God had already made financial provisions for my business. Therefore, I had made the decision to bring in a business partner without God's approval. No, not this time! God had sent a spirit to give me a warning that would not be overlooked. If not for God's warning and protection I would have been in a world of mess dealing with such a man. My emotions of fear and insecurity blinded me from seeing that I was making the same mistake again. I saw myself as being inadequate to do the job alone, even though I had all the knowledge. But the fear of failure consumed me to such a degree that I succumb to my fear. God had equipped me with the knowledge and financial provisions that I needed so what more did I need to feel approved? I had been validated and endorsed by the Almighty. That alone should have been enough.

Another valuable lesson I learned: we jumped to the wrong conclusions about why people come into our lives and we make more of it than we should. Some people are in our lives for just a season, some for a lifetime, and some just for a reason. We allow people to have and take positions and stakes in our lives that they have not earned, learned, or discerned. Because I was at a very dark place in my life at the time, I assumed this lady was sent by God as a new business partner but that was not true. We make these wrong assumptions at times and try to make a relationship or situation that was never meant to be usually because of our own vulnerabilities. This lady's purpose in my life was to set me back on my course and nothing more. There are some of us who still have individuals in our lives who are unfit, undeserving, and their time has expired yet we refused to let them go. We are constantly trying to force people and situations to fit where they were never meant to be in the first place. It's time to release and stop holding onto someone or something that has no purpose in your life. Some people will be a sentence in your life, some people will be a chapter in your life, some people will be a footnote in your lives, but in the end, you are the author of the book, it is your life so you decide where the period goes.

In life when things do not go our way, we tend to get angry, frustrated, disappointed and discouraged, often questioning God, why it did not turn out in our favor. At that time, it's often hard to filter through all the thoughts and emotions that we are experiencing so we tend to dwell on our shortcomings and failures. Due to my financial state at that time, the expectation of immediate change and the effort I put in, I expected to get what I desired on the first attempt. I allowed my circumstances to alter my thoughts and emotions prohibiting myself from seeing things from another perspective. The truth is that I was solely responsible for my delay. I was the one who took it upon myself to invite someone into my business opportunity. I had not previously consulted or prayed to God for His approval concerning the partnership. Instead, I allowed my emotions to dictate my actions. I truly believe that if I had not entered into this agreement with Lot, that I would have been approved the first time. So, if there is anyone out there like me, the next time you are in a situation that did not turn out the way you desired and you decide to question God, question yourself first. What decisions have I made in the past could be the cause of my delay? Have I allowed someone that doesn't benefit me to take a position in my life? Did I make the right choice by accepting this position? Are my negative thoughts of myself causing my own self-destruction? These are just a few of the questions that I ask, but you know the question that directly relates to your situation.

One final note let's just consider if God had not intervened. I would have been in partnership with a phony and a liar, worse than my first business partner. When things do not go our way, our first thoughts should not be that we have been defeated. Instead, we should have confidence that God is working it out in our favor and appreciate that he has knowledge we are not privy to at the time. So, when you get a "Yes" thank God and when you get a "No" thank God. I am so grateful now for the first "No" because I cannot imagine the turmoil that I would have had to endure with such a man as my business partner. "No, not this time!" "And we know that all things work together for good to them that love God, to them who are the called according to *his* purpose." (Romans 8:28, King James Version)

HIGHLIGHTS

- Pay attention to the signs, your intuitions, and your dreams
- God will reveal the truth but it's up to you to receive it
- Do not look to man to be your answer or your source
- Do not jump at the first sight of opportunity without deliberation
- Embrace the answer "No" but with an expectation
- It's our own actions that delay our "Yes"

My perception then:	I did not believe in myself.
Message:	In some instances, the answer no should be viewed as a favorable response. And sometimes deception can be disguised as hope. What appears to look like an opportunity is not always an opportunity. Fear can make you vulnerable to deceit, fabrication, and schemes. If not careful your fears will be the gateway to allowing the enemy to position themselves in your life.
How this experience affected my future:	I used self-discovery to bring awareness to my insecurities and fears so I could overcome them in my present life.
My perception now:	It was my own mirror reflection of myself that created my distorted reality.

CHAPTER

Nineteen
Faith

Sometimes life would get so hard that I felt like God could not possibly be in this with me. Because if He was, this would not be so hard for me, but I would later learn that was not true. I traveled to North Carolina only expecting to be there for the holiday weekend, Memorial Day 2012. I was so excited about having the opportunity to get away and enjoy time with my family and not think about the financial issues I was facing back in Florida. My business had been active for the past 6 months but was yet to yield enough income to cover the overhead costs of the business. I became stressed and somewhat frustrated because things had not happened as soon as I had hoped especially since my only financial source had just depleted. That source was my unemployment and I received my final check that May 2012. It's was crucial to me that my business at least start covering the overhead of the business since my unemployment check had been sustaining it so far.

I was overwhelmed with fear of how I would be able to maintain my business and my personal expenses now since I had exhausted all sources of income. I had zero dollars coming in now. I was doing my best to hold onto my faith and stay hopeful regardless of what my situation looked like, which was not easy at times for me to do. But that ounce of faith that I had I held onto with everything within me to keep me from throwing in the towel and giving up. Now it was Memorial Day weekend, the same weekend I realized I would no longer be able to maintain my high credit rating. All I wanted to think about was seeing my family and friends and enjoy eating all the food from the cookouts and forgetting about the issues facing me back in Florida. During my drive, remember in an earlier chapter, my other god, I stated I had such a positive attitude, sharing my testimonies with friends and praising God for all that he had already done. Then out of nowhere my tenants hit me with not being able to pay the rent which almost ruined my trip completely. This would be only the beginning of the matters I would have to face over the next twenty-five days.

My tenants called me about the rent, and it was as if the air had been knocked out of my body. My tenants were supposed to have paid the rent by the first of May, however, they promised me that they would have it by the end of the month. When they called me during my trip, they informed me that they did not have the rent money and asked if I could absolve May's rent and allow them to start new on June 1st. The answer was absolutely not. Now with my already limited funds, I had made the decision to take out court papers on my tenants who obviously cannot afford my house, which would cost more money. The mortgage company was not going to allow me to just forget about paying the mortgage for the month of May. And I did not have the income to cover for the mortgage, so for the first time since we purchased the house my mortgage was going to be late and there was absolutely nothing, I could do about it. And I had to be three months late before the lender would allow me to apply for the mortgage assistance program. I knew this was going to affect my A-1 credit. And since I could no longer cover it, I knew it was only a matter of months before my credit score would be completely ruined. My credit, the one thing I was trying to hold onto and had put so much reliance in, was now just a fading dream. I felt a great sense of desperation come over me. Financial restoration for me appeared to be a thing of the past, but I held onto a glimmer of hope believing that God would still come through for me somehow.

The saying, "If it's not one thing it is another," I experienced it myself. Also, during my trip, I received a "email" notification that the fee for my storage unit in North Carolina was doubling. I could barely pay for the fee now, so there was no way I could afford it anymore, especially since I had no income. I realized that the best solution for me was to move the furniture and store it in my other home. But where was I going to get the funds for a rental truck? I had already spent funds for court costs and now this. There was another voice saying, "You cannot get blood out of a turnip," meaning I had no personal funds to make this happen and no known sources to retrieve it. Anyway, I contacted the rental truck office in good faith and spoke with a representative and was quoted a little under $200 to rent the vehicle. It seemed as if everything was sinking all around me and I was in the middle and it was only a matter of time before I would be swallowed up. The pressure was really getting to me, and it seemed like I could not win from losing. I felt like the harder I tried, the worse it got. No current income, business yet to yield, my credit was already in jeopardy, and now my possessions was at stake. I had no one else to call on but God. "Call to me and I will answer you and tell you great and unsearchable things you do not know (Jeremiah 33:3, New International Version)." I cried out to God with a heavy heart and told him that I needed $200 for a rental truck to move my furniture. Once I had talked with God, my flesh still had some uneasiness, but my spirit had an expectation of God coming through for me. The following day I came up with the first $100 when I purchased an item on my Lowes account for a friend and she paid me back in cash. I thanked God for giving me access to the $100 and told him that all I needed was another $100. That same day, I arrived at my home in Freetown, which was next door to my mother's home. I walked over to my mom's house and my mom's best friend, Sarah, was outside in the yard. I walked over to speak and hug her but before she let me go, she grabbed my hand and put something in it. I thanked her for it and told her how much I appreciated it. I knew it was money. I figured it was about $20 and I said, God, we are getting close. But as I walked away and opened my hand it was a hundred-dollar bill. Sarah had no idea how her gesture impacted my life that day. I started crying uncontrollably, but they were not tears of sorrow but tears of joy. I went into my house and just began thanking God for how he came through for me again.

Now it was in the middle of June and I was on my way back to Florida after being in North Carolina for two extra weeks. The actual date of my return was June 13th. I left that morning from North Carolina for the 560 miles drive to Florida. I reflected on all that I had been through over the past days but what stood out most was how God had intervened on my behalf. After traveling about six hours I had arrived in Jacksonville, Florida less than two hours and a half from my destination. I had planned on staying with my friends Abigail and David for the next few days under the impression that my cousins who had allowed me to stay with them were hosting guests from out of town. So, my intentions were to stay with Abigail and David from that Wednesday to Sunday until my cousin's guests had left. As I was traveling through Jacksonville at a speed of 75 mph, I heard a loud thump. I thought I had run over something. I looked in my rearview mirror and saw nothing. I continued traveling at the same speed, give or take a few mph. I was about 30 minutes outside of Kissimmee traveling in the middle lane and a loud demanding voice spoke to me and said, "Pull over now!" The voice startled me, so I pulled over to the side of the road. And as soon as I was clear of the ongoing traffic, my vehicle shut off. I tried to turn the ignition on, but the vehicle would not crank up. I then attempted to open the driver side door to get out of my vehicle, but the wind speeds off the vehicles passing by made it impossible for me to open it. So, I moved over into the passenger seat and got out through the passenger door. Once I got in front of my vehicle, I had to brace myself, the winds from the vehicles were almost blowing me over. I pulled up the hood and engine was steaming. I contacted Nathan and told him what had happened and explained what I saw occurring under the hood. He told me it appeared as if the head gaskets had been blown. I knew enough about vehicles to know the engine was gone, but I tried to hold onto a little hope. At the same time on the opposite side of I-4, another vehicle had broken down and a tow truck was there towing it off. I thanked God that at least I had AAA and then I called AAA requesting a tow. I did my best to report my location to the attendee, but I was not sure because there was no mile marker in sight. Approximately five minutes later the tow truck driver called me and asked if I just pulled off the road about ten minutes ago and he stated some other landmark as a reference that I cannot remember now, but I said yes that was me. He said, I know exactly where you are, I was just there picking up another vehicle, I should be back there in thirty or forty-minutes time. Wow! God is so amazing that he had positioned me at the right place at the right time so that the tow driver would recognize my vehicle and know my exact location.

While waiting on the tow truck driver, I sat in my vehicle. I wanted to cry, but I held back the tears. I kept taking long deep breaths determined not to give the devil any satisfaction. I thought about everything I had gone through the past few weeks and how God was right there for me.

I thought about how God expected me to respond. So, then I started thanking him again that I had AAA, that I had pulled off the road in time, but most importantly, that I was still alive and breathing with no injuries. I realized how this could have played out differently. If I had not pulled over at that exact moment when the Holy Spirit spoke and my vehicle had shut down in the middle lane of I-4, there was no way the vehicles behind me could have stopped in time. At the speed we were all traveling, I would have been hit from behind with immense force. It would have been almost impossible for me to escape being hit and possibly even killed. But the Holy Spirit warned me to get off the highway to safety and I believe the Holy Spirit saved my life yet again that day.

Once I arrived at Abigail and David's apartment complex, the tow truck unloaded my vehicle. He looked under the hood and noticed that the engine cooling fan had blown off and broken into pieces. Also, I observed that the oil was watery, so I knew that the gaskets were blown. Nathan had taught me that. I walked into my friend's apartment. I had already called and told them about my situation. I had to figure out how I would respond to what had just happened. With no money and with no income from my business yet, I felt I had two choices to make; have a pity party or have a praising party. I chose to praise. I started just thanking God for my new vehicle. I kept reciting it over and over. When I would take a break, the devil would say how are you going to pay for it? And then darkness, a heavy weight would hover over me and try to press me down, but I would respond I'm not going to worry, and I would then feel a release of pressure. Every time I felt that feeling coming on, I just continued to thank God for my new vehicle. The following day, I went to the dealership. I had visited the dealership two months earlier, claiming that I was going to get it. I knew my vehicle at the time could not stand many more miles. So, I had previously decided on the Hybrid because of the 100,000-mile warranty and 35 to 40 miles per gallon but was planning on waiting until my business had started earning before purchasing it.

Once I arrived at the dealership, the sales representatives recognized me from my last visit. They informed me that they had a program that previous owners could get $3000 rebate. We agreed on the numbers and they ran my credit. I only had one late payment on my credit by this time, so I did not have to put any money down and my first payment would not be until August 1st. What an amazing God, the vehicle of my choice, with a rebate and 45 days before first payment. So, I walked out of the dealership with my brand new 2012 Hybrid. Grateful again how everything had worked out because I realized that within a few more months my credit might have impeded me from purchasing the vehicle without any money down or purchase at all. Then it came to me while I still had A-one credit I better get pre-qualified for an apartment and give them a move in date of August 1st. Why August 1st? I was just believing and hoping by faith that on August 1st my company would have some revenue. I looked at apartments that weekend and then continued Monday and Tuesday. Every place I looked at did not feel right. When I was about to give up for on that Tuesday, one of my staff told me to check out this area called Metro Place. At the moment she said it, I had just passed the road, so I turned around and proceeded to drive to the area. When I approached the area, I was amazed. It was like a hidden city from its surrounding. It had gorgeous buildings that were beautifully painted, a stunning green golf course, all apartment complexes with manicured yards, a shopping center with brick pavement, and lighted, clean and spacious sidewalks with people jogging and riding bicycles, as if they have no cares in this world. I said now this is where I want to live. It was close to my office and less than 10 minutes from the tourist's area and amusement parks. I immediately fell in love with the neighborhood. So, I went to the grocery store to find an apartment guide for the area to view some of the apartment complexes. I walked in the store and the only guides left were all in Spanish. As I walked out of the door, I saw a place called Apartment Finders. I walked in and looked up at the clock and it was 5:55 pm. I said to myself I'm just in time to get an apartment guide before they close. I asked the first lady within my vicinity if they had an apartment guide for the area. They said no but, "We can help you find what you are looking for." I sat down in the chair in front of the lady's desk and she asked me to give her a description of what type of apartment I was looking for and the price range. With no current income and limited funds in my account, I spoke from the desires of my heart. I told her I was looking for a one-bedroom apartment with granite kitchen and bathroom counter tops, a stainless-steel refrigerator and stove, and brand-new carpet. All four ladies in the office must have been eavesdropping because they all said at the same time, we saw that apartment today. A lady in the back of the office--not the one I was sitting in front of—said, "I'm calling the complex now to see if you can come see it." Once she got off the phone, she said the representative at the apartment complex told her a man came in and filled out an application but did not put down a deposit. She further stated that the apartment representative said if I could come right now, she would show it to me because they close at 6 pm. The ladies in the office were cheering for me, "Go, go, go you're going to get it!" Keep in mind I only came into this office less than 5 minutes ago. You would have thought these ladies have been working with me for weeks to find an apartment. So, I left their office and proceeded to the apartment complex. I did not feel pressured about the man getting this apartment. I just wanted to see what it looked like. The day was Tuesday, June 19th and I had no intentions of moving until August 1st. And August the 1st was my faith date. Once I got to the apartment complex, the lady transported me by golf cart to the apartment. I walked into the apartment and I was amazed to see that it was everything I wanted. It had a stainless-steel side by side refrigerator, granite countertops in kitchen and bathroom and brand-new carpet. It was as if I had made a wish list and every wish was granted. I thought to myself, I'll get the next one that's available in August. She asked if I liked it and I said yes. She said, well you can have this one. I said, "Oh, no!" I'm sorry I do not plan to move in until August. She said all you will pay is two hundred dollars to move in, July rent is free, and your first-month rent is not due until August 1st. My heart started palpitating. I did not know what to say. Things were just happening so fast it appeared as if everything and everyone was working together to ensure that I got this apartment. She asked me to fill out an application so she could run my credit and I did. I agreed, still having no idea what I was going to decide. However, within a few minutes, I was approved for the apartment. When I left the office, I began asking God what I was supposed to do, am I supposed to take this apartment or not? I had no income, just brought a new car five days ago on my faith account, and now an apartment which is double my car payment, which would have to also be put on my faith account. This was all just happening too fast and my current living arrangements was still up in the air. I had planned on going back to my cousins this night, but I was unable to contact them. I had keys to their home, but I did not feel comfortable going back after being gone for so many days without contacting them first. I'm sure they did not have an issue with it. I was just uncomfortable doing so. So, I went back to Abigail and David that night and asked them to stay two more nights. I told them they would not have to worry about me bothering them about staying anymore because I had found an apartment. I was so elated. I showed Abigail the brochures and she was astonished. She knew of all the things that I had desired of my apartment because I had claimed them on several occasions. Abigail said, "You got everything you asked for!" I smiled and expressed to her

188

how blessed I felt and how good God is to me. She asked her husband, David, if I could stay and he said of course. I fell asleep that night with such gratitude, knowing that I would be in my own place and believing I had only two more days before I would be in my own apartment.

I woke up the following morning and the digital clock displayed 4:13 am. I looked at it and then fell back to sleep. I woke up again at around 5 am. The Holy Spirit said, read 4:13. The Holy Spirit did not say chapter 4 of what book, but the first book that came to mind was Matthew. However, my spirit said Luke. I grabbed my cell phone and Googled Luke 4:13. "When the devil had finished all this tempting, he left him until an opportune time. (New International Version)". I took that as a sign that all the struggles I had been going through was coming to an end and my worrying would cease. Well, the next morning I woke up to loud arguing and screaming. I could hear what sounded like boxes being thrown in the adjacent room, loud voices yelling and then finally I heard a door slam. I waited a few minutes before I got up and walked out of the guest bedroom to see what was going on. As I opened the room door to peak out, I witnessed Abigail throwing boxes from one side of the living room to another. The boxes were brought in by David who worked at the Salvation Army. They had given him a lot of free items. As soon as Abigail saw me, she said, "We are never going to get out of the ghetto!" Then she said to me, pray to your God now and see if he will stop David for driving without a license. Hmm, I thought to myself, David has been nice to me why would I do that? And, we have all worshipped God together and given him praises. Why is He suddenly only my God?

I went back into the guest room and laid down for a few more minutes until it was time for me to get dressed for work. When I got ready to leave, I asked Abigail if she needed me to take her anywhere before I went to work, and she said no. As I approached the door, she asked if I was taking my clothes. I thought to myself, Wow! It did not take a rocket scientist to know I was being kicked out. I promptly went back to the bedroom with a smile on my face and grabbed my bag. Abigail then asked if she could have my key because David had taken hers. I knew he had not taken her key, but this was her nice way of saying you are no longer welcome here. As I left her apartment, walking towards my vehicle, I just started laughing. What had just happened did not bother me at all. I was at peace. The verse the Holy Spirit had led me to read that morning had already prepared me for this situation. I went to my office and obtained the rest of the paperwork that I would need for the final approval of my apartment. I had told my first cousin, Chloe, about what had happened with Abigail and she volunteered to give me a portion of the money so I could move in immediately. So along with the funds and final paperwork, I gave it to the apartment representative, and she gave me my keys that day, so I ended up moving in one day earlier. I felt so favored and blessed. I called the electric company and had the electric transferred from the apartment complex to my name. That evening I went to Walmart and purchased me an air mattress, towels, washcloths and a few other items. I set my air mattress up in the middle of my living room and that night I fell asleep with a grateful heart knowing that in less than a week from arriving back into Florida I now had a new car and new apartment. I do recall hearing that voice that asked me the question, how are you going to pay for all this? My response was, "Do not ask me, ask God. He is the one who told me to get them."

The following day David called me. He apologized for Abigail's behavior. He told me that she had woken up that previous morning listening to Joyce Meyer talking about a well running dry. She could not understand how I could get a brand-new car and a new apartment in a luxurious neighborhood so quickly. She felt she had been suffering for years and I had been here less than six months and God had blessed me. I told him not to worry; that I figured that out when she said, were never going to get off the ghetto. I also told him that if I was in her shoes, who knows, I might be envious to not knowing all the facts. Abigail had no idea how long I had been suffering. She could only relate to the time I had been in Florida. Despite the ending of our relationship, for the season God allowed Abigail and David to be in my life, they were awesome associates and I will always be forever grateful. God showed me that some people will be in my life for a season and some a lifetime, so I choose not to worry about people that have been moved out of my life. I am a true friend, willing to go the extra mile for my friends. However, some people's motives are not noble. I simply appreciate the time we had together and move on.

"No test or temptation that comes your way is beyond the course of what others have had to face. All you need to remember is that God will never let you down; he'll never let you be pushed past your limit; he'll always be there to help you come through it" (1 Corinthians, 10:13 Message). Did I have reasons to be concerned about issues that had to be addressed those 25 days? Yes, I did. But given what I know, I wish I would have had a more trusting attitude towards God. I made the statement earlier on, "Sometimes it would get so hard that I felt like God could not possibly be in this with me because if He was, then this would not be so hard for me," but what I realize is that I made it harder for myself. God had already prepared me a way of escape and the people he would use to get it done. God had positioned everything, so I could receive what I needed and all I had to do was ask Him, believe that He would do it, and praise Him in advance for doing so. My mistake was that I allowed all my issues to compound and I focused on the situation that I perceived as adverse, but what I discovered is that adversity is often necessary to bring about positive change.

I had made a god out of my credit score; therefore, I had to deal with the consequences of my actions. "Thou shalt have no other gods before me" (Exodus 20:3, King James Version). I received the email about the rental property and the storage unit during a time I was already scheduled to be in town. Therefore, I did not have to make an unnecessary trip. I had to extend my stay a few weeks to handle these concerns, but who knows, God may have been protecting me from unforeseen danger if I had left earlier. Yes, it cost money I did not have initially to relocate the furniture. However, God touched the hearts of others to provide me with it. Yes, my vehicle did break down, but it ran for two more hours after I heard the gaskets blow allowing me to get closer to home. Yes, my engine was completely shot, but it happened at a convenient time allowing me time to purchase a new vehicle before my credit score was drastically affected. It also prompted me to search for and lease an apartment before my desired time after considering how my credit score would affect my approval. "And we know that all things work together for good to them that love God, to them who are the called according to *his* purpose" (Romans 8:28, King James Version).

I wasted time worrying and stressing about issues my Father had already attended to. I will admit that it gets hard sometimes when new issues arise, and we forget about the situations that God just brought us through. We have been programmed to expect the worst making it almost impossible for us to digest the word of God. "Finally, brethren, whatsoever things are true, whatsoever things *are* honest, whatsoever things *are* just, whatsoever things *are* pure, whatsoever things *are* lovely, whatsoever things *are* of good report; if *there be* any virtue, and if *there be* any praise, think on these things" (Phil 4:8, King James Version). Looking back now, I wish that I had the confidence to handle every situation as I did when I went into the Apartment Finder's office. Without even second guessing myself, I confidently provided the ladies with a list of all the things I desired for my apartment with an expectancy with no current income and only a couple of dollars in my account. And we all know the result of my request. I received my every desire. So, I believe that when we are facing an issue that is beyond our control that we should do the following:

1. Ask God for help (only if it is His will)

2. Believe that he will come through for us

3. Praise him in advance for working it out

4. Act as if your request has already been granted

5. Do not allow distractions to stop you from believing in your request

6. Cast down any thought that does not align with your request

7. Believe that you are worthy to receive it

Lastly, what do I mean by God's will? The Bible states: "Beloved, I wish above all things that thou mayest prosper and be in health, even as thy soul prospereth" (John 3:2, King James Version). "With long life will I satisfy him, and shew him my salvation" (Psalms 91:16, King James Version). "For your shame *ye shall have* double; and *for* confusion, they shall rejoice in their portion: therefore in their land, they shall possess the double: everlasting joy shall be unto them" (Isaiah 61:7, King James Version). "And he shall be like a tree planted by the rivers of water, that bringeth forth his fruit in his season; his leaf also shall not wither; and whatsoever he doeth shall prosper" (Psalms 1:3, King James Version). These are just a few of the verses that express His will for us. However, praying to have others' spouses, possessions and praying for harm against another is not God's will for us.

My perception then:	I knew without a doubt that God had led me to relocate to Florida and open my business, but I could not understand why I was facing so many obstacles since He himself had ordained me to open it and manage it.
Message:	Situations are going to arise in our life that will be a verse to our current state, but we should not be discouraged or dismayed instead we must face it head-on with the assurance that God is in the midst of our situation. The reason we get tired, weary and overwhelmed by our situations is a direct result of us using our physical strength as opposed to the weapon that God has designed for us to utilize when engaging in battle. We are to confront our situation with the Word of God in order to conquer and defeat the obstacle that we are facing with expectancy that God will deliver the final resolution.
How this experience affected my future:	During times when I felt as if I was in the dark about the outcome of my situation, I would reflect on how God in the past had intervened on my behalf.
My perception now:	Adversity should not be faced with anxiety or fear but from a position of boldness in knowing I have been bestowed the power by God to defeat and conquer it.

CHAPTER

Twenty
Cooler Full of Fish

*I*t was October 2012 and it was that time of the year when the fish are biting in the oceans of North Carolina. It was one of my favorite times of the year. I had to make a trip back home again to North Carolina to represent myself against the tenants that were renting my house. Having to constantly take my tenants to court was getting really old. I prayed this was the last time that I would have to make a trip for this reason, but I also thought about the enjoyment I would have during this trip. During these long trips from Florida to North Carolina and back, I would often converse with God. I found these trips to be some of the most peaceful drives as I communicated with my Father in Heaven. I recall one of the conversations during this trip that I had with my Father when I made a statement and then asked Him this question: God I know that you will bless what you have instructed me to do, but how will I know if you agree with and bless what I desire? I am confident in knowing that  when you speak to my spirit, and I do as you instruct me that you will deliver. So my real question is, "God, when I have ideas and desires that came through the channel of my mind and I want to receive it by faith, are you going to fulfill them if they were not directly spoken to my spirit?

I had just visited North Carolina the previous month for the birth of my dog, Cocoa's, six puppies and to take out the court papers on my tenants for the late rent again. And, of course, this trip was a result of the papers that were taken out last month. One good thing: I was driving a rental car and did not have to put more miles on my new vehicle. But on the other hand, I was not driving my vehicle because it was involved in an accident on the previous trip back to Florida in September. As you are aware, I had just purchased a new car four months prior, in June. After getting close to the halfway mark to Florida while I was traveling South on highway 95, the accident occurred. As I was driving through a small town in Georgia, I saw an RV approximately three-fourths of a mile away on the opposite side of the road swerving from side to another. The RV, of course, was traveling 95 North and both sides seemed to be keeping up with or exceeding the 70-mph speed limit. As both of our vehicles traveled in opposite directions facing each other, I noticed that the tire broke away from the exterior of the RV. I thought to myself, this cannot possibly be happening. The tire hit the road picked up momentum and jumped over two lanes. The tire appeared to be traveling at a speed greater than the vehicles on the highway. I could see the spare tire coming directly towards me. I braced myself and stayed focused. I knew there was no way to avoid a collision because I was in the left lane and other vehicles were in the middle lane stopping me from moving over causing a vehicle collision. The tire then jumped over the guard rail and hit the bar rail on my vehicle that separates my windshield and driver's side window. After the first impact with my vehicle, it collided with the top of the hood and then jumped over two more lanes into a ditch then landing in the trees. Just a little to the right it would have crashed through my windshield or a little to the left it would have crashed through my driver's side window. I pulled over to the side of the road. My heart was pounding. I knew immediately without a doubt that an Angel of God had deterred the tire from hitting me head on. I could not help but imagine what would have happened if the tire had broken through my windshield and hit me directly in my face shattering the windshield forcing the pieces of glass in my eyes.

I noticed that RV had pulled over also, but we were almost a mile apart. I waited to see if they would come back, but after a few minutes they just drove off. I called 911 and reported the incident. Two sheriff deputies came to the scene and took a report, but of course, I was not able to provide them with any identifying information with exception of vehicle type and color. There was no way that I could have possibly seen the RV's plate number, so I just filed the report with the limited information I had, but I gave them a detailed description of what had occurred. The deputies informed me that they would file the report but then apologized for not being more helpful. They insisted that I drive to a public place and park for a few minutes to get the edge off after being in, what they considered, could have been a tragic accident. I knobbed my head in agreement with the deputies, thanked them for their assistance, and then drove off. As I proceeded to get back on the highway, I continued to praise God over and over for protecting me again.

I did not take the advice of the deputies because I realized that everything was going to be alright. There was one area in my life that my faith was strong. I was confident that my life would be protected, and nothing was going to happen because I am yet to finish what God had called me to do. As I drove down the highway, I pondered over the life and death situations that I faced in the past that God had intervened. The first thing I thought about was when I was around seven years old, I was in the horse stables racking up hay and the dust from the hay caused an allergic reaction. I had passed out unable to breathe for a few minutes before my grandfather came and rescued me. When I revived, I was fatigue, my eyes were swollen, throat was itchy, nose runny and I couldn't stop sneezing. I was taken to the doctor and given a prescription for an allergy I didn't know I even had. When I was 19 years old, I was bitten by a baby copperhead whose venom was as potent as an adult copperhead. However, the baby copperhead had only got one fang in my foot therefore I only suffered a few symptoms. My leg was swollen, and I had to walk on crutches for about two weeks along with having a few hot flashes. I thanked God for not allowing the snake's fangs to penetrate in my foot which could have resulted into a totally different outcome. And then, how could I ever forget my experience in the New England state when on three different occasion women tried to physically harm me, yet God protected me. Next, my most emotional experience when my baby died inside of me and had been poisoning my bloodstream leaving me on the brink of death, God did not allow me to die. After that, when the Holy Spirit warned me to get off the road right before my vehicle's engine blew. And finally, all the times I pleaded for God to allow me to be with Him. I realized a long time ago that if God was ready for me, I would have already been taken. So, I was confident that nothing was going to happen until I had completed what he had asked me to do.

I recall the time I was traveling by airplane with Sapphira, her spouse, and Canaan at the time to the City of Lights. We had seats sitting directly across from each other, so we were able to talk and pass time. The flight was about seven hours in total however during the last two hours there was great turbulence. The plane began to shudder a few times and then felt as if it was dropping out of the sky into violent wind patches. The Captain informed us that everything was fine; however, we would have to endure the turbulence for a longer than normal period. By that time, Sapphira, her spouse and Canaan had all stopped talking holding onto their seats fearing for their dear life. Since it was obvious to me from their facial and body expression that they were too nervous to continue talking, I asked the flight attendant for a blanket. I sat my chair into a lounging position, covered my body with the blanket and closed my eyes. I fell asleep. They said within moments I was sleep and looked so peaceful. They were amazed at how I could sleep under the circumstances. I must have really been comfortable and into a deep sleep because Canaan nudged me to tell me that I was snoring. I looked at him in contempt, as if to say, I cannot believe you woke me up out of my good sleep. I rearranged my body in the chair and went back to sleep again. I guess it was a little while later when Canaan nudged me again, informing me that the plane was getting ready to land. I woke up to notice that all three of them were looking at me strangely as if there was something wrong. I asked them if I was snoring. Sapphira asked me, "How could you sleep with all the bumping and shaking of this plane?" I responded, "I know nothing was going to happen with me on board." They all just looked at me in disbelief, but one thing was certain, I was well rested, and they looked exhausted.

Once I had finished traveling down memory lane, I contacted my insurance agent and reported my claim. I was once a liability adjuster for an Insurance Company, so I knew the claim would be paid up under comprehensive instead of collision and I would not be liable for the incident. Well, when I checked on my comprehensive limits. I had a $250 deductible. I could not believe that I had agreed to that because for years I've always carried $250 deductive on collision and $100 on comprehensive. However, I immediately recalled when the mishap occurred. When I purchased my new vehicle, I obtained the coverage over the phone while at the car dealership, but somehow neglected to confirm the coverage that had been added. I asked myself, how could I have made such a mistake? Before I could catch myself I began verbally abusing myself but then I took a deep breath came to my senses and said, "I could have been in the hospital or even dead, so I'm not going to allow this mistake to consume me." The real reason I was upset, I barely had enough money to cover my expenses. I felt I could not afford to make mistakes like this to generate more financial burdens for my situation. Instead of me blaming myself, I should have been more focused on my blessing even amid mishap. Sometimes, it's so easy to lose sight of the blessing when it is in conjunction with pre-existing issues. Therefore, it's so important that we are grounded in the word of God. "That is why I tell you not to worry about everyday life—whether you have enough food and drink, or enough clothes to wear. Isn't life more than food and your body more than clothing? Look at the birds. They don't plant or harvest or store food in barns, for your heavenly Father feeds them. And aren't you far more valuable to him than they are" (Matthew 6:25-26, New Living Translation).

It was the second Thursday in the month, and I was traveling to North Carolina to attend the court hearing for my tenants, but all I could think about was sitting on that ocean pier fishing. It had been a while since I have had the opportunity to go fishing and I was really yearning for it. The past few times that I had gone, I did not even catch enough to comment on my catch, but this time was going to be different for me. From the moment I left Florida, I believed I was going to catch a cooler full of fish. "Brethren, I count not myself to have apprehended: but this one thing I do, forgetting those things which are behind, and reaching forth unto those things which are before" (Phil 3:13, King James Version). I thought about it all the way to North Carolina and everyone that I spoke to, I told them also that I was going to catch a cooler full of fish. I had planned to stay with my friend in the city so I would be close to the courthouse and leave right after heading to my hometown, to pack my vehicle, get dressed, and then go straight to the ocean. I planned to stay all Friday night at the ocean and leave on Saturday evening. Well, after about nine hours of driving, I finally arrived at my friend's home late that evening. Once I arrived, we decided to go out and grab a bite to eat but did not stay out too long because I was exhausted. When we returned to my friend's home, we talked for a few more minutes but we both had to retire to bed because we had to wake up early the next morning. Before falling asleep I thought about how nice it was to have a friend living in the area and not having to worry about being alone or having a place to stay while I was in town. But most of all it was a pleasure seeing my friend face to face. Since I moved to Florida, our visits were now precious time. Times like this cause me to reflect on what's important in life. I realized I needed to focus more on what is going right than focusing on what was going wrong. It's the obvious blessings that we tend to take for granted like the gift of friendship. In life, we get so caught up worrying about the day to day distraction in life that we never take time to appreciate the people who are right there in front of us.

Friday was here and it was court day, but most importantly I was excited about catching my cooler full of fish. I arrived at the courtroom around 8:45 am and immediately made eye contact with my tenants. They looked away as if they were ashamed of being in this predicament and a part of me felt a little sorry for them but the other part of me realized that my mortgage company would not take sorry as a payment. I had no desire to evict them I just wanted them to start making their rent payments on time so I would not have to continue traveling back and forth to North Carolina to take out eviction papers and appear for court hearings. There were a few cases before us and then they called our case. Once our case was called and I pleaded my case and my tenants pleaded their case. However, prior to coming to court, the tenants had paid the rent, therefore, I was unable to evict them even if I wanted to. However, they were instructed to reimburse me for the court fees. After court, I called them over to the side to talk with them face to face. I explained to them that this was costing me too much money to travel back and forth to North Carolina, but I would if I had to because of principle. I also informed them that I did not like having to take them to court and that I understand everyone has problems, but the mortgage company is not accepting excuses from me. They apologized for being late and said that they really wanted the house and assured me that things were going to get better. I asked them, "Do you really want the house?" They said, yes. I asked them to please step aside in the corner and I told them I was going to pray for them. First, this was totally out of character for me because I had insecurities about my abilities to pray out loud; therefore, I knew it was a greater power working within me. That day, I humbly and confidently prayed on behalf of my tenants openly in the corner of the courthouse waiting area. After I prayed for them, it was amazing how our demeanors completely changed towards each other. Before I was feeling some kind of way towards them because they were late with their first rental payment and then their non-payment in May was the cause of my first late payment with my mortgage company which in turn was the initial decline in my credit score. However, on that day I prayed for them it allowed me to release all the frustration and aggravation I had towards them. I felt like a refreshed person that had been rejuvenated and released from the clutches of repulsion. It was also evident by their response to me that they had also been relieved, and they no longer viewed me as the wicked landlord. As we proceeded to exit the courthouse heading towards the elevator, we continued our conversation. The wife began talking about the Bible verses that I had posted on the wall in a room in my house when they first viewed it. I told her that was my meditation room and I had tried to memorize every verse that was posted on my wall so that I could to hide the words in my heart. As we rode down the elevator, the conversation was getting better and better. It was so good that afterwards we stood in front of the courthouse and talked for about another ten minutes. After talking with me face to face for a few minutes, they realized that I was really an approachable and genuine person. During the conversation, the wife asked me: if she ever got depressed could she call me sometimes. I said, yes most certainly. "A word fitly spoken is like apples of gold in pictures of silver. 12 As an earring of gold, and an ornament of fine gold, so is a wise reprove upon an obedient ear" (Proverbs 25:11-12, King James Version). I hugged them both I told them goodbye and I wished them blessings with the house, but I insisted I had to go now because I was heading to the ocean to catch my cooler full of fish. As I walked to my vehicle, I thought about how a simple prayer broke down the barriers of tension and created a harmonious atmosphere with less judgment and more compassion between three people. "For where two or three are gathered together in my name, there am I in the midst of them" (Matthew 18:20, King James Version). Prayer is one of the most powerful weapon God has given us, but it is often pushed aside and discarded as invisible and futile.

After leaving the courthouse, I had two more stops to make before heading to Freetown: the gas station and the bank. The friend I had stayed with the previous night was struggling a little financially, so I took over half of the money from court fees and put in her bank account. I put aside the rest for my gas. "Every man shall give as he is able, according to the blessing of the LORD thy God which he hath given thee" (Deuteronomy 16:17, King James Version). I was ready to go fishing now. I was going to catch my cooler full of fish! I felt good about praying for my tenants and having the opportunity to bless a friend, but now, nothing was as exciting to me as catching my cooler full of fish. My day was going great and I was back on the highway traveling towards Freetown. I said I was going to catch my cooler full of fish, I spoke it, I believed it, and I felt it. "For verily I say unto you, that whosoever shall say unto this mountain, be thou removed, and be thou cast into the sea; and shall not doubt in his heart, but shall believe that those things which he saith shall come to pass; he shall have whatsoever he saith" (Mark 11:23, King James Version). I was driving down the highway thrilled about being on the pier in a few short hours then I received a phone call from my mother. She said she could not go fishing with me because she was tired, and she had a lot do. I responded, ok but she had dampened my spirit. After I hung up the phone, for about 15 seconds I was disappointed. Then I rebuked that emotion and said out loud, "I'm going to the ocean and I will catch my cooler full of fish and I do not care if I have to go all by myself." "Let thine eyes look right on, and let thine eyelids look straight before thee. 26 Ponder the path of thy feet, and let all thy ways be established" (Proverbs 4:25-26, King James Version). When I arrived at my house in my hometown, I began preparing for my fishing trip. Andrew, a friend agreed to go with me and drive. He had a prior engagement and wanted to be back Saturday before 2:30 pm which was a reasonable offer, so, I compromised and agreed with leaving at that time. While we were in the yard packing up the vehicle, my mother came over and said she would go but she would have to be back early enough to clean the church in the morning. I said, "Oh no, I cannot be rushed to catch my cooler full of fish." We would just be getting there around midnight and having to leave a few hours later would have been a wasted trip. My mother shook her head and asked, "Do you even know if the fish are biting?" I said, "They will when I get there." It was a common practice that we would call down to the pier shop and ask one of the staff if the fish were biting. However, I could feel in my spirit that I was going to catch my cooler full of fish, so there was no need for me to call and ask anyone. I told my mom if she really wanted to go, I would help her clean the church that night before we left for the ocean so she could go. "And do not forget to do good and to share with others, for with such sacrifices God is pleased" (Hebrews 13:16, New International Version).

My mother and I headed to the church to clean it up which was less than 10 minutes away. As soon as we arrived, I started with the vacuuming while she cleaned the kitchen, dining hall, and bathrooms. I was vacuuming the carpet making sure I did not miss one spot, leaving lines as proof that it had been vacuumed. I was vacuuming between the church pews and dusting them all at the same time. I was also singing and praising God for the cooler full of fish that I was going to catch. It was not long before my mother had finished all her duties, so she came out to see if I was finished. I would have been finished, but I decided to go up on the choir stand behind the pulpit and give that area a more detailed cleaning. When my mother made eye contact with me, she looked at me and the expression on her face said it all: What is she cleaning up there? I was cleaning that church like Jesus was coming back that next day. I was cleaning areas she said she had never cleaned. My OCD was kicking in and I wanted it to look perfect. And I was not going to quit until it did. Around 8 pm we had finally finished. The church was clean and now it was time to go home and get dressed preparing for the agonizing cold winds of the North Carolina Ocean waters so I could catch my cooler full of fish.

Mom and I headed back home to get dressed and finish packing the vehicle with our fishing gear and personal supplies. My wardrobe consisted of three pairs of socks one pair battery heated, thermal underwear, sweatpants, jeans, camisole, tee shirt, long sleeve shirt, sweatshirt, jacket, toboggan, my overall suit, and boots. I was prepared I did not want anything to stop me from realizing my goal. Andrew had already loaded up most of the items in the vehicle, so we did not have much to do. It was close to 9 pm and we were ready to get on the road. My cooler full of fish was waiting for me and I could feel it. I could hardly wait to get out on that pier and start fishing. The thought of catching my cooler full of fish had consumed my thoughts and now the time had come. The drive from the house to the pier was about an hour and a half distance between the two. I had been waiting for this day for weeks; it had been a while since I had been able to go fishing after relocating to the Sunshine state. And fishing for me is one of the most peaceful and relaxing hobbies that I have. I was truly looking forward to it.

Finally, around 10:20 pm, we arrived at the pier parking lot. I rushed out of the vehicle and immediately started grabbing my fishing gear. Now, all we needed to do was walk to the pier shop, check in, pay the fee to fish, and purchase some bait. Once our items were paid for, I was leading the pack. I could not get on that pier fast enough. We found a spot next to an associate from our neighboring hometown and we settled next to her. I unzipped my rod and reel bag, grabbed out my broken-down rod and begin attaching it together. As soon as my rods and reels were attached, I added my weigh and three hooks to my fishing line. Then I baited my hook and cast my rod out into the ocean. In less than five minutes after getting on the pier, my line was in the water waiting on my fish to bite my hook. I had finally made it. I was elated. And now all I had to do was to be patient. It was around 10:40 pm and it was a little chilly, even with all my covering. The first hour went by; no bites. But I still believed. The second hour goes by; no bites. I'm still confident. The third hour goes; by no bites. I'm still praising God. It was now around 1:30 am and the wind chill was increasingly getting colder and I was becoming sleepy. I told God that if they did not bite within the next hour that I was going to take a nap, but I would be back. I survived until 2:30 am and still no fish were in sight, so I gave into the cold and sleep and went into the vehicle to take a nap. As soon as my body warmed up, I fell asleep and remained there until 7 am the next morning.

I woke up that morning eager to get back on the pier. I was ready to go catch my cooler full of fish. I felt like SpongeBob heading to the Krusty Krab saying, "I'm Ready, I'm Ready, I'm Ready." I left my mom and Andrew in the car still sleeping. I stopped by the shop to use the restroom to freshen up, then purchased some hot chocolate, and headed straight for the pier again, confident that today my cooler would be full. Well, once I got to the pier, the fisherman who were already there said they were getting a bite every now and then, but really nothing much happening. Finally, around 8 am my mom came back to the pier. Andrew had gone to get us some breakfast. By that time, I had caught two or three small fishes. The fishes were quiet. Every now and then a fish would bite someone's hook, so they found other things to do to pass time. My mom had started a conversation with the people fishing beside us and discovered they lived in the town next to her. It was not unusual to meet people we knew on the pier it was one of the closest piers to fish for people that lived in our area. I recall one of the people asking Mom how long we had planned to stay, and I responded, "until my cooler was full of fish." They all laughed and said, I guess you'll be here for a while then. I guess since the fish were not being lured to our bait, everyone was bored. My co-fishermen on the left side of the pier decided I would be the target of their jokes because I refused to take my line out of the water and stop fishing. Most of them had given up and pulled their lines out of the water, but I kept my line in and was adamant that I was not leaving the pier until my cooler was full even if that meant I had to catch a ride back home with someone else.

My mother had taken her line out of the water and she spent most of her time on the pier eating up all the food that was supposed to last her throughout the day. She was also having a great time talking to her neighbors and shaking her head in disbelief when she looked at me. My sister called my mom on her cell phone while we were on the pier. I heard my mom say, "you know your crazy sister." I assume my sister's next question was when we were leaving because her response was, "when Hannah catches her cooler full of fish, I guess." Her next question must have been, how many fish has she already caught because my mom's response was, "the bottom of her cooler is not even covered." Of course, the group on the left side had heard the conversation also, so they teamed up against me and started mocking me about me. It was all in good fun. I was laughing and smiling and saying in my mind at the same time, I bind the powers, principalities, rulers of darkness of this world, and spiritual wickedness in high places and render them harmless and ineffective against me. Casting down imaginations, and every high thing that exalteth itself against the knowledge of God and bringing into captivity every thought to the obedience of Christ. We were all having a great time joking but at the same time, I was quoting the word of God against ever negative comments they spoke against bringing my belief into fruition.

I decided to go quickly to the pier shop to use the restroom before the fish started biting and get some more hot chocolate because it was still a little chilly on the pier. Once I arrived at the pier shop, I looked up at the clock and observed that it was 10:30 am. I said God I had planned on leaving at 2:30 pm that's only four hours away. I heard a voice say, "I only need a second." So, I went back to the pier still confident that I was going to catch my cooler full of fish. I bent down on my right knee and put my right elbow on the bench on the pier and laid my head in my right hand. I began to pray and thank God for the fish that we were going to catch. While I was praying, I could hear them laughing at me but the more they laughed the more I praised God. "Bear with me while I speak, and after I have spoken, mock on" (Job 21:3, New International Version). With a sarcastic tone, one of them said, pray for us too while you're down there. Once I got up, I smiled and informed them that I had prayed for them. Teasing me, they asked me if I had any idea when the fish were coming. I just smiled and said, soon. I threw my line back in the ocean and refused to allow their mockery of me to distract me from catching my cooler full of fish. While I stood there patiently waiting for the fish to start biting, I could not help but ponder on the words, "I only need a second," which gave me even more assurance that I was going to achieve my goal. I knew it was the Holy Spirit that had spoken to me because Satan never has anything good or positive to say.

While I continued to wait patiently with my line still in the water, I found myself observing the actions of others as they also waited for the hopeful tide to guide the fish along the shore of the pier into our awaited traps. I had set up my fishing gear up and personal supplies near the middle of the pier. The shop, of course, was on one end near the shore and the other end was the edge of the pier leading out into the ocean. I watched as the people found things to do to pass the time as they awaited the moment their rod would be pulled downward into the ocean. The fishermen, children, and the spectators, everyone was doing their own little thing. Some adults and children were lying on the pier trying to catch a little nap, others taking a few minutes to cure the growling stomachs, some heading for the long-awaited restroom break, other placing music and dancing, others creating conversations with strangers they would have never likely talked to off the pier, visitors sightseeing on a fishing pier for the very first time and lastly the group to my left laughing at me for praying and believing that the fish were going to come in schools. For those who are not familiar with fishing lingo, fish swim in groups are called "schools." The truth is, whether I caught my cooler full of fish or not, I was having a great time enjoying the moment, but I refused to allow the hecklers dampen my spirit and shake my belief. I'm not sure of the exact time, but somewhere between 11:30 am and 12 noon, as I stood looking down towards the end of the pier. I observed as rods were being grabbed and lines were being pulled into the ocean with fish on every line. It was like a domino effect, which started at one end of the pier and proceeded until it reached the shore of the pier. It was an amazing sight to see all the fishermen pulling up so many fish in a matter of seconds. The time had come, and I was ready to receive my blessing. However, the fishermen on my left side, the "Jokers," or we can call them the "Non-Believers" were not privy to the first school of fish because their rods were prompted up against the pier rails. The Jokers were now racing for the moment to cast their lines back into the ocean. Everyone who had a line and a hook in the ocean was pulling up one or more fish and I was included.

Before I could even process what was occurring, I felt a tug at my line. Then, waiting just two seconds, I pulled in my line and I had hooked two fish. One of the fish jumped off my hook once I got it on the pier and I removed the other one and threw both in the cooler. Within seconds, I baited my hook and cast my line in again. As soon as my line hit the water, I felt another tug and I reeled my line in having hooked two more fish. I grabbed each fish one at a time and remove the hook from their mouths and threw them in my cooler. I baited my hook again and I told The Jokers I was going to try for a triple-double. Again, as soon as my hook hit the water, I could feel the pull. I reeled in my line again and two fish were hooked. Just as soon as I got the fish on the pier, they jumped off my hook and landed on the pier. Andrew helped pick them up and threw them in the cooler for me. Bait was still on my hook so I asked The Jokers if they thought I could do a quadruple. I threw my line in, and as soon as it hit the water, I felt it yank. I reeled my line doubles again. The same thing happened as soon as I got them over the pier; the fish jumped off my hook. By this time, a few bystanders were watching me, so they picked up my fish and threw them in the cooler for me. They said, just keep on fishing. I told The Jokers that I was going to try for a quintuple. I baited my hook and cast my line and as soon as it hit the water, I felt the jerk again. I reeled my line in and it was a double again. Five times straight I had pulled in two fishes at the same time. More speculators walking on the pier had stopped to watch me in action. They were amazed at how quick I was pulling up the fishes. Lines across the ocean were casting their lines over right in front of me trying to get in my spot. They would get a bite and pull up one fish but not two at a time. Cast number six as it hit the water, I felt a strong yank. I began to reel in my line, but this time it was taking all my strength to reel it in. I just kept reeling and reeling. The Jokers said, leave some fish for us. I just smiled and kept on reeling. Finally, I got the fish above the water and I could see that three fishes had been hooked, but I still had to get them up on the pier. My back was feeling the pain of the struggle trying to pull all three fishes up at once, but I refused to allow the pain to hinder me. I kept reeling and reeling. You would have thought it was a shark that had taken the bait. After several minutes of struggling, I got them over on the pier. There was a little boy along with his parents and other fishermen watching me the entire time as I tried to reel in the three fishes. Once I got them out of the water, the expression on the little boy's face was priceless as he stood there in amazement. He asked if he could take the fish off my hooks for me and I said, yes, with much gratitude. Once he got them off, I thanked him, but he was more interested in playing with them, so I told him to enjoy himself. I was so exhausted but not enough to quit, so I continued fishing. After a few moments, the little boy's parents informed him it was time to go so he reluctantly put all three fish in my cooler with a frown on his face. He pleaded with his parents to stay a little longer, but his parents told him it was time to leave.

The Jokers on the left side that were laughing at me made the statement, "you should have prayed for us too while you were down there on your knees." I responded, "I did." The man on the right that was fishing alongside his wife said, "It's obvious that you are blessed and highly favored." I smiled and said, thank you and said yes, I am. This is pretty much how the rest of my fishing day went. I cannot describe the joy I felt that God had shown up for me that day and set me above the rest. Everyone wanted to know what bait I was using, I told them I was using the same bait as them. One of The Jokers made the statement, "she prayed for her fish, but she did not pray for anyone else." I just shook my head and said, "I did pray for you, too, but you just did not believe." For everyone that was watching me that day, it looked as if I had flying fish around me with how fast they were coming up out of the water. I was the star on the pier that day people were stopping to watch me and asking to assist me. When I would pull my fish up, the ones that did not jump onto the pier bystanders were there to take them off my hook. They did not want me to stop fishing for a moment. They appeared to be more excited than I was; they wanted my line in the water. The Jokers demanded I go to the restroom or somewhere and take a break so they could catch some fish. I reassured them I was not leaving until my cooler was full of fish.

My cooler full of fish was no longer just a spoken word or a belief but a manifestation in my reality. In less than two and a half hours after the school of fish came, my 45-quart cooler was completely full. Physically my right arm was completely worn out, my legs were exhausted, my back was sore, my hands and fingers were cramped, and my stomach was growling, but I was engulfed with an awesome feeling of gratitude. I had never pulled up as many fish non-stop in my lifetime. People continued to stop and watch in amazement until I finally stopped. God had shown up for me and elevated me for all The Jokers to witness my faith being fulfilled that day on the pier. Jesus' parables on fishing written in the Bible thousands of years ago is an actual narrative that has occurred in my life here in the 21st century. This was the best fishing day of my life. "So shall my word be that goeth forth out of my mouth: it shall not return unto me void, but it shall accomplish that which I please, and it shall prosper in the thing whereto I sent it" (Isaiah 55:11, King James Version). God had validated his word for me that day in front of hundreds of people and I praised him giving him all the glory that day on the pier. "Every word of God proves true; he is a shield to those who take refuge in him" (Proverbs 30:5, New Living Translation).

My God is an on-time God; never late and never too early. God provided me with an answer to my question on my drive down using my fishing experience as the moral of the story. The question was, "God I have ideas and desires that came through the channel of my mind that I want to have faith to receive but I'm not sure if you are going to fulfill them or not if they were not directly spoken to my spirit." And God said, "The words that I speak to your heart to do and you follow through with I will bless." But God then emphasized that He did not put in my heart that I would catch the cooler full of fish that I just spoke it and believed it. And God said it was your faith that made it happen. God knew my heart's motive for asking the question, so he further responded, it's OK to believe for things that you want personally in life you deserve to have them. When God spoke these words to me tears gushed down my face, realizing that I had been deceived all these years into believing a lie. God contradicted the two lies that Satan had always led me to believe and validated in my thoughts, as a result, I allowed them to penetrate my heart.

Satan's Lies

1st Lie: You are not worthy to receive God's blessings
2nd Lie: If God blesses you, you will not serve him like you once did

My Scenario

God had spoken to my spirit in 2003 and told me that I was going to be a millionaire. As soon as God had finished speaking to my heart, I heard another voice speak to my mind and said, "If you become a millionaire, you know you will not serve God anymore. You'll be too busy enjoying your wealth and you will not pray as much as you do now." I did not want to lose my relationship with God, so oblivious to the fact that I was being deceived, I unknowingly trusted the words of Satan instead of God. Therefore, I decided it was best for me not to believe I would be a millionaire. I would rather just make enough money to live comfortably so I could always be close to God. "The thief cometh not, but for to steal, and to kill, and to destroy: I am come that they might have life and that they might have it more abundantly" (John 10:10, King James Version).

During this period in my life, I was still a baby in Christ still learning his voice but now it is clear God speaks to our spirits and Satan speaks to our minds. Therefore, any thoughts that do not line up with the word of God is likely the words of Satan himself trying to deceive you as he deceived me for so many years. "Casting down imaginations, and every high thing that exalteth itself against the knowledge of God, and bringing into captivity every thought to the obedience of Christ" (2 Corinthians 10:5, King James Version). Today, many Christians still believe that God is closer to the poor and far from the wealthy, which is a lie from Satan.

I have changed my mindset and now I believe God's will for my life. I am a millionaire just waiting for it to come into fruition. I realize my prosperity is not going to affect my relationship with God because God's word says he wishes me to be prosperous. "Beloved, I wish above all things that thou mayest prosper and be in health, even as thy soul prospereth" (3 John 1:2, King James Version).

Throughout most of my life, Satan's lies had limited me from asking God for what I desired and prevented me from receiving the gifts that God desired for me to have. God's response to me exposed Satan's lies for me clearly to see how Satan had been manipulating me into me believing I was not worthy and incapable of handling the blessings that God has in store for me.

After I had processed all that had occurred that weekend, I asked God another question. God, why was my faith so unrelenting in believing I was going to catch that cooler full of fish? God instructed me to write down everything I did before my fishing trip. So, I began to reflect on all the things that occurred. I recalled waking up daily speaking it out loud and believing this time it would be different than the past fishing trips. I prayed for and blessed others during my waiting period. I refused to allow others' intentions to distract me by making a stand to go alone if necessary. I did an unselfish act that gave another an opportunity to participate in the trip. I refused to be persuaded by other people's disbelief and only allowed the word of God to penetrate and align with my thoughts. And I thanked God and praised him for what was going to happen. So, here is the list of my actions and reactions before and leading up to my cooler full of fishes trip:

➤ I repeatedly spoke it, believed it and expected it

➤ I did not allow past failures to influence my present

- ➢ I was a blessing to others in my waiting period.

- ➢ I refused to be influenced or swayed by the inactions of others

- ➢ I made a few sacrifices on the way

- ➢ I continued to believe in the middle of opposition and mockery

- ➢ I rebuked every thought that did not line up with what I had expected to happen

- ➢ I praised God continuously

Once I had completed my list, I was amazed at everything I had done because while I was doing it, I had not put a lot of thought into it. It was not until God instructed me to write it down that it I understood what had happened. God said, "Use this plan in every aspect of your life and nothing will be shall be impossible for you." I had been given a strategic faith plan to follow. When I returned to Florida after my fishing trip, still glowing over the outcome, I returned the rental vehicle and picked up my vehicle. I had to pay the $250 deductible, but I was thankful to God that I had the funds to pay it. By that time, I had finally forgiven myself for making the mistake with my comprehensive deductible and decided to continue to focus more on the positive aspect: the fact that I had not been injured or better yet killed. Well to my surprise about three months later, that December I received a phone call from an insurance claims adjuster. She caught me off guard because I was unclear why an adjuster would be calling me. My claim had been settled months ago and I had not been involved in any recent accidents. She then explained the purpose of her call. She stated that her insured had filed a claim and reported that their spare tire had disengaged from their vehicle and hit my vehicle. I was stunned to hear those words come out of her mouth I was not expecting them. She asked if my vehicle had been repaired and I replied, yes. She then stated that she wanted my insurance information and the deductible amount I had to pay so she could reimburse me and my insurance company. Still in total awe, I asked how she found me. She replied that after her policyholders had filed the claim providing her with all the information and she then tracked down the accident report that the sheriff deputies had filed. Tears of joy were streaming down my face knowing that I really serve a mighty God. I had written this situation off and never expected to hear from the RV owners. Yet they set out in search to find me to right a wrong. "For the Lord God is a sun and shield: the

Lord will give grace and glory: no good thing will he withhold from them that walk uprightly" (Psalms 84:11, King James Version). This incident is another example of how God is continuously working behind the scenes when all seems forgotten and lost. What an awesome and mighty God we serve?

My perception then:	God would bless whatever He spoke to my spirit if I obeyed but was not sure if my desires would be His will for my life.
	I had contempt for my tenants for inconveniencing me and causing my credit score to decline.
	I believed despite past experiences that I was going to catch my cooler full of fish.
	How could I make the mistake of not securing the lower deductible for my vehicle coverage knowing the financial strands I was under?

Message:	God is delighted to give us the desires of our heart if it is in alignment with his word so believe in your dreams. However, praying for vengeance on others and for what belongs to another is not in alignment with God's word so find a verse(s) that aligns with your desire and hold that word in your heart. Prayer has the power to activate forgiveness, break down barriers in relationships, relieve stress and tensions and restore unity amid turmoil. If you have a desire or dream, speak it, believe it and do not allow doubt to take root. Do not allow anything or anyone to distract you. Make up your mind to stand alone if you must. Understand you might have to make a few sacrifices on the way and lend a helping hand to others on your way up. Stand strong and rejoice in the face of opposition and mockery. Lastly, but most importantly, always praise God continuously. In life it may seem like every door has been closed and the decision is final however God has the power to open every closed door and reversed any decision he chooses to on our behalf.
How this experience affected my future:	I found it hard sometimes to have faith in my desires because I was afraid to believe and then if they did not come into fruition, I was fearful that I might have questioned my faith or maybe even lost it. I am not so quick to criticize and judge people instead I try to make a conscious effort to pray for them. I reflect on this faith plan when dealing with desires I want to manifest into my reality. During instances when I found it hard to let go of the outcome of a situation, I recall how the owner of the RV found me just to right a wrong.

My perception now:	God wants above all that my soul be prosperous, my health be prosperous, my relationships be prosperous, my finances be prosperous and everything I touch to be prosperous.
	Prayer is the most powerful gift God has given us, yet it is not what is most used when we are faced with conflict. Our first line of protection is to satisfy our flesh. Our flesh craves immediate gratifications and believes it can bring about the desired change which is a trick of the enemy. Satan secretly initiates havoc on our lives and creates the conflict in our minds that we encounter. He then attempts to blind us from the truth by producing thoughts in our minds of failed supplications to God with intentions of alleviating the purpose and the power of prayer. Satan does have power in the earth, but God has given us authority here on earth over satan. Now when faced with difficulties or obstacles in my everyday life I go into my secret place and I pray with authority using the word of God to bring about my desired change knowing that I have been given authority over the enemy to overcome his schemes in my life.
	The moment I believed and declared that I was going to catch my cooler full of fish that God orchestrated my footsteps so through my experience I would demonstrate to myself and others the result of unrelenting faith.
	In life, we will all make mistakes and there is no reason to criticize yourself too much, instead, we should take responsibility for our action and move forward.

CHAPTER
Twenty One

I Will Still Go

My perception for most of my life was that I was unwanted and unloved, which was far from the truth. God has always loved me and has never left my side. He was there from my infancy, as a toddler, early childhood, middle childhood, late childhood, adolescence, early adulthood, and now. He was there with me during every tear, heartache, disappointment, and every achievement. In the past, I felt alone—as if I did not even belong—and that the best place for me was with God. I felt that in heaven, I would finally be loved and accepted. But the truth is God has always loved me and made His presence known in my life, but subconsciously I felt as if his presence was only temporary. Because I had not identified the roots of my problems, when God had shown up for me, it was distorted by my flawed belief system. So, the truth is, no matter how many times God showed up for me, my traumas impeded my ability to completely  receive his blessing due to my fear of Him changing his mind on me and rescinding His blessings from me. I had been holding God to the same standards as man unknowingly, expecting him to react the same way my family members responded to me in my childhood. God had revealed to me that the fears I had attributed to Him all those years which affected every aspect of my life were displayed emotions towards Him.

I recall a discussion I had with my friend, Esther, about some of the thoughts that I was processing at the time. And I shared with her several of my testimonies when God had shown up for me in the past. However, this current dilemma weighed heavily on my mind so we processed further why my faith would not support God showing up for me this time as he had always done. Then she asked a question which resonated with me. "What does it look like when God does not show up?" Esther asked. I pondered the question for a moment and then responded, "I do not know because he has always shown up." My response stopped me in my tracks and caused me to meditate. And in a minute's notice, it appeared as if a light switch was turned on inside of me. My past experiences never revealed a time that God was not there for me, although I continued to question His loyalty in my life. I had no evidence as an adult of a time when my prayers went unanswered. I deduced God not appearing due to the feelings of abandonment established by core family members during my childhood. Also, I realized I was holding God accountable for allowing me to be born into a family that did not have my best interest at heart.

Seven Dollars & a Half Tank of Gas

My first month in Florida, while I was still in the process of setting up my business, I had no extra income to spare. It was on a Thursday afternoon and I received an email from my banking institution notifying me that I had seven dollars in my account. This was the lowest my bank account had been in my adulthood that I could recall. In a panic, I looked at my gas gauge to evaluate the amount of gas I had left in my gas tank. I immediately became scared and worried about what I was going to do concerning putting gas in my vehicle. I was living with my distant cousin and his family at the time, but I dare not ask them for anything. They had already gone above and beyond by allowing me to live with them. Also, I did not want to call and ask any of my family members in fear of them disagreeing with my decision to move to Florida and start a business. And it would be a couple of weeks before I would get my next unemployment check. In frustration and fear, I said to God, "I told You that I did not want to open this type of business again but You said you would be the CEO and take care of me so I said I will go. Now I have only seven dollars in my bank account and a half tank of gas, I need You!" I could not believe I had allowed myself to get in such a place, broke, frustrated, afraid and miles away from home. After a few minutes, I finally calmed down. I reflected on all the other times God had come through for me, so then I wiped away my tears, stopped my pity party and began to thank God. Less than 5 minutes after all of this happen, I received two phone calls: one from my sister, Zipporah, and one from my best friend, Ruth. I shared a little with Ruth about my situation, but I did not share it with Zipporah. I had always been the giver in my family and now I was facing unfamiliar territory. Now I was the one in need but refused to speak to anyone in my family in fear of being judged. I did not want anyone to question my decision to step out on faith, move to Florida, and open a business. My heart could not handle any criticism from anyone, so I spoke only to my Father about what I was going through who had instructed me to make the journey.

The following day, Zipporah called and informed me that she had heard on the News that there was an issue with the bank I patronized regarding transactions and I needed to check my account. I responded, "Ok". I thought to myself, they cannot do any damage to my account, seven dollars will not help them that much. The next day, Saturday, Abigail, David and I were at the park serving pancakes to a group of homeless people in the local area. That was usually my Saturday morning routine with my associates. As I was engaged in serving the homeless people, I received another phone call from Zipporah. I thought something must be wrong with her calling me this much. However, nothing was wrong, she just inquired if I had checked my bank account. I did a half chuckle and told her I had not checked it because I had no worries about them taking money from my account. She insisted that I check the account, so I told her to hold on as I opened my bank app from my cell phone to check the balance while she held on. To my surprise, a couple of hundred dollars had been deposited into my account. I was overwhelmed with gratitude and I thanked her and her husband, Moses for their kind gesture. All that time, she had just been using the News of accounts being hacked as a mask to get me to check my account. I held back my tears of joy until the phone call ended. But as soon as the phone disconnected, the tears started flowing down and I was overwhelmed with the feeling of gratitude. God had come through for me again. To appreciate the story, you must know my sister, Zipporah. She is tight with money and she does not spend frivolously. Zipporah has always given me gifts, but neither she nor anyone else has ever had to loan me money, so this really meant a lot to me that God would use her. Zipporah would later explain to me about how this all came about. She said she and Moses, had agreed to give me the funds a few months prior. They both discussed how I had always given and that now I was the one in need of help. On that Friday, the day after I received the email alert from my backing institution, she said she heard a loud voice say, "Go now and put the money in Hannah's account." Zipporah stated it startled her so much that she jumped up to her feet and immediately got into her car and drove to the bank to deposit the money in my account. I never told my sister that I needed financial assistance. God spoke to her directly on my behalf. God proved to me again that He was my source and He will touch the heart of whomever He desired to act on my behalf without needing my help.

The Haircut

I have discovered that there is no request too small that God will not respond to. Now during this period, I had just recently moved into my new apartment after having purchased a new vehicle and leased an apartment on faith. I had absolutely no income at all coming at the time. I remember it was a Monday morning. I had only $20 to carry me throughout the week. The previous night, I had shampooed, conditioned, blow dried, and flat ironed my hair, in preparation for the start of the week. On that Monday morning, I woke up and then prepared to go into the office for a few hours and handle a few administrative duties. I was looking in my bathroom mirror. As I unwrapped my hair, I could not overlook the fact that my split ends looked horrible. The previous night, after all the work I had done on my hair, it appeared as if I had wasted my time. To understand my discontent, think of what it looks like when a beautiful lawn has been mowed, but the mower neglects to weed eat and trim it. As I looked in the mirror, I said, God, I only have $20 for the week but I really need a haircut when you get the chance. Afterward, I left for my office to complete the few items I had on my agenda for the day. About four hours later, I returned to my apartment complex, but before going to my apartment, I heard a voice say, "Go to your mailbox." I immediately recognized that it was the voice of the Holy Spirit because I knew my flesh could not stand the sight of my mailbox. The thought of my mail made me nauseous. My mailbox, to me, had become like kryptonite to Superman. This was my first time in my adulthood that I could not afford to pay my bills. I was so accustomed to paying my bills on time and maintaining a high credit score; however, now that was a thing of the past for me. Regardless of how I felt, I still went because I was afraid of the consequences if I was disobedient to the Holy Spirit. So, I drove to the mailbox, but not without voicing my feelings. I stated I will go to the mailbox and clear out the junk mail, but I am leaving those bills in there. I do not have the money to pay them, so I am not going to take them into my apartment, constantly see them and become even more depressed. I opened my mailbox and begin sorting out the mail, removing all the junk mail, bills, and advertisements. Then I began placing the bills back into the mailbox. However, one piece of mail caught my attention. It was a postcard advertising the Grand Opening of a hair salon in my neighborhood with $3.95 haircuts. I held tightly onto the postcard as I threw the junk mail in the trash. As soon as I put the last piece of mail in the trash, I proceeded to my car. I drove less than a half of a mile down the road to the new salon and graciously received my $3.95 haircut. This haircut meant so much to me because God responded to something that was important to me at the time. Although it may seem small to others but to me it was priceless. He did not deem that it was vain; instead, He had it waiting for me before I even asked for it.

The Hug

I recall one day while I was in my apartment and the darkness was trying to overtake me again. I did not know how much more I could take being all alone, financially strained, and wondering if I had made the right decision. I knew God had instructed me to move to Florida, but I started questioning whether if I had misheard Him about my decision to move and open the business. I was going through all these emotional changes, but all I truly wanted at the time was to feel my Father's arms around me. So, I said to my Father, I know that you are a spirit and you cannot hold me in the flesh, but I just wish somehow you could find a way just to hug and hold me like you did before. I need to feel You. I spoke like a child, as if I was the little three-year-old Hannah speaking. I cried and communed with God until I was so exhausted that I laid down and fell asleep. A few days later, after my conversation with God, I went to church as usual, but this day would be different than all the other days. The church I attended at the time had a membership of about 1200 people. This day I was sitting in the middle section of the congregation about 15 rows from the front of the church in the middle of the row. During praise and worship service, a lady that I had never recognized before walked from the front of the church down the middle aisle and then pointed her finger in the direction of the area where I was seated. It appeared that she was pointing at me, so to be sure, I looked to my left, then to my right and then made eye contact with her again. She shook her head in a nodding fashion of sideways as she said, no, you. I was not able to hear her, but I read her lips. I then proceeded to the middle aisle where she was standing. Once I got close enough to her, she grabbed me and started hugging me and holding me so tight that I would have to struggle just to break free from her grip. She said God told me to tell you that He loves you, He has not forgotten about you and He just told me to hug you. She also said, "God said to tell you that He hears all your prayers." I know the lady continued to speak to me, but honestly, after she said, 'He loves you, He has not forgotten about you, to hug you and He hears all your prayers,' I was in complete astonishment so what she said next was just a blur. I felt as if I was frozen in time. The very words that I had spoken to God in the privacy of my apartment were being recited to me. God's confirmation that He loves me, He has not forgotten about me, the hug and He hears all of my prayers destroyed all the remaining barriers of doubt that surrounded my heart. The realization that He loved me so much that He sent someone to physically hug me filled my heart with unspeakable joy. God gave me great assurance knowing that He was my comforter.

The Prayer

I recall the time I prayed for my brother-in-law, Moses to get a raise. It had become a ritual for me to pray for someone(s) three times a day, morning, noon, and evening prayers. Some days I found it hard to pray for others because I felt it was meaningless and that I sounded ridiculous when praying but I would still go and pray because I had made a commitment. During this evening prayer, I asked God to bless Moses for being supportive of my sister, Zipporah by encouraging her to pursue her dream of starting her own business. Then, I thanked God for doing it. But once I finished praying, and as I was getting up off my knees, I said to God, that was the worst sounding prayer ever. I was critical of the words I had used and the statements I had to formulate when speaking with God. I felt like my prayer made no sense and the words I used were so premature. I further stated, "I am going to need your help because I have to do better than this!" My perfectionist spirit had crept in, front and center. The very next day, I gave a testimony to a group at work about my conservation with God. I expressed to them how I depicted the words used in my prayer resonated with me. On my way home that afternoon, I called Zipporah just to chitchat to pass time as I drove home. Her first comment to me was, you know I do not usually tell people stuff like this, but Moses got a raise today. My sister is private and can appear introverted at times. She said, Moses' supervisor called him in and just said we are just going to give you a raise. I was in complete awe; my mouth was wide open as I was driving down the road. I could not speak at all for a few seconds. I thought to myself, God that was quick. After I regained my composure, I said to Zipporah, I prayed for Moses yesterday evening to get a raise and that I complained to God about how bad my prayer sounded. God had again confirmed to me that He had heard my prayer. He also made it clear to my spirit that when I prayed it was not about how great I sounded, or the words I used, it was about where it came from, the pureness of my heart. I responded, "I understand God." God showed me I was worthy and deserving by answering my prayer so promptly. He also showed me I was enough by acknowledging that he recognized the pureness of my heart. After that day, I became less concerned about how I sounded or the words I used. I just prayed from my heart and self was moved.

Home

Every now and then, I would revert to my old feelings, questioning my choices and my importance whenever I would face difficult struggles in life and wondering if I missed God's directions. On this one day, I was feeling a great sense of loneliness again with no close family or friends around and wondering what's God's purpose for relocating me. I had faced so many obstacles since I had arrived in Florida and a part of me wanted to give up, but the other part of me knew that God would be there for me. So, I cried out to God in despair asking him to help me see my purpose and to give me the strength to hold on. I felt again as if maybe I had been lying to myself about what I had believed that God had sent me to Florida; that maybe I had made it all up in my head. However, even with all those negative thoughts, I was too fearful to turn away from Him because of a moment of weakness. Focusing all my attention on God, I began praying and inquiring of the Lord for answers. I prayed so long and hard that after a while I prostrated on the floor and I felt myself fall into a completely relaxed state as if I was in a comatose stage. While lying there, I found myself in a familiar place knowing, without a doubt, I had been here before. I could not see my surrounding with my natural eye, but my spirit recognized this place as heaven. At the same time, a spirit of peace came all over my body and the emptiness that I once felt vanished. I could not help but to contemplate on God's word, "Before I formed you in the womb I knew you before you were born I set you apart; I appointed you as a prophet to the nations" (Jer. 1:5, New International Version). Then a scene from my life flashed in my memory, one I had no remembrance of. God showed Him and I having a conversation about me coming down to Earth. In this conversation, God revealed to me all the emotions that I would encounter when I arrived at my new home on Earth. God said to me, "it's going to get hard sometimes, you will want to give up, you will feel that you're all alone, and you will feel like I've abandoned you, but I promise I will always be there for you." Even with His warnings, without hesitation, I stated, "I will still go." I could not remember the conversation that God had shown me, but I did recognize I was finally back home. I finally had the awakening experience of knowing my purpose and my heritage. I had been selected by my Father to help others here on Earth who would be lost to return to Him. After years of wandering and wondering, feeling like I did not belong, I had found my way back home.

All the hurt and pain I had undergone over the years did not seem to matter anymore. God had shielded me from Satan's deadly attacks over my life and I had endured and overcome all his satanic attacks to prevent me from discovering the truth.

> *The truth is God is my father, Heaven is my home, I am deeply loved, and that I have always belonged.*

The moment my spirit recognized God as my real Father it seemed as if my heart had melted. A breath of fresh air was blown into me and my body became weightless and free. The emptiness that I had once felt for all the years had disappeared; it was restored with love, joy, and peace. It was my least concern who had hurt me, betrayed me or rejected me. The only emotion I felt towards those that had caused me pain was LOVE. Every negative word that was spoken over me, every negative experience that I suffered, sleepless nights that I endured, and every painful tear that I cried was worth it. Through them that inflicted my most pain, they helped me find my way back home and I will forever be grateful.

Visibility

In my life, I have allowed my traumas to obstruct my view of the truth so it's hard to see the truth sometimes when it's right in front of me. Most of the time we are so blinded that we are not capable of receiving the truth however God has a way of bringing things to light when we are ready to accept it. Visibility is defined in several different ways however I am going to focus on two meanings; first, the capability of being easily observed and second, providing a clear, unobstructed view (The Free Dictionary). An example of the meaning; capability of being easily observed, is a pastor with high visibility. Another example of the meaning; providing a clear, unobstructed view, is an airport runway with good visibility. One is referring to a person in a position and the other is referring to a thing that you can see clearly with your own eyes. Most people determine how they feel based on their position. It's either you are a victim or a victor. While most of us determine the truth based on what we see visually, your current position usually determines how you discern what you see, your perspective.

My final chapter will summarize the roots of my problems, true origins of my four fears that I attributed to God innocently. I will also show the interpretations of my parallels of God and man and my parallels of God as my Father. Here again are my four fears I equated to God. First, I feared that God might change his mind about me.   Second, I feared that God was going to take everything away from me. Third, I feared that God did not love me. Fourth, I feared that the words in the Bible applied to everyone else but me. I had previously written and titled these next four experiences long before the book was near completion and I was not sure how they would fit in any chapter of my book. The Seven Dollars & a Half Tank of Gas, The Haircut, The Hug and The Prayer were all heavily weighed on me to write about these experiences and the four fears in my final chapter, but I could not see the correlation at all. However, I continued to write in obedience to the spirit, asking God to help me make sense out of this. When I completed the editing of the four experiences, God spoke to me and revealed to me their meanings. He used these four life experiences in correlation with my four fears and revealed how He is my source and His presence will always exist in my life. This revelation overrode my flawed belief system and assured me that God will never leave me, He has blessings stored for me, He loves me, I am worthy, and I am enough.

Parallels of God and Man

➢ The root: I paralleled that since my stepfather changed his mind on me when he separated from my mother that God might also change his mind towards me.

➢ The root: I interpreted that because each time my grandmother brought me a gift and then took it back when she got upset with me that God would rescind his blessings also if I made a mistake.

➢ The root: My closest relatives neglected to show me affection and love so I could not equate how God could find me worthy to love if my own blood relatives did not.

➢ The root: I never felt important or worthy, so I believed the scriptures in the Bible applied to people who were deserving of them.

Parallels of God as My Father

➢ In the Seven Dollars & a Half Tank of Gas experience, God revealed the correlation with the feeling I had towards my stepfather changing his mind towards me and Him changing his mind on me. When I was down to my last seven dollars and half of tank of gas, God showed up for me. God had touched my sister's heart months ago to give me the money, but she decided to hold onto it for a little while longer. But when I needed it the most, God spoke to my sister and compelled her to put the money in my account immediately. God proved to me that His word would not return void and He will touch the heart of whomever to get me what I need.

➢ In the experience with The Haircut, God revealed the correlation of my gifts being taken from me by my grandmother and Him taking everything from me. When I only had $20 to last me throughout the entire week and I asked God for a haircut, before I even asked, he already had an inexpensive haircut advertisement in my mailbox. God proved to me that he knows what I desire even before I ask. God showed me that he has no intentions on taking anything from me, He has blessings stored and waiting on me.

- ➢ In the experience with The Hug, God revealed the correlation of my relatives not loving me and Him not loving me. When the darkness tried to overtake me again and I requested that God give me a hug expressing to Him that I needed to feel him, he sent an Angel. The Angel stated that Gods said, He loves you, He has not forgotten about you and He told me to hug you. God proved to me that He hears my prayers. He showed me that He loved me so much that He sent an angel in the flesh to single me out in a full congregation and show me how much He does.

- ➢ In the experience with The Prayer, God revealed the correlation of me feeling unworthy and unimportant and the word of God not applying to me. When I prayed for Moses to get a raise, once I finished praying, I felt as if my prayer was inadequate, not eloquent enough. God validated I was worthy and deserving by answering my prayer so promptly and providing me feedback. He affirmed I was enough by acknowledging that he recognized the pureness of my heart.

"These trials will show that your faith is genuine. It is being tested as fire tests and purifies gold—though your faith is far more precious than mere gold. So, when your faith remains strong through many trials, it will bring you much praise and glory and honor on the day when Jesus Christ is revealed to the whole world" (1 Peter 1:7, New Living Translation). Acknowledging the root of our problems is the first step in the healing process. The second step is accepting our journey of trials as tests and not as misfortunes. The challenging and traumatic life experiences that we may have endured do not define us, but our ability to overcome our circumstances does. We have the choice to be characterized as a victim or a victor. The third step is forgiveness; however, some individuals find this hard to process for different reasons. Some people believe it will release the individual(s) from any fault, some feel it will give the individual(s) permission to do it again, others it gives the person a false sense of control over the situation by not forgiving, and others are resistant to forgiving because they feel the individual(s) should suffer more. However, this perception or belief is not true. Forgiveness is not for others, but for us. We are the benefactors of forgiveness. Forgiveness allows us to heal, grow and initiates the opportunity for progress. Holding onto hurts stagnates moving forward and creates the fertilizer for bitterness to breed. In addition, forgiveness allows us to reclaim our power, overcome fear, and we will no longer be controlled by our emotions but by our heart. "There is no love without forgiveness, and there is no forgiveness without love (McGill, no date)." Love is the greatest gift of all. "If I have the gift of prophecy and can fathom all mysteries and all knowledge, and if I have a faith that can move mountains, but do not have love, I am nothing. 3 If I give all I possess to the poor and give over my body to hardship that I may boast, but do not have love, I gain nothing" (1Cor. 1:2-3, New International Version)."And now these three remain: faith, hope, and love. But the greatest of these is love" (1Cor. 1:13, New International Version).

My perception then:	I deduced the chance of God not appearing with the feeling of abandonment established by core family members during my childhood.
Message:	God is always with us even in the worst moments of our lives when we feel defenseless, alone, forgotten and unloved. Our hurtful and painful life experiences can hold us in captivity in our minds and cause us to accept the emotional effects as our truths. However, if we can trust God with the pain, we have endured he will restore all that has been lost. God has given us the power to conquer all our hurts and fears through him. And these same fears that we once suffered can be nullified and used for the good of helping others. The power of daily communication with God and the power of prayer is the vehicle for manifestation in our lives. If you have a heart for God nothing is too small, too big, minimal, or vain for him to grant you. God loves for us to ask for the small things in life. It's the little things that build our faith to ask for the bigger things that we desire in life.
How this experience affected my future:	The more obstacles and setbacks in life I faced the more my faith grew. It was through my journey of setbacks, failures, and disappointments that I found my greatest strength and my faith flourished. If it had not been for the opportunity to experience these events in life my faith would have never been tested for evidence of growth or endurance.

My perception now:	Parents, spouses, children, and friends are vessels that God uses to bring about his blessings, but they should not be exalted. The difficult life experiences I faced as a child was only a test to prove that I had the ability to overcome any circumstances. The individuals that were used to bring about some of the most painful experiences in my life were only vessels used to help me discover the power within me. And for those same individuals, I am grateful for their part in my life. God is my source, heaven is my home, I am deeply loved, and I belong. Everything I ever needed and desired He provided for me. God has always been by my side and has never left me. God is my assurance and I am confident that his presence is always with me and he guides my life.

BIBLIOGRAPHY

Bartholomew, K. (1991) *Attachment Styles Among Young Adults: A Test of a Four-Category Model.*

Suval, Lauren. (Sept. 20, 2012) *What Drives our Needs for Approval?* Psych Central.

McGill, Bryant. H. (Date Unknown). *Simple Reminders.*

http://bryantmcgill.com/20140712021309.html